Secrets whispered in laughter, tears, and inward prayer tell the true story of Elisabeth Amalia Eugenia. She was Empress of Austria, Queen of Hungary, the most beautiful princess of the nineteenth century.

Written in love and passionate wrath by her dearest friend, "my little girl"—this personal vindication of Empress Elisabeth is said to be the only true portrayal of that career so bitterly criticized.

"To me she talked without restraint during our long rides, our endless tramps in the mountains and forests....I heard wellnigh every detail of her existence."

Share this intimacy with the Empress. A tenderness and emotion stifled by fools and locked by fate in the pitiless intrigue of the Hapsburg reign.

But death is not the end of her story. It never is.

The Empress lives. The same elite soul reincarnated in this century.

> Beyond the gates
>   Of darkness flies
> The soul
>   Into a timeless sea
> To reappear
>   By grand design.
> The eyes
>   Within a new disguise
> Betray the secret that
>   The One is born again.
>
>   Forget me not...

"I was trying to reason myself into going to sleep again in spite of all, when a very slight rustle attracted my attention and made me shudder from head to foot. It was so slight that none but ears sharpened by fear could have perceived it, and yet there it was—a soft, silky, gliding, undulating motion of something invisible gradually approaching my bed."

"If anybody ever felt regret for past indiscretions, surely this great ruler, before whom multitudes bowed, did so now, and shame as well as remorse filled his cup of bitterness to the very brim. The true character of his wife began to dawn upon him; he knew that since all eternity many women, both handsome and highly born, had suffered, and were suffering from the same indignities which he had put upon Elisabeth."

". . . Touching her hunter slightly with her spur as she spoke. . . . 'Sir Launcelot' laying his length out in his mighty strides, and my pretty chestnut racing her best by his side. They dashed neck to neck on the damp moss at a rattling pace, breaking straight for the open. . . . The pace became tremendous as we reached the short grass of the Pùsztá. Here a high fence towered, there a brook rushed angrily, but we stopped at nothing; and both horses, their mettle roused, needed no touch of stick or spur, and rose in the air with bounds that knew no obstacles."

"It was then, also, that she wrote a little poem about the famous legend which connects every misfortune happening to the House of Hapsburg with the appearance upon the scene of a raven. . . ."

Forget Me Not

The True Story of
Elisabeth of Austria
and the Mysterious
Hapsburg Curse

SUMMIT
UNIVERSITY PRESS®
LOS ANGELES

This work was originally published in 1899, one year following the tragic assassination of Elisabeth, Empress of Austria. It was written by her closest companion as a vindication of the malicious investigations and numerous press reports which attempted to establish a false idea of Elisabeth's personality. The author chose to remain anonymous.

FORGET ME NOT
Contains complete text of hardcover edition
The Martyrdom of an Empress.

Copyright © 1981 Summit University Press

Library of Congress Catalog Card Number: 81-85400
International Standard Book Number: 0-916766-51-9

Printed in the United States of America
First Printing

Cover design adapted from the original allegorical marble picture of the Empress by Robert Weigel, 1901.

THE EMPRESS AT THE AGE OF SIXTY—
JUST BEFORE HER ASSASSINATION

TO

MY EMPRESS

IN LOVING AND DEVOTED MEMORY

OF YEARS GONE-BYE

ILLUSTRATIONS

Forget Me Not

CHAPTER I

"Let them talk, let them slander, let them think what they please about me—I am used to it; it does not hurt me as it did at first; I do not care! And you, my little girl, do not take it to heart; do not try to fight my battles; do not let bitterness come into your life through me, for that, indeed, would give me pain."

The Empress stopped her restless pacing up and down the room, and, putting her slender hands upon my shoulders, she looked deep into my eyes with those glorious dark-blue orbs of hers, and added, gently:

"You are so young—hardly older than I was when I married. Do not allow my clouds to obscure your sky; you will have enough of your own!"

How well she understood the passionate wrath I felt when witnessing the continual prejudices displayed towards her was shown clearly to me by these few words. I was then very young—very inexperienced, truly—but she was all in all to me, and the depth of my love and admiration for her pure, noble, peerless nature bridged over the difference existing in our years, and I was happy in the thought that already at that time I had become wellnigh her only confidante and truest friend.

Perhaps it was the singular similarity of our fates which at first drew us so closely together—a similarity which arose from the sweeping contempt with which the haughty Viennese aristocracy had enveloped us both at different periods and under different circumstances; probably, also, because neither of us was of what is called "royal birth," and because neither of us was Austrian born. Moreover, we heartily disliked pomp and pageantry, the empty, vapid amusements of social life, with its hurry and fever, its fussing and fuming, its seething caldron of calumny kept boiling by malice and envy; and both found no pleasure whatsoever in chatting and scandal-mongering with other women, preferring horses and dogs to the company of most human beings! Last, but not least, alas! we had alike failed to find in matrimony what we foolishly fancied we had a right to expect from it, and scorned the very thought of seeking consolation after the fashion common to so many women when thus disappointed.

Be all this as it may, we certainly breathed an atmosphere of our own, and held aloof from others as much as possible in these years of close intimacy that make it possible for me to-day, now that she has gone to a sphere worthier of her, to give to the world the only true portrayal of the so much maligned and cruelly treated woman, who was the one faultless figure, the one perfect being among the past and present sovereignty of Europe.

That very morning Elisabeth had been kindly informed, by one of the good souls who formed her *entourage*, that her refusal to be present at the Corpus-Christi procession along the magnificently decorated streets of Vienna had given much offence, and had caused a renewal of the rumors long since set afloat concerning her sanity. Of course this had only been hinted at in her presence, but she was far too shrewd and quick-witted not to have gathered instantly the true meaning of these veiled allusions, and she easily foresaw what persecutions would follow.

"Cannot they leave me alone?" she continued, stamping her little foot impatiently. "All I ask of humanity is that it should not interfere with me; and yet all my actions are the subject of uncharitable comment and of cruel criticism. Can you tell me why I should thus be persecuted?"

The face of the Empress was flushed with vexation, and her straight, exquisitely pencilled dark brows contracted ominously.

"I am going away," she continued. "Let us be off to Gödöllő, where at least I am not continually under a microscope, and where I can fancy that I am a woman like all others, and not some extraordinary insect created for the malicious investigations and observations of the public."

The rays of the setting sun, slanting through the tall windows of her bedroom, caught the bright, golden strains of her magnificent coronal of brown hair, and made a sort of halo about her head. She gazed for a moment at the vivid tints of the sky, and then, sighing wearily, she resumed her monotonous walk from one end of the great room to the other.

This scene is so present to my mind, in spite of the many years which have elapsed since it took place, that when I close my eyes I seem still to see the Empress as she looked on that day, with the pained expression which did not mar the beauty of her face, but only emphasized the

angelic suavity of her features, and made her
look, in the trailing white draperies of her dinner-
gown, like some creature belonging to another
world than ours, far removed from our petty,
narrow-minded, shackled sphere.

The fair body of the Empress now lies at rest,
but our minds are too gross to know whether her
spirit is not still tormented by the oppressive
sense of injustice which made her life a long
martyrdom; and yet not a pen is grasped to
vindicate her memory, not a voice raised to refute
the inane calumnies which from start to finish
have pursued her during the entire course of her
career as a sovereign. I consider, therefore, that I
am but discharging a debt of honor in placing
before the public a true and authentic version of
that career, so nobly accomplished, so bitterly
criticised always.

That this work is also one of love may serve to
heap coals of fire upon the heads of those who
knew her well, too, but who took a fiendish
delight in lending color, by their words and attitude, to the ever-recurring and increasing society
and press reports which strove to give the masses
an entirely false idea of the Empress's personality, and which mercilessly placed her in the pil-
lory of an unfair and ignorant judgment.

Among many other things, as I have just mentioned, she was accused of having an unbalanced
mind. This was a cruel mistake, for there was no
more accomplished, level-headed, and sagacious
woman in the length and breadth of Europe than
she. But her horror of the shams and the narrow
conventionalities of modern existence made her
avoid, as much as she could, the requirements of
a bauble-loving, vulgar social system—truly an

unpardonable crime in the eyes of both classes and masses, and one which has led society to punish it by screaming over the very house-tops that the Empress's mind was "unbalanced." Would to Heaven that there were in this sad planet of ours more such "unbalanced" minds and less of those who, from a worldly point of view, are so admirably constructed that they find their greatest joy in tearing to shreds whatever they are unable to understand—namely, that which soars so immensely above them!

The void left by her death is one which can never be filled. She was too perfect, too different from other women, not to arouse the bitterest criticisms on their part. There were times when the temptation to cast off all trammels and ceremonies became too strong for her to withstand; it was then that she went away on her long, restless travels, freeing herself thus from the horrible incubus of perpetual show and parade.

Since an incurable sorrow befell her, ten years ago, she was almost perpetually on the wing; the iron was in her soul, the knotted cords about her waist, but she always bore a brave countenance, for she could not endure that the world should pity her. She was never heard to say an unkind thing or known to do one. Generous to a fault, she had not a trace of selfishness in her grand nature, and always spared those about her as much as possible. But she did not understand the art of forgetting, of laughing and dancing when her heart was full of sorrow; she did not take kindly to fools and their follies, and refused to make a perpetual show-figure of herself for the benefit of a pageant-loving public. Those were her crimes. How unpardonable they were

every sensible worldling will readily understand.
Her lovely face and her luminous eyes were
accused of being too sad. Alas! it was the sadness
of a noble nature that has borne the burden of
other people's sins, faults, and lack of comprehension.

She expected death at any moment, and
looked upon it more in the light of a deliverance
than in that of a dreaded foe. This, and this alone,
brings a shade of comfort to the hearts of those
whom she loved and who loved her, for now they
know that at least she has in a measure found
repose, and that the throbbing and aching
despair which tortured the latter portion of her
life has been lulled by the mighty hand of the
Great Consoler.

Cold and impassive and mute as she was
believed to be, the Empress possessed so warm a
heart, so enthusiastic a soul, that when one had
once succeeded in reaching her inner nature
through its frigid envelope, one could easily imagine what the sufferings must have been which
brought about this stifling of all outward sign of
tenderness and emotion. To me she talked without restraint, during our long rides on the
Hungarian Pùsztá, our endless tramps in the
mountains and forests of Upper Austria and
Carinthia, and also at night, when she was supposed to have retired, and when we sat alone in
the library, which invariably formed a portion of
her private apartments wherever she went. Thus I
heard wellnigh every detail of her existence, from
the moment when, a girl of sixteen, she united
herself to the handsome and dashing young
sovereign who had fallen in love at first sight with
her matchless beauty.

This marriage between the ruler of a great country and the little daughter of the impoverished Duke Maximilian, in Bavaria, is one of the most poetical and romantic pages of modern history. It has been often told, but has thereby lost none of its charm, for it is too sweetly quaint and unique ever to become vulgarized by repetition.

Little Princess Elisabeth was literally idolized in Bavaria, and to this day the peasants who hang her picture as that of a saint in all their cottages still call her "Unsere Kaiserin" (Our Empress), forgetful of the fact that this title now belongs to the Empress of Germany. I may add that Emperor William and his consort are by no means beloved or admired in the dominions of their ally, the King of Bavaria. In those far-off days Elisabeth enjoyed an almost unlimited amount of liberty, and was called by everybody "The Rose of Possenhoffen," Possenhoffen being the name of Duke Maximilian's castle and estate. She ran about like a young fawn, untrammelled and unwatched, for the Duke was by no means a wealthy man, and all his disposable means were lavished upon the education of his older daughters and of his sons, who he expected would all make brilliant marriages. And thus did lovely Princess "Cinderella" stay at home and roam about at her own sweet will under the grand old trees of the great forests, sometimes on the pony which was her great pride and joy and which rejoiced in the name of "Punch," often on foot, indulging her passion for wild flowers and fruit, and coming home with her arms full of mountain treasures, her lips stained by the juice of berries, which she gathered amid the undergrowth of the osmunda-bushes and the trailing ivy, and her

luxuriant hair tossed upon her shoulders, surrounding her entire form with a wavy cloud of
brightness. She hunted and shot with her brothers, especially with Prince Karl-Theodore, who
was her favorite. At that time the young fellow
was already a budding philanthropist, and, with
the assistance of his dear little sister, would
attend to the ills and aches of the peasants, giving
decided signs of the genius which was to make
him later one of the cleverest doctors and oculists
of our day.

The magnificent medical establishment now
managed by Duke Charles-Theodore is situated
at Kreuth, on the slopes of Hohenstein, one of the
Bavarian Alps, overlooking the lovely Tegernsee.
Early in the eighth century the Benedictine
monks, who had their head-quarters at Tegernsee, obtained possession of all the land in that
neighborhood. The good fathers, skilful doctors in
their way, were not long in discovering the cura-
tive qualities of the little sulphur springs on the
Hohenstein plateau. They built by the side of it a
hospital, to which the delicate members of the
Order used to retire from time to time to recruit
their strength. As years passed this hospital was
replaced by a much larger one, and even up to
1803, when the Order was dissolved, Kreuth
remained the regular health resort of the Benedictine monks. The hospital was then turned into a
farm-house. In 1813, however, it was rebuilt by
King Max of Bavaria, who restored the old *bade-
haus* (bath house) and erected yet another one. So
long as he lived the place was used as a convales-
cent home, and when at his death it passed into
the hands of his widow, it was with the condition
attached to it that a certain number of poor

people should every year be hospitably entertained there. It was his wish that Kreuth should
remain a charitable institution.

At Meran the Duke has established also a
large hospital and sanitarium, with the assistance of his sister-in-law, Archduchess Maria-
Theresa of Austria. Indeed, there is no end to the
good which he has done in every direction, and
his medical and charitable labors are boundless.
He is especially famous for the many cures which
he has effected upon people threatened with
blindness.

Elisabeth was forever coming into the
peasants' homes and doing them some kind turn
or other. When the rain and storms of November
set in she would run right among them for shelter, and would sit down beside the hearth and
drink a glass of milk, chatting away just as if she
were one of themselves. Her greatest sorrow was
that she had not much pocket-money to make her
humble friends presents with, and so during the
long winter evenings she was in the habit of
making up with her own deft fingers some warm
clothing for the many little children who were her
dearest protégés, and all sorts of pretty little gifts,
which are preserved as relics, and in some
instances under glass cases, in the châlets which
nestle around Possenhoffen. Her skill as a rider is
proverbial in Bavaria, and the peasants still
relate, with considerable relish, how she jumped
over some perilous obstacles which had never
been attempted by anybody before and have
never been cleared since.

The young girl had even then this intense love
of nature and fine scenery which distinguished
her throughout her life. Buchensteiner, who was

her favorite guide in later years during her long
mountaineering expeditions in the Tyrol, said,
when speaking about her: "Often, when I take
people over the mountains, I wonder what they
came there for. They do not seem to give the
beautiful spectacle before them a thought, and
the blue sky above their heads, as well as the
green-clad slopes of the high hills, or the awe-
inspiring abysses which yawn before their feet,
seem to make no impression upon them. But
when her Majesty came to some point from which
there was a more than usually fine view to
admire, my heart felt like bursting with joy as I
watched her gazing into the far distance, with a
look upon her face just as if she were inwardly
praying. Once, I remember, I took her to a very
romantically situated and lonely farm, away up
in the mountains. This farm, though belonging to
the Crown, was in the hands of a family composed of seven brothers and seven sisters—this
sounds like a fairy tale, doesn't it? but still it is
so—and the mistress and manager of them all
was the elder sister, a masterful kind of a wench,
who had a will of her own and who ordered
everybody about just as a general does his troops.
It was on a warm summer afternoon that we
reached this particular corner of the Tyrolese
Alps, and her Majesty, who was tired and thirsty,
sat down on a fallen tree-trunk to rest. The
mistress of the farm, who was standing at the
door of the cow-stables, inquired if she would not
like her to fetch out a chair; but the Empress
declined this offer, and asked if she could have a
glass of milk to drink.

"'Milk is not good for you, you are too warm,'
replied the 'Sennerin,' and running into the house

she soon came back with a stone bottle and a glass, into which she poured some 'Kirschwasser!' This made the Empress laugh, and giving me the glass to drink, she again asked for some milk, and followed the girl into the stable to watch her milk a fine black cow, for, according to the 'Sennerin,' 'Cold milk would not do at all, but newly drawn would not hurt!' She stood looking at her visitor while the latter drank the large bowlful provided for her; and when, after thanking her before proceeding upon her walk, the Empress handed her a gold piece, the 'Sennerin,' amazed at the amount paid for such a homely luxury, turned to me and whispered, 'Who is she, to give so much for a mouthful of milk?' 'The Empress,' I chuckled. 'The blessing of the saints be on us!' exclaimed the startled girl. 'What, the Empress! and I let her pay for the milk, although the farm and the cows and everything around here belong to her?'

"Then glancing after the slender, black-robed figure which was beginning to disappear under the drooping boughs of the pine-trees, she continued: 'That's a piece of money I'll never spend. I'll bore a hole through it and wear it round my neck, for I know it will bring me good luck.'"

For many years the Empress revisited her old home at Possenhoffen every summer, and, when there, resumed her wanderings in forest and on mountain and her visits to the peasants, just as if she had not changed her position as a poor little princess for the rank and status of a great and powerful empress. She used to say that she was never so happy as when in Bavaria, and the good people there declare to this day that had she come to take up her abode in their midst after the tragedy of Mayerling, which so completely broke her heart, she would have found consolation, and would not have become, as she did, a wanderer on the face of the earth in search of change from the monotony of her everlasting sufferings.

Nevertheless, after the catastrophe which brought about the death of her cousin, King Louis of Bavaria, who had always been, in spite of his mad and erratic ways, a great favorite of hers, she feared to go back to Bavaria, lest it should recall to her mind the shocking scene of which she was almost a witness; for at the time when it occurred she was staying at a castle on the opposite shore of Lake Starnberg, practically within view of the spot where the drowning took place, and just about where the King would have landed had he succeeded, as was evidently his intention, in swimming across. The death of the handsome King of Bavaria, in the Starnberg "See," has been often told, and yet, like this ill-fated monarch's life, it is so romantic and extraordinary that it is still a frequent topic of conversation at Munich.

The King had been for some time becoming more and more difficult to manage, and had accordingly to be continually watched for fear of his doing himself or others some injury. His one idea was to escape from his attendants and to try to get over the frontier, for he was convinced that he would then be safe from any further danger of incarceration. Accordingly, one evening he persuaded the doctor under whose immediate care he was to permit him to take his post-prandial stroll along the edge of the water. The moon was shining brightly, and the glitter of its rays on the lake, which had always possessed a powerful

attraction for Louis, seemed to fill him with
extreme delight. He broke out into exclamations
of enthusiasm as he watched the fleeting shadows of the tall reeds which swayed above the
rippling surface at his feet, and affectionately
linking his arm into that of his physician, he
entreated him to send away the two servants who
were following them at a short distance, "in
order," as he said, "that these menials might not
mar his perfect enjoyment of this lovely night-
stroll." Confident that his turbulent patient was
in an unusually manageable mood, the doctor
granted this request, and chatting pleasantly
with his royal charge, he continued his promenade. Suddenly, without the slightest warning,
the King made a bound and precipitated the
unfortunate physician under the water, and
jumping in after him held him beneath the surface until his struggles ceased. He thereupon
started to swim across the lake, imagining that
on the opposite shore he would find plenty of
assistance, as he was aware that the peasantry
were so fond of him that they had been on the
point of rising *en masse* throughout the kingdom
when they heard of his being placed under
restraint. After he had swum a few strokes, however, congestion, due to his immersion in water of
a very low temperature immediately after a heavy
meal, supervened. This serves to explain how it
was that when his corpse was found his lungs
were free from water, whereas the contrary was
the case with those of the doctor.

Notwithstanding her proximity, the news of
this awful incident did not reach the Empress
until the next afternoon. Strangely enough,
during the previous night she had alarmed her

attendants by an agonized scream soon after
retiring to her bed. On hurrying to her chamber,
her women found her terror-stricken, she having
just awakened from a dream in which she had
seen King Louis standing by her bedside, his
clothes dripping with water, which ran in such
quantities from his hair and garments that she
fancied that she was going to be drowned thereby. When she received the news, she caused
herself to be rowed across the lake to her cousin's
castle, and demanded to see his body. She had
not seen him for some time, for his mental and
physical condition had been such that visitors,
even when belonging to his family, were not
allowed by his medical attendants to be brought
into his presence, and she was much shocked by
the change which his long mental trouble and
awful death had worked. She laid a bunch of
white blossoms between his folded hands, and
knelt down in prayer by his side, requesting all
those present to leave the room. For nearly an
hour they awaited her return, and at length,
alarmed beyond measure, the Grand-Mistress of
her household ventured to enter the apartment,
where she found the Empress stretched upon the
floor and apparently lifeless. It was only with
the greatest difficulty that she was restored to
consciousness, and when at length she opened
her eyes, she stared wildly about her for some
moments, and then cried, in a shaking voice:

"For God's sake, release the King from the
mortuary chapel. He is not really dead; he is only
pretending to be so, in order to be left in peace
and quietness, and not to be tormented any
longer."

Her nerves were so shattered by this dismal

affair that it was feared that she might be stricken down by some serious illness, and the impression produced upon her by this last and terrible proof of the madness of her cousin preyed upon her mind for a very long time. This is more than sufficiently proved by the fact that when the physicians who went to Mayerling to perform the autopsy upon Crown Prince Rudolph returned to the Hofburg, and declared that he had given himself death in a moment of temporary mental aberration, she sought out the Emperor, and entering his study, in her long black sweeping garments, she held out towards him her little quivering hands and said, with a sob:

"Franz, pardon me; I had no right to marry. Madness is in my family, and I have brought it into yours."

Poor, tender-hearted woman, always ready to take all blame upon herself, she yet knew well that it is not in the younger but in the elder branch of the House of Wittelsbach that there has been, and still is, lunacy, and it was with a great deal of trouble that the Emperor comforted her by gently and tenderly saying:

"You brought nothing but what is good and sweet with you when you married me, and I, my dear, have never been worthy of you in any way."

Possenhoffen was a truly befitting place for the imperial idyl which preceded the marriage of Franz-Joseph and Elisabeth. Every one knows how the Emperor, soon after his arrival at his future father-in-law's castle to celebrate his betrothal with Duke Maximilian's eldest daughter, met under the dense shadows of the parklike woods a child, clothed in a short white frock, with

a wonderful mass of wavy, silken, chestnut hair
falling about her slim girlish figure, down to her
tiny feet, and with a brace of large white deer-
hounds leaping about her. With a child's impul-
siveness she threw her arms about the neck of
this imperial cousin of whom she had heard so
often, as of a new brother that was to be, but
whom she had never met, and merely recognized
from the portraits she had seen of him. The
sorcery of her luminous sapphire-hued eyes, the
witchery of a smile which later on became celebrated throughout Europe for its radiant charm,
combined to rob the young monarch of his
heart.

He linked her arm within his and tried to
draw her towards the castle, but the young Princess would not allow this.

"They would be awfully angry with me if I
mixed with the grown-up ones," she said, laughing. "They have all to be married away before I
am allowed to appear."

"That's what we are going to see," replied the
deeply smitten Emperor. "Go and dress for dinner and meet me in the hall before I go down, my
sweet! I'll manage the rest."

Completely subjugated, the young girl flew
towards the great old building, while the Emperor
marched off to his rooms, vowing to himself that
he would win that little fairy princess in spite of
all objections that might be put forward. Just as,
after terminating his elaborate toilet, he was
about to step into the hall, he heard two voices
proceeding from behind a door, which was not
quite closed. The louder and angrier of the two
was saying:

"Please don't, Princess; you know that you

have been forbidden to let yourself be seen."

"I shall do so, just the same, Countess," murmured the other voice, which Franz-Joseph recognized as belonging to Elisabeth. The door opened wide, and the charming girl, followed by a lady-in-waiting, whose flashing eyes and ruffled gray locks denoted the greatest agitation, appeared in the hall.

"Let us go down together, my cousin," said the Emperor, offering Elisabeth his arm; and in spite of the frowns and entreaties of the old Countess, he drew the radiant creature, who had grown as white as a moonbeam, towards the broad flight of steps leading down to the terrace, where Duke Maximilian and Duchess Ludovica of Bavaria were waiting, surrounded by all their other children, the appearance of their august guest. At the sight of the handsome young couple a look of surprise, chagrin, and thorough disapproval started from the eyes of all present; but it was too late to interfere, for the mischief was done, and that same evening, closeted with the Duke, the Emperor declared to him that his plans had altered and formally asked from the infuriated old gentleman the favor of his youngest daughter's hand.

A scene of much violence took place. Both men were overbearing and quick-tempered, and the affront put upon his eldest daughter could not but seem difficult of acceptance to the old Duke. The Emperor, at last losing all patience, sprang from his chair and declared in his most fiery manner that, should his request be rejected, he would start instantly for his own dominions, and marry neither one nor the other of his host's fair daughters; nor for the matter of that would he

marry at all, little heeding the future of his
empire, since the wound at his heart would not
heal sufficiently to permit of his ever thinking of
any woman but that one girl whom he had met
for the first time a few hours previously!

Thus forced from his last intrenchments, the
Duke reluctantly yielded, much to the astonishment of his family and *entourage,* for he was an
extraordinarily obstinate old gentleman in general. During that time the little Princess, whose
heart had been awakened by the first kiss of
"Prince Charming," was sobbing in her narrow
white bed and comparing herself anew to Cinderella, for she had not as yet made her début at her
father's small court, and she could not but dread
the consequences of her incredible disobedience
to her parent's orders.

She would, so she thought, in all probability,
not again see the stalwart, blue-eyed youth who
had called her "My lovely little cousin," and
whose caressing looks and tender words had
created so deep an impression upon her. Little did
she guess that he was to be the magician who
would transform her peaceful, lonely life into the
most brilliant of earthly lots, and, more is the
pity, also the saddest which has ever been the
portion of an imperial lady.

These details were given to me by a dear
old woman who was the Empress's nurse from
earliest childhood, and who died not so very long
ago. She it was who told me of this, the girl's first
sorrow, and of that night when at last, exhausted
by such unusual weeping, she fell back on her
pillows, sleeping the dreamless sleep of innocent
unhappiness under the moon-rays which stole
through the stained glass of her windows and

glittered on her long, wet eyelashes.

"Ah, my darling, my beauty; how much too pretty and too sweet and too pure she was for all that was to come!" the old woman often said to me.

"And on her bridal-day how delicate and dainty and like an angel she looked, in spite of the weight of her court-mantle and of the heavy jewels bruising her tender flesh! But she was happy then; they had not yet crushed all joy out of her heart. She thought that life was one long festival, one endless chain of enchantment; that all people were good, and that the boundless wealth of her consort would be a magic wand with which to conjure away all the miseries of the earth wherever she went, poor child—poor little silly, loving child!"

And then large tears would roll over the withered cheeks of the old dame, and she would clench her thin hands and pour out such a torrent of maledictions upon those who had wrecked her "little child's hopes," that I could but stand by her side shuddering and thinking of my own ideals which lay already dying at my feet.

This new betrothal of the Emperor was of short duration, and within a few weeks from the fateful day on which he had met his "little Elsa" their nuptials were celebrated with all the pomp and splendor that the most magnificent and ceremonial-loving court of Europe could lend to such espousals. At the moment when the young monarch slipped the golden circlet upon her finger the bride grew deadly pale, and glanced at the magnificent crowd which filled the sacred edifice with a gleam of anxiety and pain in her eyes. Did she at that moment foresee that these gorgeously

clad nobles, headed by the members of her husband's family and by those of her own, were
already hatching the plots which were to turn her
treasures into mere dross and ashes? None can
say, for with the instinctive dignity and courage
which never failed her, she raised her drooping
head and faced the rest of the ordeal without
flinching.

The marriage ceremony was celebrated on the
24th of April, 1854, by Prince Archbishop Raus-
cher, and during a whole week Vienna was given
over to the most magnificent series of feasts
which its ancient walls had ever witnessed. Soon
afterwards the imperial couple undertook a round
of visits throughout their dominions, extending
their voyage to Hungary, Lombardy, and Venice,
where the beauty of the Empress created the
greatest possible impression.

How happy these two young, handsome, and
kind-hearted people could have been had not
Archduchess Sophia interfered!

If ever there was an indisputable example of
the harm which can be worked by a mother-
in-law's jealous influence upon the future existence of a loving couple, it is to be found in the
relations which almost at once established themselves between the imperial pair and the grim
Archduchess, who was known at court under the
title of "Madame Mère" (Madame Mother).

Clever as few women are, the Archduchess
possessed a real genius for management. A
remarkable tactician, she had over her son a
sway which she never dreamed of surrendering
into other hands, and little did she care whether
her interference was likely to imperil the happiness of her child so long as she herself, in a

political and in a private capacity, reigned
supreme. She hated her daughter-in-law, whom
she alluded to as "that pretty wax-doll;" and,
heedless of the girl's feelings, she deliberately set
her aside, making it impossible for her to assume
her natural place towards court and country.
Indeed, she went so far, at last, as to insinuate
herself absolutely between those two idyllic lovers, who would but for her overbearing selfishness have, perchance, enjoyed the perfect bliss of
a well-assorted union.

Of course, at that time Elisabeth was very
much in love with her "Franz," not perhaps in
the way suggested by this vastly comprehensive
expression; for if the Empress possessed one
fault—many would call it a virtue—it was an
absolute lack of human passion. She had married, not in the least knowing what marriage
meant, and her extreme youth, combined with
that spirituality which causes the senses to sleep
sometimes forever, made it impossible for her to
share her imperial lover's ardent feelings. The
obligations of such a love had no charm for her;
indeed, as I heard it from her own lips, they at
first frightened her. She was a quaint combination of an angel and a goddess, a Greek
nymph and a Christian virgin blended in one; her
mother-in-law described her as a child, narrowly
educated, lacking in comprehension and sympathy, and who ought to be more than satisfied with
the high estate, boundless wealth, and brilliant
surroundings which had now become hers!

Infinitely cold, very cruel and tenacious, and
an *intrigante* (intriguer) in the full sense of the
word, the Archduchess showed plainly the
immense scorn which she felt at seeing her son,

one of the mightiest rulers of this world, fall more
and more under the sway of a mere child of
sixteen. Her only comfort lay in the one belief that
he would soon tire of his new plaything, become
satiated with the peach when once the bloom had
been rubbed from it, and cease to hearken to the
song of the little bird which she deemed had but
one note in its répertoire, and would sing it so
constantly that its owner would feel ready to
wring its tender little throat into silence.

She knew well that her boy had inherited the
flightiness and inconstancy of his race, and upon
this knowledge did she build her plan of battle.
Yet although contemptuous of what she termed
his momentary weakness, she nevertheless
attached herself more closely to him than she had
ever done before; she forced him to seek her
advice, nay, she pressed her opinion upon him
ceaselessly and worked untiringly both by day
and night to maintain the supremacy which she
cherished above all other things.

Having ascended the throne at a moment
when the country was shaken to its very centre,
the Emperor had from the beginning, in spite of
his extreme youth, shown a statecraft, a good
sense, and an energy which will hardly be appreciated until the history of our century is written.
During the first years of his reign he had, however, naturally enough, turned for support in the
hours of discouragement and of fatigue to the
dauntless strength of mind which his mother
possessed in so high a degree, and during the
dark days when his vast empire all but slipped
from his grasp he was glad to feel her at his side,
urging him on, and helping him as no other coun-
sellor could have done. This the Archduchess

utilized later, when peace was restored and when she had nothing greater to dread than the too absorbing love of a maiden, which she feared might prove an obstacle to the continuance of her former position with regard to the great ruler who was her favorite child. She loved him too, undoubtedly, but she loved power better still, and her despotism became wellnigh unbearable after the advent of Elisabeth at the court, where she had until then played the leading rôle.

"Uneasy lies the head that wears a crown!" Surely this old maxim was never more pathetically verified than by the life of Emperor Franz-Joseph of Austria. None can deny that the cup of bitterness of this unfortunate monarch, who for half a century has now worn the Hapsburg crown of thorns, and who ever since the day when, in 1848, he was forced by his mother to become the ruler of Austria-Hungary in lieu of his uncle, Emperor Ferdinand, "the kind-hearted," has been filled to overflowing. Misfortunes and catastrophes have overtaken him from all sides. He saw his Italian provinces wrenched from him by Napoleon III., who dictated peace to him on his own terms after Solferino and Magenta. The six weeks' war which he waged with Germany ended for him at Sadowa with humiliation and sorrow. He lost his beloved brother Maximilian in an ignominious fashion in Mexico; his only son, the pride and joy of his heart, was taken from him by an unrelenting fate and under circumstances which made his death especially painful for the Emperor to endure; his sister-in-law, the Duchess d'Alençon, to whom he was devotedly attached, was burned alive at the appalling conflagration of the Bazar de la Charité; his favorite niece, the Queen Regent of Spain, was humbled into the dust by the failure of her subjects to hold their own in the war against America; and, to cap the climax of his distress, his beautiful and lovely consort was foully slain by the knife of an Anarchist.

Surely such a series of calamities was not deserved by Franz-Joseph, for his sins have been, after all, but the faults of a man whose position was so exalted, whose rank so high, and whose personal charm so great, that he would have needed a resolution more than human to resist the countless temptations continually thrown in his way. One can say of him that he has been and still is the most popular and sincerely beloved monarch in all Christendom, beloved, too, by both rich and poor, by the high-born and by the humbler classes. To the latter in particular he has been always accessible, ever ready to lend an ear to their personal troubles and grievances, and eager to redress them. Nothing is more character-istic of this than the scenes which take place in his antechamber on Monday and Thursday mornings when he is at Vienna. The great ante-room is thronged with cardinals and prelates, with generals and statesmen, with great nobles and magnates, and mingling with all these high and mighty personages are Bohemian brick-layers, miserable creatures from the poorer quar-ters of Vienna, and village priests, all waiting to submit their troubles, their sorrows, their wrongs, and their grievances to "unsern Guten Kaiser" (our good Emperor). I need scarcely add that, very much in accordance with the teachings of the New Testament, it is the village priest who is generally received before the scarlet-robed

EMPEROR FRANZ-JOSEPH AT THE TIME OF HIS
ACCESSION TO THE AUSTRIAN THRONE IN 1848

cardinal, the poorly clad peasant before the cabinet minister in his gold-embroidered uniform, and the farmer before the great territorial magnate.

Gay and thoughtless as was Franz-Joseph before he ascended the throne, he proved thereafter that he really meant what he said when, on the early morning of December 2, 1848, after his father had informed him that Emperor Ferdinand had abdicated and that he, Archduke Francis-Charles, renounced his right of succession to the throne in favor of his eldest son, he pronounced the historic sentence, "Good-bye to the days of my youth."

Franz-Joseph was born on the 18th of August, 1830, during the reign of his grandfather, Emperor Francis, and was from the very day of his birth regarded, especially by his mother, Archduchess Sophia, as being the natural heir to the crown, for his father's elder brother, Ferdinand, who occupied the throne of Austria-Hungary from 1835 until 1848, had no children, and was always in an extremely delicate state of health. On March 13, 1848, revolution broke out in Vienna. Prince Metternich, who had until then been absolute master of all the foreign affairs of the country, was compelled to fly, and poor, weak Emperor Ferdinand granted his people a constitutional government, including more or less liberty of the press, the so-called right of public meetings, etc. Nevertheless, Vienna was by no means pacified or quieted; Lombardy and Venetia broke out into open rebellion, the King of Sardinia declared war against Austria, and the great Austrian leader, Field-Marshal Radetzky, was forced to evacuate Milan. It was at this

moment that Franz-Joseph joined the Austrian
army at Verona, and displayed such personal
courage during the many bloody engagements
which devasted Lombardy during the month of
May that Radetzky expressed his opinion with
regard to the certainty of the young Archduke
becoming one of the greatest generals of his day.
In the meanwhile Emperor Ferdinand and his
court had left Vienna for Innsbruck, in the Tyrol,
and, pressed hard by the machinations of Archduchess Sophia, finally decided to relinquish the
reins of government to the stronger and younger
hands of his nephew, Franz-Joseph. The ceremony of abdication took place on December 2,
1848, at the Archiepiscopal Palace of Olmütz, in
the presence of Archduchess Sophia, Archduke
Francis-Charles, her husband, the Cabinet Ministers of the Empire, Prince Windischgratz, Count
Grünne, the Banus of Croatia, Baron Jellachich,
who was one of the most ardent followers of Archduchess Sophia, and several important members
of the imperial family.

Solemnly and impressively, although in a
slightly trembling voice, Emperor Ferdinand pronounced the words which made him pass from
the rank of a ruling sovereign to that of a mere
onlooker upon the doings of his country:

"For very weighty reasons we have irrevocably decided to lay down our Imperial Crown in
favor of our beloved nephew, the Most Serene
Archduke Franz-Joseph, whom we hereby declare to be of age. Our beloved brother, the Most
Serene Archduke Francis-Charles, father of our
above-mentioned most serene nephew, having
irrevocably renounced his right of succession to a
throne which belongs to him by right, according

ARCHDUCHESS SOPHIA AND THE EMPEROR WHEN A BABY

to the fundamental laws of our family, and of the state, in favor of his above-mentioned son, Franz-Joseph."

Surely never did a monarch ascend his throne under more difficult circumstances than did this young man, whose pleasure-loving, gay disposition made him bitterly regret the conditions which forced upon his shoulders so crushing a weight of responsibility.

The country was in a state of seething rebellion from one end to the other; the Hungarian Dictator, Kossuth, had declared that the Hapsburg Dynasty had forfeited its right to the crown of Hungary; in Vienna the population had adopted a sullen attitude of defiance, under the martial law instituted there, as well as at Prague; and in the Italian provinces the most awful civil war raged, for the hatred existing between the Italians and Austrians had grown to a white-heat.

It would take too long, and would turn this work into too historical a one, to follow here, step by step, the various stages through which Austria and Hungary passed before at last peace was, after a fashion, restored.

Suffice it therefore to state that in 1853 matters had sufficiently quieted down to render admissible the words of the young Emperor, who said:

"I think that now my reign may become one of peace."

This was, however, to be far from the case, for hardly had the Emperor tried to console himself for past troubles with dreams of this new era, when on February 18, 1853, his own career came within an ace of being cut short for evermore. While Franz-Joseph was walking on the old fortifications of the inner town of Vienna, a Hungarian of the name of Joseph Libenyi threw himself upon the young monarch and plunged a long dagger into the back of his neck. Fortunately the stiff military collar of the Emperor's coat somewhat paralyzed the violence of the stroke. But it was nevertheless a most dangerous wound, and Count O'Donnel, who was then aide-de-camp to the Emperor, and who had accompanied him on that morning, fearing that the weapon might have been poisoned, courageously sucked the wound. The Emperor, who had until that moment remained upright, and entreated the crowd, which had immediately gathered, not to hurt his would-be assassin, fell fainting to the ground.

It is on the spot where this *attentate* (criminal attempt) took place that now stands the "Votiv-Kirche," which is one of the finest and most severely and magnificently Gothic churches in the whole world.

None can deny that Franz-Joseph must have been endowed with more than ordinary sagacity and tact to be able to subdue the many turbulent peoples under his rule, and to obtain over them an authority which is really enormous. His way of speaking with those who seek an audience from him, his apparent interest in the most trivial details concerning those who are favored by an interview with him, are very characteristic. At the reception of delegations, his Majesty makes a point of wearing a Hungarian uniform to receive Magyars; that of an Austrian officer when greeting his Cisleithan subjects, and the uniform of a Polish regiment when welcoming Poles. On these occasions he speaks to more than a hundred people in rapid succession, and every one of his

remarks shows a thorough acquaintance with all
the affairs, great and small, of the monarchy.
Foreign affairs and railway tariffs, commercial
treaties and parliamentary procedure, the army,
the navy, agriculture, the budget, the troublesome young Czechs, and the poor Jewish population in Galicia—all form the subjects of his kindly
and paternal remarks. Nor is the comic element
always wanting in these conversations. Once,
when addressing a Polish delegate, Franz-Joseph
asked how things were going on in Galicia. "Oh,
sire, we are suffering from a dreadful plague of
field-mice," answered the delegate, ruefully. "Ah,
das ist recht fatal" (Ah, that is very unfortunate),
answered the Emperor, with a smile.

All these things are trifles, yet they mean a
good deal, for every delegate comes away happy
after having spoken with the Emperor, and feeling that his Majesty is quite as much interested in
his particular business, whatever that may be, as
he is himself. If he had a grievance, he has had an
opportunity of making it known. If he had a favor
to ask, the chance of so doing has been given to
him. Now multiply the impression produced upon
one hundred and twenty delegates a thousand or
a hundred thousand fold, by remembering that
twice a week the Emperor is accessible to all
classes of his subjects, and the result may be
easily imagined. Any one who has serious business with him may see him, and speak with him
quite alone, without even a secretary being present. The applicant, whatever may be his station,
is ushered into a study and finds the Emperor in
a plain uniform, without a single decoration. He
may say what he likes, sure of being hearkened
to with patient attention. The scenes that have

been enacted in the Emperor's private chamber
no chronicler will ever tell. Of the acts of kindness, mercy, and charity shown, of the swift
redress of wrongs, of the shrewd, soldierly advice
given, and of the imperial magnanimity displayed
at all times, no record has been kept, excepting in
the Emperor's own memory, if even there.

The war with Italy, in 1859, almost broke his
Majesty's proud heart; and after the peace of Villa
Franca, which was signed by Franz-Joseph and
Napoleon III. on July 11th, and confirmed at
Zurich in the following November, the Emperor
returned to Vienna in a very sad and dejected
mood. There can be no doubt whatsoever that on
the luckless battle-fields of Italy he had courted
death. After Solferino, as he was retreating with
his escort, a French battery opened fire on the
imperial party. The Emperor checked his charger,
and remained as motionless as a statue carved
out of stone under the burning shower of iron
which fell about him. Death, however, strongly
resembles a coquette, and evades those who seek
her. Thus was the unfortunate sovereign, who
has since been called "Franz-Joseph the Un-
lucky," spared, so that he might drain to the very
dregs his cup of misfortune and sorrow.

One of the heaviest of these sorrows was
caused by the stormy days of 1866, when
Bismarck defeated the Austrian forces at
Sadowa; for this capped the climax of the
Emperor's humiliation, and embittered him to
such an extent that it was only in 1873, when
the first Universal International Exhibition,
which was held at Vienna, took place, that he
began to realize how much he had really done for
his country, and how prosperous it had become

in his hands. Enlightenment and progress had indeed been made to follow wherever his sceptre pointed. Trade and commerce had revived, and the city of Vienna itself was fast becoming one of the handsomest in the universe.

The one flaw in a character which was otherwise so fine was the Emperor's love for flirtations of a most pronounced description. It was believed by him, as by others who thought that they knew him well, that his love match with a princess so beautiful and so completely attractive as Elisabeth would cure him of this hereditary trait. This was, however, a lamentable error, and the origin of the Empress's first poignant sorrows is to be found in the *légèreté* (inconstancy) of her consort, whose numerous infidelities made her shed so many tears in secret.

CHAPTER II

As soon as the young couple were definitely established at Vienna, *le parti de Madame Mère* (the party of Madame Mère) grew every day stronger, covert taunts were not spared to the young Empress, who, with smiling lips and an aching heart, was made to understand that the portionless daughter of a mere non-royal duke was not worthy of the honor that had been done her. She was treated by all with a coldness and disdain calculated to break the spirit of a less courageous woman, but as she always hated to be an object of pity, she never complained to the Emperor, who, save in her gradual if very marked recoil from all those appearances in public which she could possibly avoid, and in her increasing sadness, noticed no change in her. He himself treated her with the most constant courtesy and solicitous care, but a misunderstanding arose between them, fomented by wounded pride and feeling on her side, and on his by the continual intriguing which was brought to bear upon him.

Yet Elisabeth still dearly loved the man who had come into her life to change, at first, all its dulness into fields of light and of joy; the distant sound of his step still thrilled her with delight, the very sound of his voice made her pulses beat quicker, but the spiritual and enthusiastic love

which she bore him was little by little forced back
into the innermost recesses of her heart, and the
very excess of it held her pale and silent when she
should have confided her sufferings to him, for
fear of appearing in his eyes the troublesome
child her mother-in-law told her so frequently
that she was.

It was a pity indeed that the Emperor had no
leisure, or no desire, to study his wife's character
with more care then, for he would easily have
discerned those gifts, mental and intellectual,
which make up the noblest of temperaments. He
was as yet violently, passionately in love with her
matchless beauty, but affairs of state, social suc-
cesses, out-door sports, to which he gave almost
his every free moment, and the beginning of a
vague return to his former less commendable
pleasures, widened daily the gulf which was to
force them apart more and more as time went on.
Nor can Franz-Joseph be blamed very severely
either, at that time, for this state of affairs.
Women had thrown themselves into his arms
from his earliest youth, not only for the sake of
his rank and sovereign position, but also on
account of his handsome face and presence, of
his winning manner, and of the many gifts and
talents which made him one of the most attractive of men. He consequently, in spite of his
ever singularly chivalrous ways, did not esteem
women very highly; they had flattered and
cajoled him too much for that, and wooed him
also, until something very like contempt took the
place of gratitude where they were concerned. His
wife was to him a thing apart, so lovely and pure
and innocent that she fulfilled his ideal of absolute perfection; but unfortunately he fell into the

EMPEROR FRANZ-JOSEPH IN 1855

unpardonable error of believing her to be too young, too inexperienced, and too indifferent to become his real companion and comrade.

Poor Empress! One year after her marriage her future seemed so immensely long and wearisome that she felt disheartened when she thought of it; her rank was too lofty, her riches too great for ambition to present any luring charm for her, especially as all inroads into politics were forbidden to her by "Madame Mère's" own insatiate ambition in that direction. What waste this all made of a superfine nature, sedulously forced back into apparent worthlessness!

Jealousy had not at that time entered her heart, but this also was not long to be spared her. One morning the old nurse to whom I referred before, and who had remained in her service, entered her Majesty's dressing-room at the usual hour, and not finding her there, ventured to go and seek her in the little adjoining oratory.

This small sanctuary was a favorite retreat of the Empress, and she had decorated it with that delicate taste so peculiarly her own. The walls were of alabaster, as was the tiny altar, above which hung a wonderful crucifix of onyx and silver; golden candelabra raised their perfumed candles among a wealth of snowy blossoms, and shed a soft radiance, day and night, upon a priceless triptych of Lucas von Cranach, and upon a *prie-dieu* (a prayer desk with a kneeling bench), embroidered on white velvet by Elisabeth's clever little hands.

She herself was kneeling down, with her arms leaning on the altar-rail, her magnificent hair streaming over her loose white robe, and her head buried in her hands, while convulsive sobs

shook her whole slender form. For a moment
the old woman watched her wistfully. She knew
that her darling was not happy, but she had
never seen her display such a passion of grief
as she now beheld. Moreover, she was aware of
the fact that to this daughter of an ancient race
pity seemed the last of insults, the alms thrown
to some proud, impoverished being, which
brands him as a beggar for evermore. So she
hesitated to advance and to offer her any kind of
consolation.

Impelled, however, by the adoration which she
felt for her imperial mistress, she drew slowly
nearer and touched the weeping figure. The face
which the young Empress raised towards her had
lost in a few hours all its childish bloom: it
was the pale, haggard, drawn countenance of a
woman who had left behind her all the careless
joys of youth. More lovely, perhaps, than ever
before in its tear-glazed distress, it nevertheless
struck her old and devoted attendant's heart with
terror.

"My little one—my poor darling!" she exclaimed, reverting in her amazement and sorrow
to the fashion in which she used formerly to
address her nursling. "What have they done to
you now? Oh, the wretches! the cruel monsters!
Tell me what has hurt you so."

In a broken voice, very unlike her own, the
Empress said, shudderingly: "I wish I were dead!"

The words escaped her almost unawares; evidently when they were uttered she would have
given worlds to recall them. She grew paler than
ever, her expression hardened into something like
anger, and rising from her knees, she pushed
away her trailing hair and said, impatiently:

"You mean well, but you must not ask me such questions, for I cannot bear to pain you by refusing to confide in you, and my pain is not one which I can speak of to any living soul."

And after kissing the old woman tenderly to soften the effect caused by her words, she left her standing in deepest consternation on the threshold of the oratory, while with a firm, proud step she returned to the solitude of her bedroom.

There was at that time at court a lady who for convenience sake I shall call the Countess von L——. She was a very handsome woman, in a pink and white blonde way, à la Rubens. She was not extraordinarily refined or talented, and certainly not at all ethereal, but she was very *chic* and very amusing; she dressed admirably, and was quite the rage, especially since she was known to be "Madame Mère's" especial *protégée.* At a great ball given in honor of some foreign royalties the Emperor seemed much struck by this type of sensuous beauty, and devoted more of his time to her than strict etiquette allowed. Many an unkind, if just, comment was made about this incident, and the good souls who formed the Empress's *entourage* took good care that it should assume in her eyes the maximum of the meaning it could be made to bear. She gave no outward sign of having understood these charitable allusions, but her grave, colorless face, that had already become so cold in its innocence, now assumed an entirely novel expression, so melancholy, so thoughtful, that she was immediately taxed with moodiness and sulkiness. She now seldom smiled, and when she did so it was in a chilly, half-hearted way which was painful to behold.

Her beloved hero, the husband whom she had held would be her eternal lover, was tottering upon the pedestal of virtues which she had erected for him in her soul. All the horrors of doubt and of sin fell suddenly and without warning upon her ignorance of social wickedness, and a great disgust overcame her, for she was informed by many willing and poisonous mouths that her consort's attentions were not restricted to the fair Countess, and that there were many hours in his life spent after a fashion of which he would be more than unwilling to render her an account.

For this bitter awakening of her love-dream she was also indebted to her mother-in-law. The old lady—who then, by-the-bye, considered herself only in the very prime of life, and who had by no means abdicated her rights to universal admiration—seeing that her son was more enamored with his lovely wife than she thought it safe or desirable for him to be, managed to surround him with those temptations to which a man of the world yields so easily, and the satisfaction of which he calls by the convenient name of peccadilloes.

The Archduchess was by no means an immoral woman; she even posed as an infinitely religious one; but to her the *raison d'état* (well-being of the state) was more important than all else, and she was absolutely convinced that the influence possessed by Elisabeth over the Emperor would work to no good end. That she should bear him healthy children was all that she asked of her son's young wife; the rest had no interest for her.

This question of maternity was an all-important one, and was represented as such to the Empress, who said once, sadly, to her own mother, in one of her few moments of semi-confidence:

"Should I remain childless, I wonder if Franz would follow Napoleon's example and cause our union to be annulled?"

Much horrified, the duchess-mother, who was a kind-hearted, sagacious, and loving woman, replied, gently:

"You are unreasonable, my child; you must not become morbid. Franz loves you dearly—you know it well; and as to Napoleon, savants have proved long ere this that his heart, or what served him in lieu of one, was ossified. In my opinion he was, perhaps, the greatest general that ever existed, but he was also an ambitious wretch, who sacrificed all humanity to his own desires and interests."

"Such wretches still exist," murmured the young Empress, with a heavy sigh.

"My dearest," continued her mother, "there are two sorts of women in this world—those who always get their own way, and those who never get it. You seem to me to be one of the latter: you have remarkable abilities and talents, a deep, thoughtful mind, and you do not lack character; but what you *do* lack is the power of stooping to the level of your associates, of bending yourself to the exigencies of modernism. You belong to another period, that in which saints and martyrs existed. Do not attract notice by being too obviously the first, or break your own heart by fancying yourself to be the latter."

This conversation was repeated to me by the Empress more than twenty years after it had taken place, and she then added, with a rather wan smile:

"I am afraid, my dear, that I did not follow my mother's excellent advice, for I have often been taunted with posing both as a saint and as a martyr, although, I am sure, I never believed myself burdened with two such calamities as saintliness and martyrdom."

Duchess Ludovica in Bavaria, Empress Elisabeth's mother, was one of the most sympathetic princesses in Europe. She was the sister of the Emperor's mother, Archduchess Sophia, otherwise called at the court of Vienna, "Madame Mère," but she was a perfect antithesis to her, and her kindness, sweetness of temper, as well as her talents and remarkable sagacity, were justly celebrated. A magnificent performer on the piano, the organ, and the zither, she spoke Greek and Italian with amazing fluency, and even up to the time of her death, at the advanced age of eighty-four, she spent many hours a day in study. She was a remarkably well-preserved woman—the astounding manner in which beauty remained hers to the last may be accounted for by her invariable habit of riding and driving in all kinds of weather, and by the cold baths in which she indulged twice daily. She was an excellent mother, and deeply devoted to her husband, who died shortly before her, and almost immediately after the celebration of their golden wedding.

He was a very witty and somewhat eccentric—in fact, altogether a very interesting person. Passionately fond of dogs, he treated the numerous ones which he possessed just as if they were children, much to the amusement of his courtiers. Being, moreover, endowed with an extraordinarily original turn of mind, Duke Maximilian was the hero of many an amusing anecdote.

One day when the Duke was travelling from Munich to Vienna, without submitting himself to any of the fuss which generally surrounds the voyages of princes, a gentleman, at the moment when the train was about to steam out of the station, entered the ordinary first-class carriage in which he was established. A conversation soon began between them, in the course of which the unknown mentioned that he was one of the greatest watch-makers in Austria, and ended by asking Duke Maximilian what his profession was, and why he was going to Vienna.

"Well, to tell you the truth," replied Maximilian, "I have at present no profession, and I am going to Vienna to visit my daughter and son-in-law."

"Ah, and is your son-in-law in business?"

"Yes and no; he is a pretty busy man, if that is what you want to know."

"Has he a good position?"

"Yes, a pretty good position."

"What kind of a position is it?"

"He is an emperor."

The Viennese watch-maker began to laugh loudly, thinking, of course, that his travelling companion was joking, and when they finally arrived at their destination, the vivacious merchant, without waiting until the train had completely stopped, gave a playful dig in the ducal ribs, and jumping out of the railway carriage, called out to the astounded old gentleman:

"That was a good joke of yours, but I am not so easily taken in. Good-bye, and good luck; hope to see you again soon. Don't forget to introduce me to your imperial son-in-law some day."

At dinner that evening Duke Maximilian

related his adventure to his greatly entertained
children, and the Emperor, who was then still
exceedingly fond of fun, hastened next morning
to send for the watch-maker in question. Upon
being ushered into the Emperor's presence, the
unfortunate man, who at a glance recognized,
sitting in an arm-chair beside the Emperor's
writing-table, the benevolent-looking gentleman
with whom he had travelled from Munich on the
previous day, was frightened out of his senses.
But he was soon reassured by the Emperor's kind
smile, and, moreover, delighted beyond measure
at receiving an order for some dozen or so of his
very finest watches.

"You see," laughed the sovereign, "that my
position is not a bad one, but don't you go
envying it, for it brings with it often more thorns
than roses."

There is in the palace of Laxenburg, near
Vienna, a magnificent painting representing
Duchess Ludovica surrounded by all her beautiful daughters. The Duchess was so proud of them
that when she used in early days to go out
walking with them she would exclaim:

"Voila mon attelage de poste" (Look at my
handsome team). She might indeed be well
pleased with the extreme beauty of the princesses, for all of them were singularly comely,
although Elisabeth was, and always remained,
the pearl of them all.

Princess de la Tour-et-Taxis, who died in
1891, was a woman of a great deal of personal
charm. She resembled greatly that other sister,
the unfortunate Queen of Naples, who played so
brilliant a rôle during the siege of Gaëta, when,
placing herself at the head of her husband's

beleaguered army, she walked about the ramparts under a hail of bullets and infused her indomitable courage into the hearts of the most timid by her magnificent attitude in the face of the enemy.

Countess Trani was more like the Duchess d'Alençon, whose gentle, noble-hearted nature inclined her to think everlastingly of good works, and who employed the greatest portion of her life in succoring the poor and the afflicted. It was while working for them at the Bazar de la Charité, in Paris, that the Duchess found a terrible death among raging flames. The sorrow caused by this new tragedy, which was one of so many, drove Empress Elisabeth almost to inconsolable despair.

It is claimed that when the Duchess d'Alençon was yet a young girl her awful end was predicted to her by a gypsy, who said to her:

"Do not fear water, but beware of another element, namely, the natural enemy of water, for it will attack you when you are employed on an angel's errand and will cut short your career."

The Princess who was later on to become the Queen of Naples was at that moment with her sister, and turning to the Zingara woman, she asked her to predict her own future. Peering into the girl's eyes, and then gazing for an instant into the soft palm of her little hand, the gypsy replied:

"You will become a queen, but amid blood, war, and disaster you will lose your crown in spite of the energy and courage which you will show. Fear Red Men, for it will be through them that you will ultimately be vanquished."

Subsequently, as it is shown in history, it was by Garibaldi's "Red Men" that the King and

Queen of Naples were robbed of their crown. In both cases the gypsy spoke the truth.

The tourists who visited, a few years ago, the shores of the Starnberg Lake in the Bavarian Tyrol may still remember the brief stop of the steamer at the Possenhoffen pier, and the silvery-haired old lady who was generally standing on the verdant slopes of the château grounds, acknowledging with stately courtesy the respectful salute of the captain and of his crew.

This was Duchess Ludovica. Her life was embittered by many sorrows caused to her tender mother's heart by her children's countless misfortunes. The first of these was brought about by the extraordinary conduct of King Louis of Bavaria when he jilted Princess Sophia, later Duchess d'Alençon, in so cruel a manner. The reasons for the King's conduct in this matter are not generally known. Shortly after his engagement to the Princess a very pretty actress fell violently in love with him—he was then a most remarkably good-looking young man—and so great became her passion that she decided to try to capture the monarch's heart and to supplant in his affections the charming Princess to whom he had so lately become affianced. With a view of accomplishing this praiseworthy plan she left the stage and obtained, through the influence of some high personages whom she knew, the position of reader to the Princess, this enabling her, of course, to come into personal contact with the King. As I remarked just now, this enterprising damsel was extremely beautiful, and Louis could not very well help observing her physical advantages. When he met her he used to chat and banter, without, however, forgetting in the very slightest way his allegiance to the Princess.

One fine day the *ci-devant* (former) actress hit upon the Machiavellian idea of taking from the Princess a half-hoop of turquoises shaped like forget-me-nots, one of the many presents sent by Louis to his fiancée, and of giving it to a young officer of the King's body-guard with whom she had, for that purpose, begun a mild flirtation, requesting him to wear it for her sake. The enamoured youth was only too happy to do so, and flaunted it carelessly before the very eyes of his royal master. The character of King Louis of Bavaria was even in those days an odd one, and instead of inquiring from the young man how he came to possess this jewel, he took it for granted that the Princess was untrue to him, and in a fit of almost demoniacal fury he wrote her a quite unpardonable letter, breaking off his engagement. The unhappy girl, wounded to the heart and unable to understand what had caused such an attitude on the part of her erstwhile fiancé, was further dismayed when she discovered that her fair reader had fled from the palace and had taken up her abode in a little châlet situated within the limits of the royal park. Believing, naturally enough, that the cause of the King's behavior towards herself was to be found in his preference for her *protégée*, she sent back all the presents which he had given to her, excepting of course the turquoise ring, which she believed that she must have accidentally lost. The absence of this jewel from among the others returned to him aroused the King's suspicion, and he mentioned the fact to the lady who had caused him to act so abominably towards the Princess. They were at that moment floating about on Louis's favorite

lake in one of those swan-shaped boats for which
the "Märchen-Prinz" (Fairy-tale Prince) had so
much partiality. The moon was shining high up
in the heavens and casting its silvery glory upon
the surface of the water, and the young dame
thought this a perfectly fitting *décor de scène*
(stage set) for a sensational revelation; therefore,
casting herself at her lover's feet, she confessed to
him the trick she had played upon him in order to
win his love. Here again the singular and fiery
temper of the monarch overcame him. Taking the
kneeling girl by the waist, he flung her from him
right into the lake, and without turning his head
propelled the swan-boat towards the shore. Fortunately for the drowning lady, some game-
keepers heard her cries for help and rescued her
from a watery grave. She fled from Bavaria; and
the King hastened to Possenhoffen in order to
explain matters and make his peace with Princess Sophia. He found, however, that this was an
impossible task, for she refused to see him, and
declared that she would never consent to become
the wife of a man who had mistrusted and
insulted her.

CHAPTER III

One of the accusations which has been most frequently launched at the Empress Elisabeth is that she was not a good mother. This is quite as untrue as all the other villanies alleged by her many detractors.

When her first little daughter was born the Empress felt that a brilliant ray of joy had come into her life. During the months preceding this event she had suffered as only over-sensitive natures can suffer, natures so refined, so exquisitely delicate that they find no comfort in unburdening their souls by confidence, or in heralding their wrongs by reviling others. She was ashamed of the piteous jealousy which kept growing in her heart, but she could not resist the inroads which it made into her peace of mind, until she felt nothing but a sickening despondency. The Emperor still continued to see no great alteration in her, save that which he ascribed to her naturally failing health.

She was always calm and gentle, and he was far from guessing that beneath the serious smile of the sweet mouth, which served so effectually to hide her sorrows, there throbbed the most torturing of doubts and of fears.

The birth of her child brought more cheerful and hopeful ideas in its train. "Now," she said to her mother, "my existence cannot be said to have been utterly useless; besides, children form an unbreakable tie, even between husbands and wives who are otherwise absolutely indifferent to each other."

It was a desolate kind of consolation for so young a girl, but it helped her wonderfully, until she discovered that, the baby not being of the right sex, everybody was disappointed, even the Emperor himself, who passionately desired a male heir to his crown. This was but another blow to her, and her melancholy—which her *entourage* chose to call "melancholia"—increased steadily.

The baby, on whose downy head Elisabeth had built so many hopes, was, however, not destined to remain long on this earth as a consolation and a joy to her young mother, for before she was two years old she died of some swift and terrible infant ailment at Budapesth, where her imperial parents were spending the spring. When the little coffin, covered with a shower of white roses, and containing the small corpse of tiny Archduchess Sophia-Dorothea, had been taken from her side, the Empress realized for the first time that there are worse miseries here below than disappointment and jealousy. She struggled against a feeling of utter revolt against her fate, but all her self-restraint was broken down at one stroke by the sudden appearance of a superb white dog which had been the playfellow and devoted companion of the dead baby. Flinging herself upon her knees, she threw her arms about the shaggy neck of the animal, and wept such tears as it must pain the very angels in heaven to see a human creature shed.

All her love became centred upon little Arch-duchess Gisela, who had made her appearance in the world in 1856, and also upon the hope of bearing a male heir to the crown, since this seemed to be looked upon as the most important aim of her existence. With these sentiments to sustain her drooping spirits, she tried her best to brace up against the continual malevolence of those about her. This was hard enough to bear without there being added the steady diminution of her husband's first adoring devotion.

Wearied, perhaps not entirely without cause, by his wife's silence, self-effacement, and un-spoken reproach, for his mother made it her most sacred duty to give other names to these defects, and to point out to him what a blunder he made in uniting himself to a mere beauty who had neither mind nor heart, and who was a chill as an arctic landscape, he threw himself into the whirl of the gayest society on earth. Kind and considerate he always was to Elisabeth, when they were together, but as soon as he had left her, even the memory of those great, sad, luminous eyes, the pathetic pallor of that lovely oval face, ceased to haunt him as of yore, and he thought of nothing save his many pleasures and occupa-tions—the council of ministers over which he was to preside, or the ball he was to honor with his presence.

At last, a little before she attained her twenty-first year, the Empress gave birth to a son, a beautiful child, somewhat delicate of appearance, but with whom even his irascible paternal grand-mother deigned to be satisfied.

"Nobody has seemed to need me until now, not even my little girl, who is kept away from me

so much," said poor Elisabeth; "but my boy
I shall not permit to be taken away to distant
nurseries and the care of strangers; he will need
me, and we will be happy through each other."

In this, however, she was mistaken again.
The heir apparent to one of the greatest empires
of this planet was not to be brought up by a "chit
of a girl who did not even know enough to behave
herself"—such was "Madame Mère's" charitable
verdict. The baby Archduke was, therefore, as
soon as was feasible, installed in a far-off portion
of the palace, where, as his kindly granddame
judiciously remarked, "he would be much better
than in the hands of his silly young mother." The
"silly young mother" remonstrated in vain. She
was curtly told that the boy was perfectly well
cared for, and treated in a much better and wiser
way than if she had the management of him.

The Empress nevertheless insisted upon the
loving duties of maternity, upon the consolation
it would be to her to look after her own darling, as
any other mother would be allowed to do.

"Pshaw!" replied the Archduchess, impatiently, "what consolation do you need? You are
one of the handsomest women in the world, you
have the finest jewels, and the grandest position
one can imagine; that ought to satisfy you. Do not
grow morbid and sentimental; it is in execrable
taste. Enjoy yourself, laugh and be merry; you
have played the ridiculous rôle of victim long
enough; one gets weary of watching such a performance on the part of the luckiest of all human
beings."

Thoroughly roused this time, the Empress
swept out of her mother-in-law's presence, swear-
ing to herself that, come what might, she would

"play the victim" no longer, and would follow all this good advice in so far as her nature permitted her to do so.

Far be it from me to hint that "Madame Mère" was anxious to see her son's wife take her words too literally and embark upon a life of flirtations and deceits, but still it is impossible to deny that her strange counsels might have easily worked a havoc which would have rendered her son the talk of Europe, had Elisabeth not been cast in a mould that had not one weak point in its make.

The Empress was—commonplace as the expression may seem—a thoroughly honest woman. To her delicate, fastidious taste there was a sort of horror in being compromised; it was low and common, and only good for "mundanes" belonging to the type represented by the famous Countess de L——, who, by the way, had long since been replaced in the Emperor's regard by a host of younger and yet more attractive persons.

The chilliness of temperament to which I have alluded before may have had something to do with the lovely young sovereign's remaining forever unsuliied by even so much as a questionable action. She was always as loyal to her husband in thought and in deed as if he had shown her at all times becoming fidelity. She possessed over all men who approached her a charm too complete to be ignored; for, after attracting them by her exceeding loveliness, she retained their attention and admiration by her many other remarkable qualities of conversation, wit, and brilliancy; but whenever they attempted to cross the slender barrier which separates a courtier from an outspoken admirer, they found, so to speak, a wall of ice facing them, impalpable, but absolutely

impassible. The greatest lady-killer or *blagueur*
(joker) at court never dared to hint at a possible
weakness where his fair sovereign was concerned. As for their womankind, when they were
particularly filled with jealous envy they permitted themselves unseemly jokes and predictions
with the facility which women bring into these
small and cowardly acts of revenge towards those
who are too blameless not to unconsciously
shame them; but they did not go unrebuked.
These amiable ladies were, of course, quite certain that the Empress had never shared and
would never share their follies; but none the less
they could not resist the delicate pleasure of
talking evil of one who towered immeasurably
above them in every respect.

In spite of all that was said in that line, it is,
however, an averred and irrefutable fact that at
no instant of her life has the breath of scandal
had any right to touch the Empress's pure, transparent, and unalloyed record of virtue—a record
of such perfection as has seldom been attained
by so beautiful a woman, or, for the matter of
that, by any woman, whether beautiful or the
reverse.

Once, and only once, did a man so far forget
what was due to his sovereign, and also to his
own honor, as to yield to the wellnigh irresistible
temptation of avowing to her the passion which
she had aroused in his heart. This scene, which
was related to me after many years by the unfortunate gentleman himself, took place at the
palace of Schönbrunn, the favorite summer
residence of the Emperor, in the immediate out-
skirts of Vienna. It was on the night of a state
ball, and the Empress, fatigued by the heat and

glare of the *salons,* had stepped out upon the terrace, illumed by the chastened radiance of the full-moon. She was accompanied by the young Count H——, a great noble, and at that time one of the handsomest and most dashing officers of the Emperor's body-guard. Elisabeth had at that time attained the fulness of her flawless beauty. Clad from head to foot in snowy laces, with great emeralds, her favorite gem, gleaming on her white neck and in the masses of her perfumed hair, she paced slowly up and down along the rose-covered marble balustrade, talking to her companion in that melodious low voice which had something so captivating about it. Suddenly, as they reached a secluded and shadowy corner of the long mosaic-paved walk, Count H——, losing all control over his feelings, cast himself at her feet, and confessed his love in broken, tremulous accents. He was terribly in earnest, and words came to his lips like a furious torrent let loose by the breaking up of ice in the spring—words unconsidered and unwise beyond all pardon.

He clung to the hem of her skirts, which he had grasped, his eyes sparkling like fire, his whole frame shaking with fierce emotion. With one swift movement she shook herself free, and looked at him as she might have looked at some infuriated animal which she wished to cow. He saw that she was implacably offended. It was the first time that any one had ever presumed to thus insult her.

"How dare you!" she exclaimed, almost choking with a fury which was all the more terrible because it was so foreign to her nature to yield to any outward sign of anger.

"Beloved! beloved! do not repulse me, do not send me away from you," murmured the young Count; but he talked to the empty air, for she had already moved away rapidly and had entered the palace by a side door, leaving him to stagger, blinded by tears of despair and of remorse, into the darkness of the gardens.

This regrettable incident had had a witness in an old and valued friend of the Emperor, who was of course at once informed of what had taken place. Two days later the Count was exiled to his vast possessions in the south of Hungary, and during many long years he was kept there by the orders of his imperial master.

Time flew on, bringing on its wings much pain and sorrow, as well as countless humiliations, to the Empress. More and more were her slightest actions distorted. Whenever she appeared in public at Vienna—much as she disliked doing so—she was regularly mobbed by pushing, struggling crowds wild to scan her lovely features as closely as possible, and for weeks afterwards her personal appearance, her looks, her every gesture served as a theme for the most extraordinary exaggerations and nonsensical anecdotes, which had not a bit of truth in them, nor the least right to be set afoot. Her delicate, narcissus-like complexion was said to be the result of an enamelling process; her erect, dignified bearing was dubbed with the appellations of pride and haughtiness. The common herd failed to comprehend her peculiar style of beauty, for it was of a kind which had nothing gross or ordinary about it, but was ethereal in the extreme, and which indeed was retained to the very last.

One day, at the close of a court ball, as she was walking down the steps of the Rittersaal, her long train became inadvertently entangled around the feet of the Papal Nuncio, who was standing at the head of the stairs and bowing low as she passed. Amid the covert smiles and sneers of the courtiers forming a hedge on either side of the great Hall of Ceremonies, the Empress disengaged herself with a rosy blush, but later on she was fated to hear many unseemly hints and exasperating pleasantries about this so-termed "brusque separation of Church and State!" Slight as were all these hints and unkind interpretations, yet they had the power of unnerving the Empress to an inconceivable extent, and her heart turned completely from her Austrian subjects to give itself unrestrainedly to Hungary and to the Magyars.

At last the intrigues and cabals encouraged by "Madame Mère," and by her many adherents and followers, found their fruition, and a complete estrangement—not to call it by a more severe name—arose between the young couple. The reasons for this wretched affair, as discussed then by the classes and the masses, are both too foul and too untrue to be even mentioned here. "One lends to the rich," as the old proverb goes; and although the Emperor deserved serious blame and censure, yet his crime against his lovely and innocent consort was by no means so black as it was made out to be. Nevertheless, his "flirtations" had become of so flagrant a nature that it was not in ordinary flesh and blood to overlook them, far less was it possible for a woman of the Empress's proud temper to stand the countless slights thus passed upon her.

A very unpalatable adventure, of which her husband was the hero during one of his hunting expeditions in the mountains, and of which she was immediately informed by the no doubt well-meaning and charitably intentioned wife of one of his Majesty's confidants and boon companions, broke the last restraint upon her indignation, and without informing anybody of her intentions she hurriedly left the imperial palace of Vienna for Trieste, and set sail for the Ionian Islands, on board her yacht, fully resolved never to allow her husband to approach her or to speak to her again.

The amount of scandal caused by this flight may be more easily imagined than described, and it is evident that even the Empress herself had no conception at first of the tempest of abuse she was arousing by thus abruptly departing from her usual rules of silent suffering and reserve. But when once the deed was done she would sooner have died a thousand deaths than have turned from her course. She was thoroughly unhappy, and had been so for a long time, and when a woman is unhappy she is never very wise. The step she took was extreme, but her youth seems a sufficient excuse, for in youth such wrongs as those which she had endured seem to fill earth and heaven with their magnitude; yet she brought about her head, and about the Emperor's too, a thousand hornets'-nests of slander and useless misconstruction, and there were very few, either at home or abroad, ready to admit that if the vengeance she took was perchance too drastic, it was at any rate a very dignified one.

Not quite so dignified was the pursuit which the, for the moment, remorseful Emperor at once undertook after his truant Empress.

The latter, however, was firmly resolved not to give him a chance of pleading his own cause, which, had he only known her better, he would have understood to be practically a lost one. A faithful and devoted woman, Countess X——, who had accompanied her, told me once that in all her profound experience of human nature she had never seen such a change as came at that time upon the Empress. She never regretted for one instant what she had done; she certified to the gentlewoman in question, over and over again, that she would be ready to repeat it at any moment were she called upon to ratify her choice, for it seemed to her that it was the only thing for her to do in common honor and self-defence. All the pent-up anger and disgust which her soul contained broke forth with such force that she positively frightened those about her. She hardened her heart against everybody, and even the mention of her children failed to make any impression upon her.

Naturally unselfish to a singular degree, she now dropped into the habit of one given up to that most blamable of all defects: she wrapped herself in her own bitter, poignant sorrow, to the exclusion of everything else. She faced her self-elected widowhood—the saddest of all—with a kind of strange relish, for at last she felt free to be herself, and to drop the mask of cold indifference which she had worn so long and so bravely.

When she heard that her husband had started after her and was making his way towards her place of refuge, she, without losing a minute, boarded her yacht again, and before many hours had elapsed was off to the island of Minorca. There again she was informed that his

Majesty had resolved to track her, and from thence she departed immediately, scarcely conscious of any feeling or wish save that of escaping him. She crossed the Straits of Gibraltar, and never paused until she had reached the gray expanse of the Atlantic.

Despairing of catching up with her, and moreover realizing the ridicule with which he was covering himself, the Emperor returned to his own dominions, where he arrived a sadder and wiser man.

If anybody ever felt regret for past indiscretions, surely this great ruler, before whom multitudes bowed, did so now, and shame as well as remorse filled his cup of bitterness to the very brim. The true character of his wife began to dawn upon him; he knew that since all eternity many women, both handsome and highly born, had suffered, and were suffering from the same indignities which he had put upon Elisabeth; but, from the very force of the remedy which she had chosen, he gathered that her nature had now changed to that of a proud woman, ripened by sorrow beyond her years, and that it would be almost an impossible achievement to make his peace with her. She might break, but bend she would not, whatever the strength used against her.

While he was occupied in vain regrets and in yet vainer plans of future reforms and alterations of circumstances, over which he had by his own fault momentarily lost all control, the Empress was first making a tour through the Fjords of Norway, and then a conscientious exploration of the Mediterranean coasts. Greece, Algeria, and Egypt interested her passionately, and she was able to go wherever she listed in absolute

THE EMPRESS AT THE AGE OF TWENTY-EIGHT

freedom, for she maintained when she so willed it the strictest of *incognitos.*

In Algeria she took possession of a charming villa, with blue and white awnings shading its verandas, and a broad terrace-roof, half hidden in palm and pepper trees, surrounded by a large garden, where fountains bubbled in pink marble basins. The cool, silent rooms were adorned with curious costly things of Arabian workmanship— old embroideries in dull gold and silver on a ground of silk or brocade, curious antique braziers of silver and brass, trailing draperies wrought in silks of melting hues, quaint pieces of furniture in moucharabien work, and great bronze vases, which, according to her wishes, were always filled with a wealth of flowers and plants. Arab servants, soft of tread and noiseless of movement, filled her anterooms, and some Barb horses for the carriages and for the saddle took places in her stables. In this pretty abode she attempted vainly to forget her woes, and led a life that was outwardly at least a happy one.

Alone in the dreamy repose of the large garden, alone during the balmy moonlit evenings on the marble terraces, alone in the shadowy stillness of the house, it was yet very hard, sometimes, for her to maintain her composure. She ceaselessly endeavored to conquer these tendencies to sadness by physical exhaustion. She would jump on her horse and gallop off towards the desert in the cool hours of dawn or in the starlit evenings. She had a deep veneration for this old African soil, so full of relics of the past, and was never tired of gazing at the great rolling plains of orange-colored sand, the awful grandeur of which has remained undisturbed since the beginning of the world, defying the power of man. This sight exercised a potent spell upon her mind, and the impression grew upon her that she could not fail to find calm and comfort when encircled by these seemingly endless horizons. A certain sense of awe stole gradually into her heart, and soothed her nervousness and pain. Many an hour did she spend in the saddle, dashing through the dry air in breathless and pauseless speed, borne on and on by her fleet Arab horse, sweeping by villages or peaceful Bedouin douars, passing files of camels and of laden mules on her way as she rode over the sun-scorched roads of the vast shadowless plateaux which are the ante-chambers of the great Sahara desert. She generally rode alone; of assistance she needed none. A rider of her merit could spring as lightly as a bird into her saddle, and she loved the intoxication of complete solitude and the unchecked rapidity of her flight. League after league passed away like a dream, and it was only when she felt her horse quiver under her with fatigue that she would slacken her pace and let the bridle drop upon his neck.

Days and weeks and months drifted on, and still Emperor Franz-Joseph's brilliant court remained deserted by the fair, graceful figure which had once been barely tolerated there, but which now was missed by many. "Madame Mère" began to observe that she could no longer afford to be too sure of her ground, and that when, with pious eyes raised towards an unjust Heaven, she threw out hints about her daughter-in-law's unpardonable conduct and incredible ungratefulness, a respectful silence was all that she received in return. Men who had always admired the

Empress, and who, besides, had very good reasons for knowing that she was sinned against and not sinning, even raised their voices in her defence, but, unfortunately, the truth compels me to say that *vox feminae* (the voice of woman) is often *vox Dei* (the voice of God), and almost without exception women took part against the woman who had never shown them anything but kindness, and who was now so lonely. They agreed with touching unanimity that it was her lack of amiability which had caused all the trouble, and added that the primary reason of every subsequent catastrophe was the foolishness of their sovereign—this, of course, was murmured *sotto voce* (in a low voice) behind the shelter of a fan or the fragrance of a bouquet—in throwing himself away on an unsympathetic, heartless girl, whose brain had been turned by her sudden magnificent change of circumstances.

One could write volumes about this period of Elisabeth's existence. It was during this time that, remembering only too well the many slurs concerning her "insufficient education" which had been thrust at her, she undertook to remedy this defect, for which the early age at which she had been married was alone to blame, and began to study with an earnestness seldom to be found in man or woman. She bent her supple form over black-letter folios and Latin works, Greek authors and old poets, devoting hours and hours to studying many dead and living languages. She wrote some very remarkable descriptions of her travels, and, to lighten the tedium of this labor, made hundreds of exquisite sketches of the places she visited, or played on the piano or the zither, for she was a wonderful musician. It was then also that weariness of heart from her loveless existence caused her once more to turn with all-absorbing ardor to the cherished companions of her childhood and early youth—namely, to horses and to dogs—for comfort and affection. She went out in all weathers, minding neither storm nor rain, boisterous winds, intense cold, nor burning heat. Often, drenched to the skin, she would walk or ride for days at a time, taking no harm whatever, for it is a singular fact that an absolute indifference to the consequences of physical imprudence often bestows complete immunity from all bodily ailments or accidents. Soldiers who rush out of the trenches seeking death pass unscathed through a hail of bullets, whereas the coward who cringes behind a bastion is almost certain to get his deserts, by being the first to be hit. She still possessed her sensitive horror of compassion or of comment, only now it was intensified to an almost morbid extent, and she preferred her poor empty life as a wanderer to the molestation and interference of those who had made such a wreck of her fair young days.

"You have acted as if you, and not your husband, were guilty," her mother wrote to her. "I do not deny that there is nobility in your refusing to retain the advantages of your position at court since you fancy that you no longer possess Franz's heart, but many things which the world need never have known are now public property. The higher we stand on the social ladder, the less right have we to gratify our own private vengeances, or to set ourselves free from painful obligations. Remember the good old saying, 'Noblesse oblige.' You are the integrant part of a great nation's honor; you are faithless to your trust and to the traditions of your ancestry when you thus act on the spur of personal injury and passion."

At heart Elisabeth knew that her mother was right. She acknowledged as much to me when one day, while looking together over a casket filled with old letters, she showed me the one referred to above. But yet her reply to it was couched in terms which plainly indicated that as long as she never did anything to lower her consort's high estate in the eyes of his people, and as long as her own conscience did not reproach her, she was justified in declining to exist in hypocrisy, and in what seemed to her to be moral degradation.

Her husband's offences against her were very grave, but she was forced to confess to herself, now that she had time for reflection, that they were inseparable from such a temperament as his. The mistake had been that when she had given herself to him she had not known enough of life, or of what life brings with it; of rude awakenings from preconceived ideals, of sin, of shame, and of disappointment.

As usual, public rumor excused the husband's weaknesses and distorted the wife's failings. Proud, delicate natures disdain the favor of the world, but cruel indeed is the manner in which they are made to pay for this disdain. She endeavored to school herself to forgive the Emperor's numerous so-called *affaires de coeur* (affairs of the heart), her better judgment showing her that the "Anointed of the Lord" are frequently subjected to temptations from which ordinary mortals are exempt, especially when, as in the case of her husband, they combine in their person good looks, supreme elegance, extreme chivalry of behavior, and a marvellous charm of manner. She knew that loyalty on the part of the fair sex towards the sovereign in most cases assumes a terribly demonstrative form. They ruffle their feathers and put forth all their charms for the purpose of attracting royal or imperial favor, with a tenacity which leaves no room for doubt as to their intentions. Elisabeth's deep religious feeling urged her, too, towards the side of mercy, but her pride had taken arms, and the time had not yet come when she became able to conquer it, and to relent towards her husband.

In the meanwhile the Emperor was growing more and more uncomfortable, and more and more conscience-stricken. He had for a long time xcused in his own sight his transgressions, and .rors, and follies, but the sense of his inexcusable disloyalty towards his blameless wife grew insensibly upon him, and he soon could no longer palliate or waive them off with sophistry. Swayed to and fro by conflicting emotions, at times he could scarcely resist the impulse which urged him to obtain from her, by hook or crook, an interview which would permit him to cast himself at her feet, and to implore her forgiveness and mercy; while during the hours when he was submitted to his mother's indirect, nay even direct, influence, he once more became the slave of his wilful, passionate nature, forgot for the nonce that men whose names are continually before the world should, under any circumstances, keep them clean and hold them high, cast all repentance to the wind, and believed himself quite sincerely to be the injured one.

It is unnecessary to dwell at length upon the details of this long conflict, during which there

ARCHDUKE RAINER, COUSIN OF THE EMPEROR

took place a few strictly official meetings between the imperial pair, meetings that were solely brought about to close the mouths of the people, and where, pride gaining once more its full strength, the young couple refused with lamentable obstinacy to talk together in private even for five minutes.

It goes without saying that the Empress was forced by reasons of state and of policy to make *acte de présence* (an appearance) in her husband's dominions and at her husband's court once or twice during each year. But these meteor-like visits, made almost unbearable to her by the dread of being obliged to resume her conjugal life with her husband, already called forth, from those who were not well informed as to the true situation, remarks regarding the sanity of the Empress. Tongues kept wagging in the most lively way. She was said to be erratic, unbalanced, morbid, and the world pitied the so-often-forsaken Emperor.

As soon as her official duties were discharged, Elisabeth, not heeding these slanders at all, left the country again and again, to try to regain what peace and equanimity she could muster under foreign skies. She was heard of as staying at Biarritz, San Remo, Algiers, in Egypt, Greece, or Syria. She loved the Mediterranean, and once a year at least returned to its shores. It was then that she first became enamoured of lovely Corfu.

Nearly seven years elapsed before this detestable *modus vivendi* (mode of living) came to an end. A great political event—namely, the reunion of two crowns and of two countries under the sceptre of the Emperor—made it imperative that

the august couple should once more appear hand
in hand before their subjects. Moreover, the
health of the Crown-prince was causing much
anxiety to his *entourage.* Perchance the child
missed the love and care of his "silly young
mother," so ill-replaced by a grandmother who, in
her own estimation at least, possessed all the
cardinal virtues and several more besides, but to
whom a just Providence had refused the owner-
ship of a truly womanly heart. One cannot have
everything! Anyhow, the heir apparent's extreme
delicacy inspired the far-seeing with a very natural doubt as to what might be the fate of the
dynasty if the slender thread which bound him to
existence should snap asunder, and his Majesty
was assailed on all sides by his most esteemed
councillors with entreaties for a *rapprochement*
between himself and the Empress.

   She herself was approached about the matter
by wise and clever people, who forbore to mention
to her how greatly her own interests were at
stake. This would have produced a disastrous
impression upon her. They argued, instead of
this, that her children needed her, that her continued absence from the court was injuring them
morally and physically; reasons of state were also
brought forward, and her husband's deep regret
and sorrow much magnified—although of a truth
they did exist—until that infinite yearning for
affection which is wholly outside the instincts of
the passions began to thrill in her heart anew.
She was brought gently and securely to the point
where doubts about her own reading of duty as it
should be entered her soul. She asked herself,
with agonized tears, whether in the violent scorn
of her revolted pride she had not lost sight of the

only fashion in which duty should be understood. For years she had gone upon her joyless path not caring much whether she was displaying too much vindictiveness, or whether, in cleaving so closely to the traditions of what she deemed honor, she had not forgotten the obligations of mercy and of forgiveness.

As I have stated before, she was a very religious woman, not in the outward, noisy manner of a *bigote*, but sincerely devoted to the Catholic faith, and she now allowed the first of Christian virtues—charity towards those who have hurt us most—to guide her towards pardon.

The love she had once felt for her husband stirred at those times beneath all her wrath, and echoed back in her heart. The outcome of all this was that she suffered herself to be induced to return and to take up her duties again. Many were the tears which she shed kneeling before her crucifix, in an anguish of doubt as to what she had best decide, before she came to that conclusion. But finally her surrender was complete; she realized that she could not forever arrogate to herself the right of judgment against her lord, and a great peace fell over her like a mantle.

The meeting between them had no witness save the Emperor's favorite brother. It was a sad and mournful moment. The Emperor looked older, paler, more weary than he had done when she had last seen him. She, with a beating heart and an ashen face, stood silently looking at him, without making a gesture or giving a sign of the nervous strain which she felt. He crossed the room, dropped on one knee, and bowing his handsome head over her hand, kissed it as deferentially as if he were the meanest of her subjects.

His lips were as cold and trembling as the slender fingers he held.

"Que Dieu vous garde" (May God keep you), he murmured.

She fixed her eyes upon him where he knelt, and then, with a gesture infinitely forgiving in its almost motherly tenderness, she passed her disengaged hand over his hair.

"We have both much to forgive," she said, softly.

CHAPTER IV

The ceremonies attending their coronation as King and Queen of Hungary were welcome circumstances in the official reconciliation of the two sovereigns, and greatly facilitated Elisabeth's resumption of her life at court. These magnificent ceremonies are still present to the memory of all those who witnessed them, and aroused the genuine enthusiasm of the young sovereign so vividly that never could she speak of them without emotion.

The town was crowded with Magyars from the Bakos Plain, Suabians from the mountains west of the town, Slowàks from Northern Hungary, Servians and Croatians from the southern districts, and even long-haired Saxons from Transylvania, and with different corporations, unions, and guilds carrying banners. The honored veterans of the war of 1848 to 1853 in their old uniforms, numbering in all sixty thousand persons, lined the streets from the Western Railway Station to the royal castle, a distance of six kilometres.

The royal castle of Buda is a marvel of antique architecture. It was built in 1769, and ever since 1771 the hand of St. Stephen has been preserved as a sacred relic within its ponderous walls. Every year, on the 20th of August, a

procession leaves the citadel, the relic being carried from there to the Church of Our Lady of the
Assumption, and back again, to the sound of
thrilling music, and under a veritable hail of
blossoms.

On the coronation-day, all those who had
been invited by the government or the municipal
authorities occupied seats on the official grand-
stands. When their majesties issued from the
palace on their way to the cathedral deafening
"eljens" were raised, and were kept up almost
unin*erruptedly. The Emperor and Empress rode
in a magnificent state carriage drawn by eight
white horses. At the moment that the procession
began to move, a salute of one hundred and one
minute-guns was fired from the citadel. The procession was headed by mounted police, followed
by the carriage of the governor of the city and
that of the chief of police, and was the most
brilliant pageant imaginable.

The escort of one hundred and sixty-two
aristocrats was an especially magnificent sight.
Twelve pairs of cavaliers, whose horses were led
by armor-bearers in Magyar dresses, were followed by eight mounted magnates, each of whom
carried a banner. The others all came in pairs,
each horse being led by one or two armor-bearers.
All the nobles wore the splendid dress of the
Hungarian magnate, adorned with gold embroidery and precious stones from the kálpàk—or
head-covering, which is surmounted with herons'
feathers—down to the high boots. The reins, gilt
stirrups, and the shabracks and golden scabbards of the scimitars were covered with diamonds and jewels, many of them being worth a
fortune. The imperial carriage was accompanied

THE EMPRESS AT THE TIME OF HER CORONATION
AS QUEEN OF HUNGARY

by the adjutant-general and by the Hungarian minister.

The procession was followed by six carriages containing court officials, and by several hundreds of the carriages belonging to members of the episcopacy and the aristocracy. Most of the coaches and harnesses were covered with gems and gold. The long train went at a foot pace through the gloriously decorated streets, amid the cheers of several hundred thousands of spectators. The English know how to cheer, but their "hurrahs" are not to be compared for volume of sound with the thundering shouts heard on that day. Maidens dressed in white showered flowers on the road followed by the procession, invoking blessings on the heads of their handsome sovereign and his lovely consort.

So great was the enthusiasm aroused by the appearance of the Empress-Queen, that it is scarcely wonderful if her whole heart went out anew to a people who, by the warmth of their reception, the many tokens of admiration and love bestowed upon her, presented so vivid a contrast to the manner in which the Teutonic portion of her husband's subjects had comported themselves towards her when the imperial crown had been placed upon her brow, almost thirteen years before. Her predilection for Hungary from henceforth became more than ever marked. She learned the terribly difficult Magyar language with her usual facility, devoting herself with such energy to this task that she absolutely amazed her instructors, and most of her time was spent in her marvellous Castle of Gödöllö, near Budapesth.

During the years which I had the joy of spending there near her, we wandered untiringly

together a-horse and a-foot, in the green, moss-
carpeted forests and on the boundless Pùsztá.
Everything interested her, and, like her husband's celebrated relative, Archduke Joseph,
who actually wrote a Zingari grammar and is
the greatest authority on the origin and habits
of the Tzigane people, she delighted in visiting
the camps of these copper-hued, glittering-eyed
beings, who have music and poetry born in them,
and who are to be found in the entire purity of
their race only in those still semi-barbaric
egions.

There never was, I truly believe, a rider worthy of being compared to Elisabeth. Both in the
field and in the riding-school she was absolutely
matchless with regard to seat, grace, and ability,
and although her slender, dainty build would
hardly have caused one to believe it, her strength
was very great, and there was no horse that she
could not ride when once she had made up her
mind to do so. The opinion of Franz Gebhardt on
the matter, who was the foremost rider of the
Spanish school at Vienna, is worthy of being
recorded.

He declared, many a time, that she outshone
any rider of her own sex, for she had a knack of
putting herself into immediate and almost mes-
meric communication with her horse, and of making it show off to the best advantage, never in any
way hampering it by the slightest false movement
on her part. She aroused the delight of the true
connoisseur by the perfection of her steps, *cour-
bettes, changements de pied,* and all the other
delicate and intricate secrets of the difficult art
of high-school riding.

Not the least remarkable feature of her

fondness for horses was the extraordinary, almost hypnotic, influence which she possessed over them; the most unmanageable animals would let themselves be approached and petted by her. She used to throw the colonel in command of the Reit Lehren Institut at Vienna into absolute convulsions of terror by occasionally bearing down upon him with the request to "send to the riding-school a couple of your wildest specimens for us to have a little fun with!" The hapless colonel would at first try to evade obedience, but the Empress was peremptory, and he had to give in, though his bronzed face would turn ghastly pale under its tan as he watched the slender, graceful figure of his sovereign vault into the saddle and perform wonders of horsewomanship on horses which he would not have dared to let an ordinary cavalry officer ride.

Her friendship with Eliza, the celebrated *haute-école* rider at Renz's, gave rise to much unkind comment, but the truth is that Eliza, now married to a distinguished French officer, was of unimpeachable repute, and that her admirable powers as a rider and breaker-in of horses gave her the best of introductions into the favor of the Empress.

Count P——, who is one of the wealthiest magnates in Hungary, and who breeds horseflesh on a very extensive scale, owned in 1878 a magnificent coal-black stallion possessed of so fiendish a temper that for six months his grooms had been unable to enter his box, and were forced to feed him from pails provided with six-foot-long handles. The Empress heard of this, and would not rest until we had driven over to see the Count, or, much rather, to see the Count's restive pensioner. No prayers or entreaties could prevail when the Empress had once made up her mind, and so, *nolens volens* (willing or unwilling), our host was forced to conduct us to the farther corner of his superb stables, where "Black Devil"—such was the amiable animal's name—reigned supreme.

Without a minute's hesitation, and disregarding the exclamations of horror from the on-lookers, Elisabeth walked deliberately to the box, and chirruping in a peculiar manner to its occupant, she drew back the bolt and coolly entered. Those present held their breath, expecting every moment to see the dauntless woman trampled upon and torn to pieces. No such thing, however, happened. At first the startled beast snorted and laid back its ears, but soon the great fiery eyes softened and grew tender, and the Empress was suffered to pat the dilated nostrils and arched neck.

"Come here," she called out to me; "he is as gentle as a lamb, poor old boy, but he is in bad need of a brushing up!"

Where she had gone self-respect forbade me to refuse to follow, so I promptly obeyed her command. Between us we polished up "Black Devil," and ultimately left him whinnying with fond gratitude, a vanquished tyrant! So astonished was the Count, and so relieved also at finding that no accident had happened, that he craved permission to present the dusky beauty to her Majesty. The gift was accepted, but it took a long time before the four-footed "Devil" could be induced to endure the presence of a man near him, and we had all the work we could do in attending personally to his demoniacal needs.

However, the Empress ended by obtaining such good mastery over him that he used to follow her about like a dog in the park and grounds of Gödöllö.

When we were at Gödöllö we were in the saddle as early as half-past four in the morning, guiding our horses through the tall, sweet-scented grasses, and jumping over hedges and ditches, with little variation save the changing of our mounts until the eleven o'clock *déjeuner à la fourchette* (substantial breakfast with eggs, meat, etc.).

Franz Gebhardt rode with the Empress a great deal, not only in the riding-school, but also in the plains surrounding Gödöllö, and his admiration for the Empress's *terrain reiten*, as field-riding is called in Austria, was as great as that which he felt for her performance in the riding-school. The kindness which his imperial patron showed him was boundless. She caused his daughters to be brought up at her expense, and showered gifts of all kinds upon himself and upon his family.

A very amusing incident took place during one of my sojourns at Gödöllö, where Franz Gebhardt was also staying at the time. During her high-school exercises in her private *manége* (riding-school), the Empress was in the habit of having the necessary musical accompaniment to the horse's paces played to her on a piano, which stood in the gallery, by one of her maids-of-honor, a pretty little countess, who, however, played abominably, and, for the most part, completely out of time. One morning Herr Gebhardt, who was wandering about the castle, came upon a magnificent Bösendorfer grand-piano in one of

the distant rooms of the left wing. Being passionately fond of music, and especially devoted to
Schumann, he sat down before the instrument,
and, believing himself to be entirely alone, began
to play the "Traumerei" in the most masterly
fashion. Suddenly the door was softly pushed
open, and the dainty little head of the Empress
appeared.

"I did not know that you possessed this talent,
too. Surely if you can play like that you can do me
the great pleasure of playing a few polkas for me in
the riding-school this morning. The Countess is
not here, and she will know nothing about it, for
you must understand," added the Empress, very
earnestly, that I would not have her feelings hurt
for the world. She thinks that she is doing me a
great service by her playing, and she does not
realize that she cannot play at all."

I had followed the Empress into the room, and
on learning this I could not restrain myself from
laughing outright. Herr Gebhardt, in spite of the
gravity he tried to assume, laughed too, and the
three of us finally gave way to our merriment
until the tears fairly ran down our cheeks. Thus
was it that once, and only once, during that
summer did the Empress indulge in a little good
music while on horseback; for, of course, "the
feelings of the little Countess were on no account
to be hurt."

Her wanderings over the Pùsztá would often
bring Elisabeth within sight of an encampment of
Csikos, and she never failed to stop her horse and
begin to chat with these children of the Magyar
plains, in whom she felt a peculiar interest.
She brought them welcome gifts of golden-hued
Turkish tobacco, and examined their troops of

semi-wild horses with the schooled eye of a perfect equestrienne and of an earnest admirer of
good horse-flesh, which delighted the strange
herdsmen. Picturesquely arrayed in a long, white,
linen, wide-sleeved smock, or shirt, embroidered
in vivid colors, in loose white zouave pantaloons
tucked into high boots, and with a bunch of
Pùsztá-grass and a heron's feather in the band of
his wide-brimmed hat, the Magyar Csikos presents the European counterpart of the American
cow-boy, the South American Gaucho, and the
African Bedaween. His life is spent on the vast
prairies of Hungary in tending the great herds of
semi-wild horses, the breeding of which consti-
tutes one of the most profitable and staple features of Magyar industry. His life is by no means
devoid of privations and hardship, and yet he
would not exchange it for any other that might be
offered to him. While the summer lasts he often
suffers thirst—that thirst which is one of the
terrors of prairie and desert life. His food, which
he carries about with him in the little, two-
wheeled, canvas-covered cart, which is his only
dwelling-place, frequently gives out, and sometimes he has to wait for many days before the
purveyor of the Csikos comes on his round to
replenish the stock of all the scattered members of
the strange brotherhood. Notwithstanding these
drawbacks, the life on the Pùsztá is possessed of
a freedom and charm which a true Magyar cannot resist. The innate and romantic poetry of the
immense flat landscape, green as an emerald,
with here and there a clump of low birch-trees to
vary its monotony, is to the Csikos what the
ever-rolling waves are to the sailor—indispens-
able to his happiness. The Csikos is courageous,

robust, and indifferent both to extreme cold and overpowering heat. As a rule, he is of middle height, with well-cut features, a dark skin, bright and intelligent black eyes, and the long, pointed mustache, known throughout Europe as *la mous-tache hongroise* (the Hungarian mustache). He wields the lasso with just as much mastery as does the Gaucho, and to my mind surpasses both the latter and the Western cow-boy in horseman-ship. A perfect rider, he breaks in the colts belonging to his herd without the assistance of either curb, saddle, rein, bit, or whip. Simply slinging a rope halter over the young animal's head, he conquers it by the iron pressure of his muscular legs and the magical skill with which he poises his body on the back of his fretting, curvetting steed.

Hard indeed is the destiny of the Hungarian Csikos, but fascinating also in the extreme. A little bread, a little salt pork, a flask of wine, a bag of tobacco, and, to shield him from the cold winds of the spring and late autumn, a huge *pelisse* (fur-lined coat) made of sheepskin, the wool being worn inside, and the outer leather richly embroidered in red, gold, yellow, and blue—these suffice for his comfort and happiness. I should not, however, omit from this equipage of his the piece of matting with which he shelters his fire on windy nights, and his can of paprika, or red pepper, with which he flavors the national dish of "gúlyàs," an absolute necessity to every true-born Magyar.

It can easily be imagined what a delightful change from the monotony of their every-day life it was for the Csikos to see us galloping up towards them, bringing them, so to speak, a

breath of worldly air and of novelty, as well as
many a little offering which pleased and flattered
them immensely.

After her definite return to Austria, Elisabeth,
with the buoyancy of youth, commenced to plan
out for herself a course of existence which she
decided in her mind would make up for all the
dreariness of the past years. She looked forward
to regaining completely the lost mastery of her
husband's heart and her place in her children's
lives.

A cruel fate was, however, creeping upon the
track of the ill-fated imperial couple. For hardly
had they had time to enjoy the first days of this,
their second honeymoon, when the terrible news
of the assassination of the Emperor's beloved
brother, Emperor Maximilian of Mexico, reached
them. Far away beyond the seas the unfortunate
Prince had met with a foul death at the hands of
the people whose ruler he had become at their
own urgent solicitation. For them he had abandoned a most happy life, led partly at his brother's court and partly on the lovely shores of the
Adriatic, where he owned the fairy-like Palace
of Miramar, which he had created, and of which
he was very justly proud.

This castle is a spot which appears like unto
the realization of the wildest dreams of an Oriental imagination. Perched on the extreme edge of a
rocky promontory, and built entirely of the pur-
est, most spotless marble, the snow-white building, with its background of emerald-green hills
and woods, is beyond any adequate description.
From the main terrace one looks straight down
upon the gently rippling water sixty feet below,
and so pure and transparent is it that the eye is

able to penetrate its full depth of over twenty
fathoms, and to clearly distinguish the ribbon-
like *algae*, and the pearly, many-hued *medusae*
(jelly-fish) which sway to and fro beneath the
glassy surface. When I visited Miramar with the
Empress, I was much struck by the extreme
transparency of the sea, and she—who was passionately fond of study, and had an extraordinary fund of knowledge—explained to me that
there are some oceans where under seventy-five
fathoms of water one can plainly distinguish the
pebbles and shells on the sandy bottom.

We walked often on the narrow edge of beach
below the rocky cliffs, which continue in a
seldom-interrupted line to the right of the castle
grounds, interesting ourselves in the maritime
plants and *polypi* which abound there in the
shallow pools of water. We sometimes found
clusters of pure tuft-coral, sea anemones which
looked like a perfect kaleidoscope of palest green,
soft yellow, vivid lilac, tender blue, and deep
crimson; starfishes, angel-wings, and prickly
fungi, which we collected for our little museums.
The *medusae*, whose opal rose-bordered umbrel-
las, escalloped with a band of blue, were thrown
by the gentle cerulean waves at our feet,
Elisabeth would invariably push back into the
water, saying, in her low, melodious voice:

"It is too bad to let them be scorched and
sucked up by the sun-rays; they suffer just like
any other animated being created by God's
hand."

Her continual dread of hurting somebody
or something was very characteristic of her,
and she would step out of the path she followed
to avoid crushing a beetle or an ugly caterpillar

crawling on the ground.

It would take a much cleverer pen than mine to portray the wellnigh fantastic architecture of the Palace of Miramar; for minarets fretted and carved like lace, pointed turrets, terraced roofs, adorned by groups of exquisite winged statues, mediaeval battlements, and drawbridges which savor of the fifteenth century, are mingled together in a picturesque and magnificent, if somewhat bewildering, confusion. The gardens and extensive grounds are another marvel which it is difficult to describe, so great is their beauty. The vegetation is a mixture of the European and the tropical, each plant, tree, or shrub having been carefully selected from the finest of its kind. Firs and Siberian arolla grow side by side with luxuriant bamboos and giant-leaved banana plants. French poplars and silvery olive-trees tower above great clusters of palmettos and cacti, while tall date-palms and dark-foliaged magnolias shelter with their deep, refreshing shadows strange mosses and creepers and web-like ferns brought from the far north. In every direction fountains very nearly as superb as those of Versailles cool the atmosphere with their prismatic spray, while even on the hottest day a cool promenade is to be found under the superb avenue of sycamores, which entirely shut out every ray of sunlight. This avenue leads to glass houses where orchids, born in the most equatorial regions of the world, bloom all the year round in luxuriant splendor. The interior of the castle is fully worthy of its matchless exterior, and contains many treasures of art in its high-ceiled state apartments and long galleries. The study, once Maximilian's favorite room, is an exact reproduction of the cabin on board his beautiful yacht, *The Miramar,* upon which the handsome young Prince undertook his disastrous voyage to his future empire.

It is a curious fact that Maximilian's consort, a haughty, ambitious, narrow-minded Belgian princess, should have been, during the years which preceded her own coronation as Empress of Mexico, the greatest ally of "Madame Mère" in the latter's persecution of Elisabeth. Indeed, it was the jealousy with which she was filled on account of her beautiful sister-in-law's superior rank that led her to urge her kind and somewhat weak husband to accept a sceptre which was bound to bring to him and his both disappointment and misfortune.

After the tragedy of Queretaro, Elisabeth's attitude of unselfish devotion towards her grief-stricken husband deeply touched all who witnessed it. It seemed then as if, with the exaggeration of self-censure peculiar to all generous natures, she strove to atone for any pain which she might have given him—although it was so idly given—by her long estrangement from him. She stood by his side nobly, and he found great consolation in looking for support and for comfort upon his young wife's firm and reliant nature. Her long wanderings in comparative solitude had matured her mind and brought out many qualities which, had things been otherwise, might have lain much longer dormant. Afraid of nothing, never watching for the impression which she produced, and absolutely indifferent to what both men and women thought of her, she was far above the starched and haughty social system in which, nevertheless, her whole life seemed doomed to be henceforth plunged. A ministering angel to all those who suffered, she resumed her position at court with a dignity of attitude, a kindness of heart, and a loftiness of purpose which simply amazed and silenced, for the time being at least, her worst detractors and her most bitter enemies.

In the following spring another little girl was born to the imperial couple, and from tenderest babyhood her training and education were the Empress's chief care. She was never tired of repeating to the governesses and tutors of her two elder children that she wished them to remain as much as possible unspoiled by the world! She endeavored to teach them her own love of the open air, of the great mountain solitudes, and of the influence and ways of nature.

The Crown-prince was a most interesting child, headstrong, generous, plucky, and at the same time extraordinarily tender-hearted. At ten years old his resolute air and charming manner made him a universal pet, but under the influence of his paternal grandmother he had acquired a waywardness, touched with some pride and some vanity, which pained his mother whenever she noticed it. From the moment of her return she strove and succeeded, too, at last, in preventing the evil effects of the adulation with which his entire *entourage* was eager to wait on the slightest whim of this little heir to a mighty throne. Fortunately he had many compensating qualities—he was very affectionate and sensitive, and easily moved to self-reproach. Well trained to all bodily exercises, he fell rapidly into the habit of accompanying his mother when she rode out on one of her many mettlesome horses, and she

never pleased him better than when she called
him her little comrade!

Instinctively the boy felt that his mother's
immovable calm and extreme gentleness covered
some great and mysterious suffering. He had
been so long kept away from her that at first he
felt a sort of shy reticence in her presence; but
this soon wore off, and a feeling of absolute
adoration for her crept gradually into his heart.

The motherhood in Elisabeth welled up with
extraordinary force; all her memories of past pain
and sorrow melted into an infinite tenderness for
her darlings, and their presence healed up most
of the wounds that had been dealt to her. On
the summer following baby Valérie's birth, the
Empress spent several months in her dear Upper
Austrian mountains with the Crown-prince and
his two sisters.

Many are the delightful little scenes of her
children's early years which the Empress
recorded in what she used to call her "day-book,"
and which consisted in reality of a series of
volumes wonderfully written in different languages, and interspersed with pen-and-ink and
water-color sketches, exquisitely done, to illus-
trate the various periods which she described.

Of what value must that book now be to those
whom she left behind, provided she did not put
into execution the threat, which she once made in
my presence, of destroying this treasure of souvenirs which, so she argued, contained too many
painful reminders of sorrowful days that had fled!
It is largely because I had the privilege of reading
and admiring portions of this book that I am able
to reconstruct so many incidents of Elisabeth's
life.

CHAPTER V

On a fresh cool morning the Empress was in her favorite room at the Kaiser villa at Ischl, a long, low apartment, with deep embrasures which she had filled with ferns and flowers. The furniture was of carved Indian work, and the walls were hung with old Gobelins, representing the siege of Troy, while sketches, books, and large stands filled with tall groups of flowering reeds, pampas-grass, and pink foxgloves gave this charming retreat a cosey and attractive aspect. The imperial lady had been giving the last touches to a small statuette representing a Greek shepherd-boy and his dog, which she had been modelling to while away the time.

At last, dropping her roughing chisel, she sank upon the low couch near the open window. The breeze came in through a screen of blue passion-flowers, stirring the folds of her white cashmere gown and lifting the soft waves of her hair from her forehead. She sat quite still, one shapely hand resting on the head of a huge St. Bernard dog, which was gravely sitting by her side and looking lovingly at her with his honest brown eyes.

Suddenly the door was gently pushed open, and Rudi and Gisela came into the room carrying a large basket of woven rushes between them, filled with forget-me-nots and myrtle. They came up to her, exclaiming:

"This is for you, mamma; we gathered them in our own garden."

With a smile of pleasure she took the children on her lap and kissed them tenderly. Gisela sat contentedly on the Empress's knee, nestling her golden head against her mother's breast; but Rudi, already a big boy, jumped down and began to trot about the room, looking at all the pretty knickknacks which littered the tables and cabinets.

"Mamma," said he, suddenly, "why does everybody like me better than they do Gisela?"

"Why do you think so, darling? I don't think it is the case at all."

"Oh, but indeed it is; probably I am better company than Gisela."

"What a conceited little man you are getting to be, Rudi!" exclaimed the Empress, trying to conceal her amusement; "you are a great deal too sure of your own superiority and perfection. God does not like conceited children!"

The boy looked up at his mother and smiled. "Oh," said he, quietly, "I am not afraid that God should not love me, because I love God and I do not see him, so God who sees me is sure to love me."

Astonished at this extraordinary remark, the Empress said, gently:

"It is when God sees how naughty you are sometimes that he does not love you, dear!"

"God made me, did he not, mamma? So he ought to be pleased with me," replied the little fellow, quite undisturbed. "But, mamma, why did God make ugly people like Countess X——, instead of making everybody beautiful like you?"

The Countess in question was one of her Majesty's ladies-in-waiting, and, thanks to her brusque, authoritative ways and ill-favored features, was the children's *bête noire* (a person or thing strongly detested or avoided; lit., "black beast": bugbear). The Empress could hardly repress her merriment.

"You are too young to talk of such things," said she. "Tell me what you want me to do this morning to amuse you both till papa comes in to luncheon?"

"Oh, do sing us something, mamma!" exclaimed Rudi, pleadingly.

Elisabeth walked over to a large harmonium which stood near the open window. She sat down before it, and after striking a few chords which echoed through the stillness of the chamber, she sang Schubert's "Serenade." She was a great musician, having a dreamy, mellow voice with an immense tenderness of interpretation.

The last words of the melody thrilled very sweetly through the silence. Elisabeth looked up. Rudi was leaning against the instrument. His eyes were full of tears and his face was pale.

"I am sorry that I spoke as I did just now," said he, tremulously. "It always makes me good to hear you sing, mamma." She drew him towards her and kissed him.

"Do you want me to sing again?" said she.

"Please do, mamma," said he, wistfully.

After a moment's pause her hands wandered lightly over the keys, and called up the sweet, plaintive "Volkslieder" (folk songs) she had heard so often in Austria sung by the peasants, and to

which she had listened so many times when
drifting slowly in her boat on the green waters of
the Gmünden-See. Suddenly with one deep,
plaintive sigh her voice ceased. When she raised
her eyes she saw that the Emperor had noiselessly entered the room and was standing before
her. Their eyes met with some of the old feeling
awakened into their depths, and Rudi, who was
watching them, said, suddenly:

"Papa, I think that the angels must have faces
like mamma."

Certainly his father thought so too.

On another occasion, late in the autumn, the
Empress was sitting in a room which she called
her studio with her three children about her.
This studio was of oval shape, hung with old
Flemish tapestries and with a collection of Meis-
sen china figures on carved brackets upon the
walls. On the open hearth great logs of crackling
wood were burning and all around there was, as
usual, the greatest profusion of flowers. An old
Dutch clock, which stood between two of the
windows, was half covered by an Australian
creeper, the waxy blossoms of which peeped out
through clusters of shining green leaves. Opening
out from this room there was a conservatory,
filled with camellias, gardenias, ferns, and
orchids, artistically grouped about a pink marble
fountain, in the crystal waters of which silver
and gold fishes from Madagascar were swimming, surrounded by masses of fragrant tropical
flowers in Satsuma boxes.

"Mutzerl," as baby Valérie was called, was
asleep on her mother's lap, and Rudi and Gisela
were dancing up and down the large room, which
was lighted only by the bright rays of the moon

and by the fitful gleams from the fire. The scene
had something fairy-like and unreal about it.
Gisela in her short lace petticoats was pirouetting
on the tips of her tiny feet, bounding back and
forth so lightly and gracefully that it would have
seemed in keeping with this elf-dance to see the
little silhouette suddenly glide up the broad,
slanting moonbeam which fell from the lofty
window, and disappear in the dark-blue, star-
studded sky. Her little slippers hardly made more
noise as she danced than the petals of a rose
dropping on the polished floor. There was no
other sound throughout the dim, shadowy room.
The Empress held her breath as she watched the
little girl, and Rudi, who had flung himself down
on a bearskin at Elisabeth's feet, lay quite still.
Gisela was then an uncommonly graceful child.
Her long curls, brilliant eyes, and small pink
mouth made her look like a picture by Sir Joshua
Reynolds. There was charm in every one of her
movements. Suddenly the little white shadow
alighted on the edge of a large arm-chair, and
remained poised like a dragon-fly on a willow-
branch, nodding her curly head, and pressing her
pink hands over her little beating heart.

"Brava, darling!" exclaimed Elisabeth. "You
are a regular little *ballerina.* Who taught you to
dance like that?"

"Nobody, mamma," laughed the little fairy,
and bounding through the room she sprang upon
the ottoman on which her mother was sitting,
and bent over the sleeping baby with a look of
adoring admiration upon her small features.
Marie-Valérie was an extremely pretty infant,
and, according to Rudi's statement, looked "just
like a very lovely wax doll that could breathe,

laugh, and cry, too, sometimes."

It is needless to say that she grew up to be her
mamma's pet, and indeed these two were not
often apart. "Mutzerl" had inherited her mother's
love for flowers, and as soon as she could rely
upon her strong little limbs to carry her wherever
she listed, she started miniature gardens of her
own at all the different palaces where the court
stayed in turn.

One fine summer morning "Mutzerl," now
five years old, coaxed the Empress to see her
"private grounds" at Schloss Gödöllö. These
"private grounds" were a sunny corner where she
was allowed to dig and plant at her will, and
where trees were represented often by branches
pulled from the neighboring bushes, and stuck
jauntily into the ground by the imaginative
embryo gardener. An obliging stable-boy had
taken upon himself the task of helping "Mutzerl"
in her horticultural pursuits, and, thanks to him,
the child could now boast of growing some real
flowers, planted in an orthodox fashion, an
achievement which filled her with delight and
pride. She had set her heart on presenting
"mamma" with a bouquet gathered among the
valuable specimens of geraniums, gloxinias, and
dogroses which had outlived many a revolution,
and it was for this purpose that she had been so
anxious to show her around her possessions. The
Empress duly admired all the treasures exultingly displayed to her by the enraptured little girl,
but at last ventured to observe:

"Don't you think, darling, that this garden
would be still prettier if kept a little more in
order?"

"Oh, that's Yanòs's fault," promptly answered

"Mutzerl;" "he's always meddling here!"

Elisabeth could hardly repress a smile, for Yanòs was the ill-fated stable-boy who spent his leisure hours in repairing the damage done by the wee Archduchess in her garden. She lovingly watched the child as she pulled several rosebuds from a bush, at the cost of her own tiny fingers, and brought them triumphantly to her. "Mutzerl" looked up from under her broad-leafed hat with an expression so absurdly anxious for praise, that she bent down and kissed the glowing face tenderly. "Mutzerl" held her fast around the neck for a moment, and as Elisabeth released her she said, solemnly:

"You are a very good mamma, and I love you very much."

"Why do you love me, darling?" asked the Empress, fastening the flowers in her bosom.

"Because you are so pretty and nice, and because you do all I wish."

"Do I?"

"Yes, and I want very much to ask something now."

"Well, what is it you wish, sweetheart?"

"Oh, mamma, when Christmas comes I want to have a lot of poor little children come to a Christmas-tree that I will fix all by myself."

Much touched by the sweetness of the idea, the Empress consented, of course, and "Mutzerl" laughed gleefully, and trotted through the gardens by her side perfectly contented and happy.

That same evening, Elisabeth was alone in her dressing-room, reclining in the cosey depths of a large arm-chair. Her hair was hanging in a loose luxuriance on her shoulders, and she was wrapped in a pale lilac *négligé* of softest Indian

texture, with a profusion of old lace at her throat
and arms. Her dressing-room was one of the
prettiest nooks imaginable with its silken hangings, its silver swaying lamps, its toilet-table
shrouded in Valenciennes laces, and its cut-
crystal vases full of flowers. She sat there with an
open book in her lap, the soft light from the lamps
shining on her fair skin, on her sapphire-blue
eyes, and on the shimmering wealth of her hair.
She was thinking of the little darling girl asleep in
the room next to her own, and of the pretty
instincts which already, at that early age, made
her think of giving pleasure to others. A proud
smile played about her lips as she lay back in her
chair, her head resting on her arm, with that
grace which was peculiarly charming because it
was so natural and unstudied. Suddenly she
started as a light sound reached her through the
open door of the adjoining room, from which a
faint light was streaming. She arose and stepped
into "Mutzerl's" sleeping-apartment. The little
white bed of mother-of-pearl inlaid Cairene work
looked very peaceful under the rosy glimmer of
the shaded night-lamp. The child was fast asleep,
her head thrown back on the pillow, her arms
above her head. Her wavy hair had been pushed
away from her forehead in her slumber, and she
looked even more strikingly lovely than when
awake. She had been dreaming, and even now
she moved uneasily in her sleep, ruffling her curls
with her chubby hand, and thrusting the cover-
ings from her. The Empress bent down to cover
her, and as she did so she heard her mutter:

"The little children will be happy at my
Christmas-tree."

For a moment Elisabeth stooped over the

unconscious child, gazing upon the rounded, flushed cheeks, and an ardent prayer went up from her heart:

"O God, spare my children to me, and let their lives be pure and blessed!"

Her face, whenever she was thus praying inwardly, was enough to make one think of Montgomery's exquisite verse:

"Prayer is the burden of a sigh,
    The falling of a tear,
  The upward glancing of an eye,
    When none but God is near."

CHAPTER VI

Nowhere was Christmas celebrated with so much fervor as at the Austrian court, until the time when the relentless hand of death robbed the imperial couple of their beloved Rudi. Before that supreme sorrow had overtaken them it used to be the most joyful day of the year for the Emperor and the Empress. Christmas Eve was a double feast, as it also was Elisabeth's birthday. Then, surrounded only by those she loved, the Empress's coldness and silent restraint would always vanish, her reserve break up, and she would become absolutely transformed by what touched her sympathies and her affections.

From the day of the little scene between Valérie and her mother, which I have attempted to describe in the previous chapter, there always were two Christmas-trees, one on the 23d of December, which the little Archduchess decorated with her own hands for a hundred poor children selected from among her especial *protégés*, and one on the 24th for the imperial family. The great fir-trees, glittering with gold and silver nuts, rosy-cheeked apples, and with myriads of little lights to illuminate the thousands of beautiful toys, were indeed things to admire.

At four o'clock in the afternoon of the 23d the

poor children's tree was lighted up in the Rittersaal, a splendid gallery-like room, with a lofty,
arched ceiling, where stained-glass windows,
Flemish tapestries of untold value, draperies of
tawny velvets, and great escutcheons of preciously enamelled metals half-covered the finely
carved and inlaid wainscoting. Every frame and
mirror, every one of the double row of grim
damascened sets of armor which stand on each
side of the long "'Saal" (Hall), was garlanded
with mistletoe and holly. Clusters of Christmas-
roses and banks of snow-drops peeped forth from
trailing wreaths of ivy gracefully disposed in
every available corner. In the gigantic porphyry
hearth a fire of aromatic logs burned, adding its
soft glow to the dazzling little flames of the
candles on the Christmas-tree.

When the court lackeys, in their state liveries,
had opened the doors and drawn back the heavy
portières, the troop of enraptured children thus
admitted to delights worthy of Paradise bowed
reverently, but without shyness—for they knew
that they were loved there, and heartily welcome,
too—and then ranged themselves, the boys on
the right and the girls on the left. Archduchess
Valérie was a picture to see as she advanced
towards them, a joyful smile on her young lips,
and her small hands filled with beribboned par-
cels, like some good little fairy about to distribute
her lavish gifts. Each child received warm
clothes, boots, caps, handkerchiefs, woollen
underwear, fur-lined gloves, and toys, to say
nothing of "goodies," as "Mutzerl" called bonbons of all kinds. The happy youngsters gave
expression to their ecstasy by jumps and
bounds, and shouts of merry laughter, just as

unrestrained as if they were in their own homes, instead of within the walls of the imperial palace. When the noise had somewhat subsided, the Archduchess invariably asked as her reward to hear them sing the "Kaiser's Hymn." For a minute all was still, then the grand melody would roll out under the high, emblazoned ceilings, the fresh young voices going upward, like the carol of a hundred larks, intoxicated by the mere joy of living. When these glad tones had once more dropped into silence, the doors at the lower end of the Rittersaal were thrown open, revealing a large hall where a substantial feast had been prepared.

Oh! how all those youthful eyes would widen with surprise at the sight of the long tables loaded with huge sides of cold roast-beef, haunches of venison, great plump, truffled turkeys, and enormous piles of daintily cut sandwiches. Wonderful cakes studded with candied fruit, showers of bonbons in capacious silver shells, pyramids of grapes, and peaches, pears, oranges, and pineapples, completed this gargantuesque *tout ensemble* ('altogether'), above which floated the delicate aromas of tea, coffee, bouillon, and chocolate.

Later on, when the overjoyed children had been dismissed, their little stomachs well filled and their tiny hands burdened with presents, Valérie was intrusted with another duty, equally delightful to her. The Mayor of Vienna, when Christmas was spent in the Austrian metropolis instead of at Gödöllö, as often was the case, was summoned to the Hofburg, and received at her hands a small portfolio containing the Christmas offering of the imperial couple to the city hospitals, ten thousand florins, and an order for hot-house fruit, cigars, illustrated papers, and magazines, as well as quantities of flowers.

On the 24th of December, immediately before the family dinner, after which the second Christmas-tree was to be lighted, a touching little ceremony always took place in the Empress's private *salon*. There her children and the Emperor, with a very transparent but none the less extreme assumption of secrecy, laid out a multitude of birthday *souvenirs* amid a mass of flowering plants. Then all the candelabra were lighted, and Elisabeth was solemnly led in by Valérie to receive the congratulations and embraces of those she loved best on earth. The smiles upon her sweet face, and the suspicion of a tear in her glorious eyes, were the best thanks that she could ever have offered, for they brought to their very highest point both the radiance of her beauty and the charm of her personality—

> "A perfect woman, nobly planned,
> To warn, to comfort, and command,
> And yet a spirit still and bright,
> With something of an angel light"—

and Christmas was one of the occasions selected by the Empress to instil in her children's hearts the continual thought of other people's comfort and pleasure, which was one of her own most striking characteristics.

One of the finest traits of the Empress was certainly her untiring charity, and her methods were always notable for the extreme delicacy of feeling which she showed in all things. It was she who caused the Viennese to realize the very decided difference which exists between men reduced to poverty through no fault of their own, and men whose destitution is the result of lazy or extravagant habits, and it was she who showed them how to treat the former as fellow-citizens who stand in need of help, and the latter as criminals deserving severe reproof if not punishment. Through her influence numberless families are now redeemed from misery, many youths are saved from sin, many men aided to begin new and prosperous lives.

In the year 1872 an association of 400 ladies and noblemen, belonging to the loftiest ranks of society and presided over by Elisabeth herself, was formed for the purpose of supplying wholesome dinners to the poor at the lowest possible price. Each member gave a sum of 700 florins towards the initial outlay, and with this money the first *volksküche* (people's kitchen) was opened. To-day there are fifteen of these in Vienna, and in the course of the year food is sold in them to the value of more than 1,200,000 florins.

The *volksküchen* are large rooms, with great windows letting in both sun and air, and provided with oak tables and benches, which are kept scrupulously clean. The floor is paved with marble, and at the lower end of the hall a wooden counter serves as a division from the actual kitchen, where many cooks are at work preparing food. All classes, from poor university students to ragged-looking tramps, receive a kindly welcome.

Every day over ten thousand persons dine in the *volksküchen*, and the marvellously low price at which the food is sold can only be accounted for by the huge quantities in which it is bought and prepared. The complete dinner, excellently cooked, costs two groschen, and a breakfast of coffee, bread-and-butter, and some kind of stew can be obtained in the early morning for one groschen. From six to nine in the evening supper is served at the cost of one groschen, and is generally composed of soup, cold meat, and pudding. The ladies and gentlemen who manage this superb association have done wonders. Eight or ten ladies belonging to the court circle make a point of being in each kitchen while the dinners are being served.

It is, one must confess, a rather touching sight to watch the lovely and aristocratic court beauties of Vienna, wearing snowy aprons over their elegant walking-dresses, as they distribute the food to the poor, ill-fed wretches who crowd the room. A kind smile or word of sympathy always accompanies the action. It often happens that one of these charming ministering angels grows deeply interested in the case of one or another of her guests, and thus becomes the means of doing a great deal of practical good.

It is not by a lavish and unreasonable expenditure that the Viennese secure comfort for their deserving poor, but by infinite attention to details, endless care, and hearty sympathy with suffering, for in spite of their long-kept-up animosity against the Empress, her influence has been great even at Vienna in all matters pertaining to kindness and generosity; and this good which she has worked is certainly one of the finest monuments which she has left behind her.

She was kind by temperament and by nature, and loved to see smiling, happy faces around her, and to give beautiful presents, just as she loved to do good on every possible occasion. It was not a mere sense of duty which prompted her, for all she did was performed cheerfully, silently, for the

most part almost as if she were not aware of what
she was accomplishing. Soft, conciliatory words,
small and great services rendered smilingly, without fuss or bustle, were habitual to her. She went
on her way feeling that her task was never at an
end, thinking of the morrow, of those she had not
yet succored, of the many hands there were yet to
fill, the many sorrows still to console, the countless miseries that, in spite of all she already had
done, remained to be relieved. Here, again, I am
compelled to quote some lines which suit her and
describe her admirably:

> "No simple duty was forgot,
>   Life had no dim and lonely spot
>   That did not in her sunshine share;
>   No caprice of mind,
>   No passing influence of idle time,
>   No popular show,
>   no clamor from the crowd,
>   Could move her, erring,
>   from the path of right."

Marie-Valérie remained her mother's almost
constant companion, even after she attained
maidenhood, and was being educated by the
highly gifted and talented Bishop Ronay, who
had previously been the tutor of her ill-fated
brother. From her tenderest childhood the very
atmosphere in which she moved was redolent of
fidelity, of courage, and of dignity. She grew up to
be extremely fascinating, and has not to this day
a grain of self-consciousness or of self-assertion.
Her appearance as a girl was ethereal and delicate, but that delicacy of mould sheathed nerves
of steel, and her slender, supple frame could
stand more fatigue than that of many a stronger-
looking woman. She swam like an otter, rode

almost as well as her mother, fenced and shot
with great skill, and was a sure-footed mountaineer. Her education had been pushed further
than is generally the case with young girls of her
position. She learned Latin and Greek, together
with seven or eight living languages, drew and
painted with great talent, and sang with a singular richness and power.

She has inherited all her mother's love for
sport and out-door life, and delighted, when at
Ischl, in taking long and tiring walks, for she was
never so happy as when among the mountains.
Late in the autumn she used often to don a fur-
lined riding-habit, and, mounting a pony well
used to the hills, she would wander on the frozen
paths leading to the snow-covered peaks above.
She knew every step of the way up to the spurs of
the mountains, and would ride till the ascent
grew too steep for her horse; then, leaving the
latter with her attendant Yaegers, she would seize
her alpenstock and go on her way over the
gigantic bowlders, breathing with delight the icy
blast from the lofty summits. Of course there was
danger in such expeditions, but the young Archduchess knew what she was about, and kept to
the right path regardless of the fierce winds
tearing at her clothes and of the proximity of the
yawning abysses beneath her.

The marriage of Archduchess Valérie to her
cousin, Archduke Francis-Salvator, was of unusual interest not only in her father's dominions
but also abroad, by reason of the fact that her
imperial highness had since her birth been the
favorite child of her parents, the living token of
the reconciliation brought about between them by
the statesmen of the dual empire on the eve of

their coronation as King and Queen of Hungary. Moreover, the young Archduchess, concerning whose unaffected ways and kindly heart innumerable anecdotes were current among the people, had always been a kind of second self to her mother, and her loving comforter and consoler at the time of Rudolph's death.

Much anxiety prevailed among her Majesty's *entourage* respecting the manner in which she would bear the separation when the Archduchess entered upon her married life at Castle Lichtenberg, near Wels, a garrison town some hours from Vienna, where the regiment to which the Archduke belonged was stationed. The Empress, however, as she always did in the important moments of her life, showed her sense and judgment by conquering the distress caused by this separation, and looked to the frequent visits that were to be exchanged between them to make up for the dreariness caused by the absence of her beloved girl. The marriage has turned out exceedingly well, the young couple being entirely suited to one another.

Her former teachers were right when they unanimously spoke in the warmest praise of Valérie's literary abilities, for she has given evidence thereof by the production of several poems and admirable essays which have been published and enjoy a wide-spread sale.

That the Empress, like her daughter, was a remarkable writer of prose is not so very generally known as that she wrote exquisite poetry. Upon a shrine, dedicated to the Blessed Virgin, near Ischl, there are inscribed a few short verses by her, so beautiful and so touching that those who see them come nearer to reading aright the

soulful nature of the Kaiserin than it has been
given to most of those who knew her to do. It is
untranslatable; at least, I humbly confess that I
would be unable to do so without destroying its
delicate charm and deep, pious feeling. I therefore
give it here in the original German, just as
Elisabeth of Austria wrote it:

> "O breite deine Arme aus
> Maria, die wir grüssen;
> Leg, schützend, sie auf dieses Haus
> Im Thal zu deinen Füssen.
> O segne dieses kleine Nest,
> Mag rings der Sturm auch wüthen,
> In deinem Schutze steht es fest,
> Voll Gnaden wirst du's hüten."*

Once Archduchess Marie-Valérie surprised
her parents by composing, for the Empress's
birthday, a charming piece which she, together
with Archduchess Sophia-Marguerite, and Prince
and Princess Auersperg, enacted on a beautifully
decorated stage which they had caused to be
erected in one of the state apartments of the
Hofburg. At the end of the representation Archduchess Valérie appeared upon the scene, alone,
wearing the conventional costume given to the
figure which represents Austria, with a crown
on her head and a sceptre in her hand, and
pronounced the epilogue, consisting of some
verses also composed by herself, and which gave
expression to her love, respect, and gratitude
towards the Empress.

The latter, with tears of pleasure in her eyes,

---

*("O stretch out your arms / Mary, whom we greet; / Placing them, protect-
ingly, over this house / In the valley at your feet. / O bless this little nest, /
Although the storm rages round us, / In your protection it stands fast, / With
full mercy, you will guard it.")

embraced her child fondly, and turning to Adolph Sonnenthal, who had superintended the whole *mise en scène* (stage directing), and who had been the teacher in dramatic art of the young Archduchess, thanked him warmly, saying:

"I have to thank you already for many and many a delightful evening spent in listening to you from my box at the Burgtheater, but to-day I must express especial gratitude for the exquisite hours which I have just enjoyed."

This little festival had taken place quite *en famille* (as a family party), nevertheless Sonnenthal was invited by the Empress to remain for the family supper. Elisabeth had a great admiration for the talent of this, one of Austria's greatest and most talented actors, and showed him marked kindness upon different occasions. While staying at San Remo she visited an Austrian lady who owns a villa there, and while being shown round the house she came upon an apartment beautifully decorated with palms and flowers.

"This," said the Empress's host, "is the room where my dear mother died, and I preserve it, as your Majesty can see, like a sort of little memorial chapel."

"Your mother was a woman of taste," replied the Empress, pointing to a marble bust of Sonnenthal which stood on a pedestal in a corner, "since she appreciated our great artist."

Alexander Strakosch was also a great favorite of Empress Elisabeth's. The late Archduke Charles-Louis told him one day, after a recitation which the genial Strakosch had given at the Archduke's beautiful castle of Wartholz:

"I wish that my sister-in-law, the Empress, could hear you," and thereupon arranged to

bring him to the Hofburg, where he was presented
to Elisabeth by the then grand mistress of her
court, Countess Kornis. In 1888, just after Strakosch's return from a tour in America, he was
requested to come to Ischl, and to appear at the
Kaiser Villa. The Emperor was present on that
occasion, and shaking him warmly by the hand,
his Majesty exclaimed:

"You have done us much honor in America
by your wonderful success."

After the evening meal, which he was asked
to share with the imperial family, and during
which both the Emperor and Empress talked in
the most gracious and amiable fashion about
America, Strakosch recited the forum scene from
"Julius Caesar." When he had finished, the
Empress said, smiling:

"It is wonderful! While you were speaking I
closed my eyes, and actually fancied myself
transported to ancient Rome."

She then asked him to recite the "Two Gren-
adiers," that beautiful poem of Heine's, and also
"The Pilgrimage to Kevelaar," and while he was
reciting it great tears ran down the Empress's
cheeks. Heine was her favorite poet, and her
reverence for him was extreme; she possessed all
his works, some of them in manuscript, and there
are many touching things that could be told
about her kindness to the great poet's family.

Marie-Valérie is her mother's imitator in being
the untiring protectress of the poor and the
afflicted, and the lessons which she learned in her
youth with regard to this have borne and are still
bearing fruit, although, perhaps, just as was the
case with Elisabeth, justice is not always done to
her by the common herd.

Ever ready to propagate cruel absurdities concerning the Empress, the short-sighted, frivolous,
and superficial society of the Austrian capital
remained only too often blind to her innumerable acts of charity. Often, in the early hours of
the morning, she would glide out of her palace
either at Vienna or at Budapesth to proceed on
errands of mercy, accompanied by a trusted,
confidential attendant. Elisabeth never knew
fear. She penetrated into the darkest, poorest,
and roughest quarters, where were huddled
together the fierce multitudes that breed anarchy
and that make revolutions. She was perfectly safe
among them. No one knew who she was, but her
courage, her gentleness, and her open-hearted
generosity caused the wretched creatures whom
she visited to regard her in the light of an angel.
They never suspected that the kind lady who
succored their cruel need was the cold, proud,
and haughty sovereign who was taxed with
heartlessness and indifference by both high and
low in the great country over which her husband
reigned. Numerous families redeemed from misery and suffering, many slovenly homes saved
from despair, many foul places purged to moral
and practical cleanliness—these were some of the
results of her Majesty's visits to the slums of
her empire. She could go unharmed where the
police would hardly venture, for the people grew
to love her, and would not willingly have hurt a
hair of her head. She helped the unfortunate
unconditionally, and consoled them just as did
her namesake, Elizabeth of Hungary, centuries
ago.

I remember many a secret errand upon which
we went together, unaccompanied by even so

much as a servant, at dusk, in the most squalid quarters of Vienna or Budapesth. Dressed in the plainest fashion possible, we wended our way through narrow alleys and ascended damp, mouldy staircases, where it hardly seemed safe to tread, in quest of the dark lodgings of the truly deserving poor, who belong to a class too proud to become actual beggars. Many a sick-bed was brightened by flowers and fruit, of which Elisabeth always insisted upon carrying her fair share. Her sweet face brought light and joy to the miserable wretches tossing their fevered bodies on dingy beds. No sore was too repulsive, no task too fatiguing for her slender, imperial hands, and instead of the cant which is used by so many when bent on such errands, she would find some encouraging, cheering words of hope and sympathy, untainted by religious exaggerations and preachings, which went straight to the hearts of the sufferers.

Sometimes our adventures in this direction were fraught with rather amusing episodes. For instance, late one evening we were riding side by side through a straggling outskirt of Pesth, followed at the regulation distance by an old and faithful groom. Passing in front of a lonely hovel separated from the main road by an apology for a garden, where some weeds and gaunt shrubs grew, we were startled by hearing the most awful screams for help proceeding from the ramshackle, crazy-looking plank building. The voice was that of a woman evidently in the greatest of distress. On the impulse of the moment we both leaped from our horses, and rushing to the door and pushing it open, we found ourselves in a villanously dirty room, where a huge ruffian of a man was dragging a woman about the floor by her luxuriant, unbound hair, kicking her vigorously as he did so. Before I realized what was happening, the Empress had laid her heavy hunting-crop about the fellow's face, and so surprised was he at our unexpected appearance and at this vigorous onslaught that he dropped his victim and stared at us in blank amazement. His astonishment was, however, as nothing to ours when the ill-used dame sprang to her feet and, putting her arms akimbo, demanded, in her shrillest Hungarian and with a torrent of invectives, what "we hussies" meant by interfering with her husband. The Empress, who possessed a considerable amount of humor, and in whom the sense of the ridiculous was singularly developed, burst into a peal of laughter, and taking from the ᵃᵈe pocket of her habit a couple of gold ten-gulden pieces, she handed them to this model benedict, exclaiming: "Beat her, my friend. Beat her all she wants. She deserves it for being so loyal to you."

Elisabeth adored children, and was gentle and motherly to rich and poor alike. At the close of the Vienna exhibition of 1873 she took into her service a little Berberine boy named Mahmoud, who had accompanied the Egyptian government mission to Austria. He had acted as page of the Cairene house which the Khedive Ismail had caused to be erected in the Prater and had presented to her imperial majesty. The little fellow, with his great black eyes, his bright and picturesque dress, and his dusky skin, looked for all the world like one of Barbedienne's enamelled bronzes. The Empress became much attached to the tiny African, and was exceedingly kind to

him. When the cruel cold of the Vienna winter
affected his lungs, accustomed as he was to the
hot winds of the African desert, and he fell ill with
pneumonia, she nursed and tended him with her
own fair hands. Mahmoud literally worshipped
his imperial mistress, and could hardly bear her
out of his sight. This intense devotion, however,
had its drawbacks, for he was morbidly jealous of
her, with all the unreasoning jealousy of a child
and the savagery of a wild little animal. He
became the playmate of young Archduchess
Valérie, and the horror of the Austrian aristocracy knew no bounds when they saw their
Empress's favorite child, who looked like a dainty
harebell with her slender figure and bright gos-
samer skirts, continually in the company of the
flat-nosed and thick-lipped African boy. The
Empress, on being informed of the indignation
which she had unwittingly aroused by her kindness to Mahmoud, whom she was accustomed to
describe as *mein kleiner schwarzer Käefer* (my
little black beetle), became imbued with the spirit
of defiance which she so often displayed where
her Austrian subjects were concerned, and she
responded to their murmurs by having the two
children—the white and the black, the imperial
princess and the slave boy—photographed together, arm in arm. Haughty, patrician, exclusive
Vienna lifted its hands to Heaven in its indignation, and this one act of hers added thousands to
the already large number of Elisabeth's detractors. Many even then began again to hint that the
Empress was not quite right in her mind, and
that her extravagances were certain signs of
latent dementia.

CHAPTER VII

Religious as was the Empress, yet she hated exaggeration in everything, and the breadth and lucidity of her mind made her regard fanaticism with a sort of horror. She was so deeply shocked by the tragic history of the Carmelite nun, Sister Barbara, which, when brought to light in 1869, was the cause of the bloody riots which took place at Cracow, that she immediately used her influence in order to have the whole horrible affair cleared up. Indeed, it was through a petition addressed to the Empress by the victim's brother that the gruesome secret of the Polish Carmelite convent was disclosed.

Sister Barbara belonged to a noble Polish family who had forced her to enter religious orders in order to prevent her from marrying a young officer of Lancers with whom she had fallen in love, but who unfortunately had neither rank, title, nor fortune. On entering the grim old convent of Cracow, she ceased all communications with her family, by her express desire, as it was believed at the time; and it was not until more than twenty years had elapsed that one of her brothers, inquiring from the religious authorities what had become of his beautiful sister, was given to understand that she was not any longer on the list of the living. Struck by the shiftiness of the answer, he proceeded to the palace of the Archbishop of Cracow, and throwing himself at the venerable prelate's feet, entreated him to find out if Sister Barbara were really living. The archbishop took steps without delay to discover the truth, but the abbess of the Carmelite convent in which Sister Barbara was supposed to have died not only refused to answer any questions about the matter, but, availing herself of the inviolability of convents, absolutely declined to allow any government official to pass the portals. In the meanwhile the brother had sent off his petition to Empress Elisabeth. She promptly sent it to the Archbishop of Cracow and with it a personal letter, begging him at once to institute a search in the convent.

The archbishop, who was a just and enlightened man, secured the assistance of the police, and surrounded by a battalion of *gendarmes* (soldiers of the police militia), commanded by Count Spauer, one of the most dashing and plucky cavalry officers of the Emperor's army, forced an entrance into the convent in spite of the invectives and desperate resistance of the infuriated nuns. The latter actually went so far as to arm themselves with stones, and the military narrowly escaped being ignominiously repulsed by these holy women, against whom, of course, they dared not draw their swords.

After a long search, the archbishop and his party descended into the dungeons, fifteen feet under the ground, where they heard low groans and moans, which sounded more bestial than human, proceeding from a half-bricked-up cell in a narrow stone passage. In this living tomb, seven paces long by six paces wide, they discovered, by the light of the torches they carried, a naked woman, with long dishevelled hair, crouching in a corner of her filthy prison. At the unaccustomed sight of light the unfortunate creature began to scream with terror, and, springing to her feet, tore at the granite walls with her talon-like nails. After much labor the bricks, which more than half closed up the entrance, were removed, and the raving inmate of the cell was approached. It was found that both her feet and hands were loosely bound with steel chains, so as to avoid the remotest possibility of escape on her part, and that her whole body was covered with ulcers, while her tangled tresses were simply alive with vermin. This was Sister Barbara Ub..k, insane, and without the power of speech— the consequences of her incarceration of over nineteen years in this chamber of physical and mental torture. The archbishop, shocked beyond measure, had the abbess brought before him, and frightened her into confessing to him that this barbarous deed had been perpetrated by her orders, and in punishment of what she called a crime committed by Sister Barbara. The "crime" in question consisted in her having, during the first year of her convent novitiate, kept up a correspondence with her former admirer, and having, it appeared, consented by letter to elope with him. This infraction of all convent rules was brought to the notice of the abbess by a nun whom poor Barbara had been forced to take into her confidence, and who was glad to ingratiate herself with the mother-superior by betraying her miserable companion. With the help of this nun, the abbess conducted Sister Barbara to the underground dungeon at the dead of night, and bound her with chains. With their own delicate hands the two women built up the entrance of the narrow prison with bricks, leaving only a square opening through which bread and water were handed three times a week. No one else was let into the dismal secret, and as the dungeon was supposed to be haunted, the moans and cries of the prisoner, if ever heard by the members of the community, were attributed to supernatural visitors, and not one of the nuns ever dared to approach the steps leading down to the subterranean part of the great building. The archbishop, whose indignation knew no bounds, placed the abbess, together with her accomplice, under arrest, in a cell guarded by sentries, until he could refer the matter to his Holiness the Pope. Sister Barbara, who meanwhile had been clothed and fed, he took to the city lunatic asylum.

When the story became known to the people of Cracow, they collected around the convent where the abbess was imprisoned and threatened to burn not only it but all the convents with which the town abounds. The military had to be called out again, and the terrible riots which ensued lasted long and caused much bloodshed. Subsequently the abbess, and the nun who had been her confidante and helpmate, were severely punished by the Pope.

In the year 1876, while on a visit to Cracow, I was taken to see the lunatic asylum where Sister Barbara had been placed. The director of the asylum asked me whether I should like to see the heroine of the riots of 1869. To this I readily acquiesced, and I was soon ushered into a large, sunny room, brightened by flowers and daintily furnished. Near the window, sitting in a large chintz-covered arm-chair, was Sister Barbara, her hands crossed in her lap and her large blue eyes staring vacantly at a cage full of canaries which stood on the window-sill. Could this placid, white-haired, aristocratic-looking woman be the same who had seven years before been rescued from an awful martyrdom, and who then had been more like a wild animal than a human being? However, it was so! Gentle treatment and good care had restored her health, but neither her reason nor her power of speech. Her attendants told me that she seemed to have forgotten all her tortures. She was now always quiet, and apparently incapable of feeling any kind of emotion; birds and flowers arrested her eye, and sometimes brought a faint smile to her still beautiful lips, but otherwise she was absolutely oblivious of her surroundings.

I spoke to her, but she took no notice of what I said, and after a few moments I left her still gazing at the little imprisoned songsters, who, perchance, reminded her of the time when she also was a captive, though in a far more dreadful cage.

The Empress was so deeply interested in what I subsequently told her of my visit to Sister Barbara that until the latter's death, which occurred some ten years later, she frequently sent flowers to the poor, forlorn creature, and also some pretty and valuable singing-birds, since birds and flowers alone had retained the power of awakening a ray of feeling in her dimmed soul.

It is hard to think that death alone should have been able to tear the veil which obscured the sight of Elisabeth's detractors. The Austrian press, from the very moment that the electric

wires flashed to Vienna the awful news of her
assassination, took upon itself to deluge her
memory with encomiums and enthusiastic praise.
A Vienna daily paper published an article, entitled
"The Misjudged Empress," in which it confessed
"that the Vienna press frequently misinterpreted
the noble motives and intentions of the Empress,
who was a highly strung, sensitive character, and
whose fine feelings, abhorrent to every form of
self-advertisement, were sometimes mistaken for
pride and dislike by the Viennese."

Some of these articles came under my notice
lately, and I cannot help feeling the bitterness of
these *post-mortem* retractions, which seem of but
very little use, and which do not in any way
modify my opinion when I said at the beginning
of this work that "not a pen is being grasped in
vindication of so many injustices." For eulogies
accorded to the dead are comprised in all funeral
ceremonies, and could corpses, lying under the
sod of our cemeteries, or beneath the flag-stones
of gorgeous mausoleums, hear the pompous
speeches pronounced by people who hated and
reviled them during their lives, they might possibly indulge in a cadaverous grin at the hypocrisy of good, generous humanity!

The multitudes which thronged the streets of
Vienna to witness the gorgeous procession following Elisabeth's coffin was composed of those
self-same mourners who accompanied, ten years
before, that of Archduke Rudolph—"Unser Rudi"
(Our Rudi)—and who wept and sobbed and tore
their hair, while in their hearts lurked the conviction that the young Prince was first an assassin
and then a suicide. Ten years, I say! It is a long
time, and yet during all those days and months

which composed them nobody has really tried to put the truth, the naked, unadorned truth, of Rudolph's responsibility in the matter before the public. One writer—who called and still calls himself a friend of the ill-fated Prince—has published a booklet about the Mayerling tragedy. But, alas, the so-called "excuses" which he puts forward to exonerate Rudolph from blame are two-edged tools, which would cut and slice what might otherwise remain sacred about his memory were that pamphlet more generally read—which, thank goodness, it is not!

Mother and son have been misunderstood, misjudged, ah, how severely! But now they are reunited, and all the sorrows and disappointments of their earthly careers have passed from them—all the unkindness done to them by so many, the small and the great. Indeed, in so far as their home life was concerned, they might both have quoted the following lines:

> "Small slights, neglect,
>   unmixed, perhaps, with hate,
> Make up in number
>   what they want in weight.
> These, and a thousand griefs
>   minute as these,
> Corrode our comfort
>   and destroy our ease."

And what about their other countless miseries?

The bond which united Rudi to his mother was a very strong one; she was so youthful and full of life and beauty that he felt towards her as if she had been but an elder and beloved sister. When apart from each other they were in the habit of corresponding daily, and many of the letters thus exchanged were exquisite bits of literature. The style of each was remarkable, and they wrote to each other in many different languages, especially in English, which they both loved to speak and to write. A letter written by Rudi at the end of the seventies from the Istrian coast, where he had gone to visit a friend, began as follows:

"MY DEAREST,—When I arrived the sun was shining brightly on the top of the pink granite cliffs, shedding its golden light over the undulating plains of the table-land, which looked like a sea of dewy grasses and odorous flowers. Far down below us there was a hazy, shimmering line that showed where the sea was breaking on the Adriatic shore. I never come so far south without wishing, more than ever, that you were with me, you who love and appreciate this beautiful part of the world so much. In this spring-tide of the year, this season of youth and of love, of bird's songs and of budding roses, I found Philip in the stately, melancholy rooms of his villa, which stands on a steeply rising slope. He was arranging pictures, tapestries, statues, bronzes, and old brocades and embroideries, in the picturesque and artistic litter which he knows so well how to produce. Outside, in the grand shady gardens, hundreds of nightingales warbled their morning sonnets in the groves of camellias and of ilex-trees. It is a delightful place. I fell at once in love with its moss-grown terraces, where miles of ivy and of clustering vines run riot beneath immense cedars and magnolias. You would be charmed with the dreamy, peaceful repose

"THE BOY," EMPRESS ELISABETH'S FAVORITE HUNTER

which reigns here supreme. I am going to ride a great deal during my stay, in order to explore the country to right and to left; it is far more poetical than your dear Ireland, mother mine, etc."

This was written shortly after the Empress's return from her first hunting-trip to Ireland. Fond as she was of hunting in her own country, yet she delighted in the time which she spent in Ireland, and when, in 1879, she first arrived on the Emerald Isle, she gave vent to a perfect burst of enthusiasm concerning the excellent conditions under which one could hunt there, and especially with regard to the dangerous obstacles with which the country is so thickly studded. She was then preserving a semi-incognito under the name of "Countess of Hohenembs," and made herself very comfortable at Summerhill, Lord Langford's residence in County Meath, which she had taken as her hunting-box. She brought with her fifty-two horses, ten of which were her especial favorites, being magnificent Irish hunters, and including "The Boy," "Jupiter," "Domino," "The Doctor," "Investment," "Beauclerc," "Lorraine," "Othello," and "Black Prince."

"Bay Middleton" was her pilot from the day of her very first hunt in Ireland. This took place on the 24th of February, 1879, the meet being at Dunshaughlin, and the field including Lord Spencer, then Viceroy of Ireland, Prince Rudolph Lichtenstein, and many other well-known riders.

February of the next year found Elisabeth back in County Meath. It was during that visit that a certain fox she was pursuing sprang over the wall of Maynooth College, and rushed across the exercise-ground, where the pious young

students were pacing to and fro. What was the
astonishment of these youths when the wall was
also cleared by a lovely woman sitting with
amazing skill a magnificent hunter, all flecked
with foam and mud. It was the Empress of
Austria, who had followed the fox through thick
and thin, and evidently also through a great deal
of water, for she was dripping wet. Dr. Walsh,
who was then principal of Maynooth College,
hurried into the grounds to receive the Empress,
who had so unwittingly and so unceremoniously
entered his domain, and observing that she was
running great danger of catching a severe cold in
her present drenched condition, offered her a
warm wrap. No feminine garment, however, was
to be found in that school for young priests, and
Elisabeth had to accept Dr. Walsh's own cloak,
which she donned, laughingly remarking that
with it a doctor's degree ought to be conferred
upon her! On the following day the Empress sent
Dr. Walsh a diamond ring of great value, and
later on presented the college with a superb silver
statue of St. George and the Dragon, as well as
with a set of magnificent vestments, but the
academic coat she insisted upon keeping in
memory of her impromptu visit. A *requiem* mass
was celebrated at the death of the Empress, for
the repose of her soul, in the college chapel, and
much emotion was shown by those present, who
still recalled the happy memories of her stay in
Ireland.

In 1881 Elisabeth rented Combermere Abbey,
in Cheshire, for part of the hunting season,
and had a splendid time while there. She was
very fond of England, Ireland, and Scotland,
and could not bear to have the British Isles

disparaged in her presence. One day somebody spoke before her of "Foggy England," and she promptly rejoined:

"You have a perfectly false idea of the place. Parts of it are simply incomparable, and as to the Isle of Wight, it is a little paradise on earth. Why, dear me, I saw fuchsias and heliotropes there as big as trees, and covered with the sweetest blossoms one can imagine. The myrtles, too, and the pomegranates and oleanders, would make one believe that one was in Greece, while those great green, velvety lawns that sweep right down to the sea could be found nowhere but in English territory."

One of the many memorials of Empress Elisabeth which will remain in Austria, and one of the most picturesque and romantic, is certainly the chapel and shrine of St. Maria-Zell, in the Styrian Alps. It is the bourne of countless pilgrimages. I mention it here because it is intimately related with the Empress's passionate love for horses, and especially with one accident which she encountered while in the saddle. It owes its origin to the efforts of the youngest daughter of Empress Elisabeth—namely, Archduchess Valérie—who, when but twelve years of age, devoted all the money that she could either save or beg from her relatives to the erection of this chapel, which she dedicated to St. Maria-Zell and to St. George as a thank-offering for the marvellous escape of her mother from death.

One day, while the Empress was riding in the immediate vicinity of the spot where the shrine now stands, she had occasion to cross a bridge rudely made of trunks of fir-trees, which spanned a deep and turbulent torrent. Somehow

or another her high-spirited horse caught one of
its hind feet between the rugged planks, and
immediately commenced to rear in its frantic
endeavors to free itself. It was only with the greatest difficulty that the Empress, perfect horse-
woman though she was, managed to retain her
seat, and to avoid being hurled into the torrent
seething among the rocks far below. At length one
of the grooms who was following her succeeded in
quieting the terrified animal sufficiently to enable
her to dismount, and after having assisted in
extricating the horse's leg from between the
planks, which had severely bruised it, she pursued her way on foot. The Empress attributed her
preservation to the special intervention on her
behalf of the Blessed Virgin of Zell, and to that of
St. George, who is the patron-saint of all horse-
men and horsewomen.

On learning of her mother's danger, Archduchess Valérie was so impressed by the account
that she immediately planned the erection of the
beautiful chapel which now covers the shrine of
St. Maria-of-Zell. Over the entrance is a marble
block bearing the following inscription composed
by the little Archduchess:

"Holy Mother and Blessed St. George,
patron of cavaliers, who can preserve us
from all danger, and by whom my mother
has been so often protected when no human
help could avail her, I pray to you both with
confidence that you will not disdain my
humble petition, and that you will always be
the saviours of the precious life which gave
life to me.

"MARIE-VALÉRIE.   *In remembrance.*"

The chapel, or church, in question is built in

Gothic style on some shelving rocks, in the midst of a dense pine-wood which partly covers the mountain-side. All around are precipices, the borders and bases of which are black with fir-trees, and a great mountain capped with snow towers above the edifice, its sides bristling with jagged rocks, chasms, and huge bowlders.

The treasury of the chapel is filled with magnificent offerings presented by the ladies belonging to the Austrian imperial family, and to the nobility. In many cases they are emblazoned with their monograms and armorial bearings. The Countess de Chambord, wife of the French Legitimist Pretender, presented a short time before her death three superb lamps of solid gold for the sanctuary, and also a huge diamond cross which had belonged to Queen Marie Antoinette. The altar-covering is of almost priceless point de Venise, and is the gift of Empress Elisabeth herself.

In the midst of all these offerings of the rich and the great is preserved the tribute of a poor peasant girl, whose history is a touching one. She was of most humble origin, and spent her days in tending her cattle on the grassy slopes around her father's alpine hut. Gay and thoughtless as a bird, she led a happy, careless life in her mountains, and sang from morn till night.

One day, however, despair filled her heart. Her betrothed, a handsome, brawny mountaineer, lay at the point of death from the effects of an injury received while out hunting chamois. Ready to sacrifice almost anything for the sake of his recovery, she cut off her superb golden hair and offered it as a votive-gift to Our Lady of Zell. The young man recovered, but, sad to relate, he was so dismayed and even disgusted at the aspect presented by his betrothed shorn of her magnificent hair, which had been one of the principal features of her beauty, that he requited her devotion with coldness, scorn, and infidelity. Broken-hearted, the poor girl retired to a cloister, but to this day her lovely golden tresses, tied with the faded blue ribbon, are preserved in the treasury of St. Maria-Zell, side by side with the diamond cross of the far more unfortunate consort of King Louis XVI. of France.

Maria-Zell is situated, as I have said, right in the heart of the Styrian Alps, far away from the beaten track of foreign tourists, who rarely find their way thither. Every year, however, from ten to twelve thousand Austrians, consisting of peasants, bourgeois, nobles, and members of the imperial family, visit the shrine for the purpose of entreating the intercession of the Blessed Virgin of Zell and of St. George. The pilgrims generally arrive in large bands. They sing as they march, and the melody of these hundreds of harmonious voices ringing out in the fresh, clear alpine air is indescribably solemn and grand. Austrians, even to the lowest class, all possess a remarkable sense of music and a deep love for it. Nature itself in the Austrian Alps is full of melody; the echoes of the rushing torrents, the songbirds warbling in the woods, the murmuring of the wind through the tall reeds which encircle the mountain lakes, all unite in a concert of the most entrancing character, and it is not surprising that the inhabitants of these poetical regions should be influenced thereby.

The costumes, too, of the pilgrims are superb, and nowhere else can such a variety and picturesqueness of garb be seen as in the processions of worshippers on their way to Maria-Zell. The Styrian women wear short skirts of heavy silk brocaded in bright colors, and caps adorned with golden filigree, which are so valuable that they are handed down by the mother to the daughter from generation to generation. The girls from the Salzkammergut, in their dark petticoats and low-cut bodices, fastened with antique silver buttons, their snow-white muslin kerchiefs and their coquettish little hats, from beneath which escape their long braids, are as pretty as pictures. They wear broad necklaces composed of many tiny gold chains, with here and there great square clasps of gold filigree studded with garnets, turquoises, and topazes.

Then there are the Hungarian women, who impart a semi-Oriental aspect to the scene; for, like the Slavonians and the Croatians, they wear robes of white linen thickly embroidered with many-hued silks, and fastened around the waist with orange, blue, and crimson ribbons, while the scarlet silk handkerchiefs so deftly wound round their dusky tresses remind one involuntarily of the Turkish fez, and the ponderous rows of huge coral and amber beads encircling their necks recall the ornaments so dear to harem women.

The statue of the Holy Virgin of Maria-Zell is literally covered with priceless jewels, which have been offered *ex voto* by wealthy pilgrims. On her head glitters a diadem of gigantic rubies and diamonds, ropes upon ropes of softly gleaming pearls encircle her neck and her waist, rings set with sparkling gems adorn her fingers and even her toes, while her cloth-of-silver robe is loaded with streams of sapphires, clusters of emeralds, and *rivières* (necklaces; lit., "rivers") of diamonds. Indeed, the statue bears striking evidence of the fact that there are no more popular saints in Austria than St. George and Our Lady of Maria-Zell.

Another very serious accident occurred to the Empress during a summer which she spent in Normandy, near the Petites-Dalles, where she had rented Monsieur Perquer's charming little château of Sassetot. She used to take long rides along the picturesque shore, and sometimes even into neighboring Brittany, where I was at the time spending the summer, and where we used to undertake long excursions together. One day, in riding home to Sassetot, Elisabeth attempted to jump one of those treacherous walls made of loose pieces of rock, which surround the fields of the Breton and Normandy peasants. The top stones gave way under the horse's feet, for the animal had jumped short, and the Empress was precipitated to the ground with extreme violence. She was riding alone on that day, and remained lying there, in a dead faint, until some laborers returning from their work found her, and recognizing in her the benefactress who had so often come to their assistance in moments of need, they carried her between them, with the utmost gentleness, to her home. The Emperor was immediately advised by telegraph of the accident, and hastened to his wife's bedside as fast as steam could take him. Of course he preserved the strictest incognito, and nobody, excepting the immediate *entourage* and Maréchal MacMahon, who was then President of the French Republic, knew of his having visited France. Fortunately the Empress's condition soon ceased to give reason for alarm, and he was enabled to return speedily

THE EMPRESS AT THE AGE OF FORTY-EIGHT—
IN COURT DRESS

to Vienna without his presence having been betrayed to any one.

To the peculiarly poetically inclined and ideal-loving Empress, Brittany was sure to become very dear, for it is *par excellence* a land of old legends, of primitive habits, a land which is still, with but few alterations, just what it used to be in the time of the Feudality. The small, quaint old Breton towns are exactly to-day what they were six hundred years ago, with the exception of a few ill-burning lamps, serving only to emphasize the darkness of the streets at night, and some funny-looking low-ceiled shops containing the queerest possible assemblage of superb antiquities and hideous modern *articles de Paris* (fancy goods). They are still surrounded by thick bastioned and cranellated walls, and by moats where wild ducks swim about on the lentil-covered muddy water, and are entered by drawbridges just as when, at the end of the fourteenth century, Duguesclin passed through them at the head of his victorious armies. The streets are narrow and ill-paved, and the sidewalks, narrower still, are completely moss-grown, and look like borders of green velvet set before the high façades of the elaborately carved granite houses.

Summer and winter Brittany is a world of flowers, for the climate is so mild that there are wild stocks blooming in the crevices of the old walls, and on the wide window-sills of almost every house, pots of basilica, geraniums, and fuchsias, which even in midwinter make lovely blotches of color, and are like the smiles of these aged buildings. During the summer the sky, although a little hazy, as it invariably is on the old Armorican coast, is as blue as an angel's

gaze—so, at least, the ancient Breton ballad terms
it. At sundown softly tinted clouds, like the flying
petals of a gigantic rose, float above the sea. The
fields are all abloom with almond-scented white
sarrazin, crimson clover, and yellow colza, while
on the heath the furze and broom burst into
countless buds, and form a sea of fragrant gold
as far as the eye can reach, sheltering under
their shaggy branches a perfect carpet of pink
heather.

The Empress confided to me her desire to
spend some days in the wildest portion of the
Morbihan, not far from Cape Finisterre. She had
heard of the place as being especially lonely, and
knowing that there was on the rugged cliffs a
half-ruined old castle which belonged to one of
my relatives, she urged me to arrange this little
fugue, which would be shared by none besides
ourselves, and four of her old servants and of
mine.

A few days after she had made this proposal
the inhabitants of the hamlet of K—— were
surprised out of their usual tranquillity by seeing
a travelling carriage stop before the crumbling
portals of the château de X——, which had not
been inhabited for many a long year. This
château is situated in one of the grandest and
most savage regions of Brittany, far from any
railroad, surrounded by barren *landes* (moors),
and possessed of nothing which could attract any
ordinary globe-trotter. To be truthful, X—— is
not the place to inspire cheerful thoughts. Its
loneliness, its storms, its poverty, are not of a
nature to make one feel particularly jolly, but it is
there, perhaps, that one can best judge this
curious and mystical country. The castle—or

rather what remains of it—faces the greenish, dangerous-looking sea, and its ivy and moss-grown towers are backed by wind-tortured pines and cork-oaks. Farther away, on the table-land, there are delightfully green nooks, great woods— almost forests—where a wealth of delicate ferns and exquisite wild flowers conceal themselves in the deep, fragrant shadow, but X—— itself is very grim and bleak, and strangely out of keeping with the effeminate and luxury-loving period in which we live.

When we arrived there it was noon-day, there was no sun, and a heavy wrack of copper-colored clouds was sweeping up from the north. The sea was high and moaning loudly as it surged around the gaunt rocks in its utter abandonment, the partially ruined castle had a desolate aspect, and a fear seized me that Elisabeth would speedily regret her desire to become more intimately acquainted with this strange part of the world. I was soon reassured, however, by seeing her making the best of everything, laughing and talking away as if she were about to enter a perfect Eldorado. As we walked up the broken stone steps and passed into the grand and solitary chambers—gloomy and cheerless, with the wind beating at the big iron-barred casements through which the gray light from without was casting a dull gleam on the furniture, which was just as Breton as Breton could be—I watched her slender, almost girlish figure with astonishment and delight.

Any other petted woman of the world would have recoiled before such a picture of comfortless-ness. Not so, however, the Empress, who walked to one of the high windows and looked out on the rock-strewn strip of sand that parted the castle from the angry-looking sea, shrouded in gray fogs, the waves rolling heavily with a deep, desolate roar upon the narrow beach between two encircling lines of jagged cliffs.

"This is splendid," said she, turning to me with eyes beaming like twin stars; "what a dear, queer old place, and how very romantic! I am expecting every minute to see a 'Farfadet' or a 'Kourigan'—that is what you call your familiar spirits here, don't you?—come dancing towards me."

"How good you are!" I exclaimed. "How on earth do you manage to keep up your spirits in this way, to always see the bright side of things? I am sure that although I am a daughter of this rugged soil, I feel just about as Crusoe did when he was cast upon his desert island."

We looked at each other for a minute and then suddenly burst into uncontrollable laughter. Attracted by these extraordinary peals of merriment, the servants, who very justly thought that probably X—— was hardly the place for elaborate court etiquette, came running in, and could hardly refrain from beginning to laugh too.

"Good heavens!" said the Empress, as soon as she could manage to recover her breath, "what in the name of wonder are we all laughing about?"

This remark did not tend to diminish our hilarity, so that the first moments of our visit, which I had begun to dread for Elisabeth, began in the most cheerful fashion possible.

Amusements, in the general acceptance of the term, there were of course none, for there was not much to see excepting a few peasant-women

wearing the prim national costume and white cap
of Brittany, as they sat knitting or mending nets
on their door-steps in the little hamlet below the
northern cliff. Out on the *landes* lean cows and
brown sheep were driven by barefooted urchins
through the short, salted grass, while far away at
sea the sardine fishing-boats with their rough,
red sails tacked to and fro wellnigh at all hours of
the night and day.

We rode and drove and walked a good deal,
and also went out upon the sea to witness the
exploits of the sardine catchers. The fishing and
preserving of these dainty little silvery morsels is
one of Brittany's greatest and most interesting
industries. For this purpose we hired one of the
ordinary strong, stanch fishermen's boats.

There was one nook in the old castle of which
we both became very fond. It was perhaps the
best preserved portion of the great pile of buildings, and was filled with memories of a glorious
past—a past when faith was of more importance
to the honest-hearted, simple-minded inhabitants
than fame, and when they used to lavish the best
of all they possessed upon the altars consecrated
by their religion. It was the private chapel of the
château. Every day we brought back from our
rambles quantities of flowers with which to adorn
the little sacred edifice.

A few nights after our arrival something occurred there which I will never forget. We had
dined late, and very simply, off some thoroughly
Breton dishes, and we were standing before a
bright fire of faggots, kindled for us in the
apartment—which, although much deterio-
rated, was the most comfortable of all the partly
dismantled suite, and served us as a kind of

sitting-room—when suddenly the Empress linked
her arm into mine, and led me through the long
gallery of the northern wing to the little low
postern-door which opened into the chapel.

The small sanctuary was dark, excepting
where an eternally burning lamp shone in front
of the altar, and where some stray moonbeams
pierced the stained windows of the right aisle
and threw patches of dim color upon the worn
mosaic floor. We gazed about us, glancing reverently at the carved mailed figure of an ancestor
of mine who had died fighting beside Duguesclin
in 1364, and whose tall form we could just
discern as he lay at rest, with his gauntleted
hands clasped on the handle of a terrible-looking
sword.

Kneeling down the Empress began to pray,
the Latin words echoing strangely under the
empty, sonorous stone vaults above. The smell of
some white roses which we had placed that day
at the foot of a marvellously beautiful statue of
the Blessed Virgin floated towards us, and a little
shudder of awe ran between my shoulders. I felt
my hand being grasped by the Empress, and as
she held it in hers she whispered:

"These have been happy days. In remembrance of them you must wear this ring, which
has never left me for many and many a year.
It will also remind you, if ever we are separated,
for good and all, that you have been very dear
to me, and that I have valued your sympathy
and friendship, as well as your devotion, more
than I can express."

Hot tears rose to my eyes, and with the hand
upon which she had just slipped the sparkling,
scintillating, square-shaped diamond—which I

have ever worn since that night—I raised her own slender fingers to my lips and kissed them tenderly and reverently.

When we went back that night to our rooms, Elisabeth stood for a moment musingly before the high stone mantel-piece of her sleeping-apartment, whereon were carved the two following lines:

> "Un chevalier, n'en doutez pas,
> Doit férir haut et parler bas."*

"Those were times," she said, "when it was worth while to live. The days of chivalry have always had a singular charm for me; all seems so tame and tasteless in this nineteenth century of ours. But here at least, within these thick, gray walls, one can imagine what the existence of the heroes of old could be, and that is why I have fallen in love with X——. Listen now to the sound of the wind roaring outside, and tell me if, with a little imagination, we cannot believe that we have been suddenly transported back five or six centuries?"

I turned towards the window, and certainly the wild spectacle of the boisterous, stormy night, seen from the high turret-chamber, lent itself to any possible imaginings. The moon was ascending rapidly above the horizon line amid a heaped-up mass of inky clouds, and the wind was rising with an alarming shriek and churning the waters into froth. Even while we were both watching, the waves began to leap in menacing fashion. They rolled in like high water walls, crashing against the rocks on which the château stood as if they were about to engulf it, and when they retreated,

---

*("A knight, make no mistake. / Must strike high and speak low.")

with a deafening roar, they scooped out deep
caverns in the pebbly shore with a noise like that
of thunder.

"Dear Lord, there will be mischief at sea
to-night," said the Empress, sadly.

"Ah yes!" I replied; "this means disaster
to any ship running along the coast, and I dare
say we will get but little sleep to-night with all
heaven and earth's artillery thus unchained
against our rock fastness!"

"Never mind, you selfish child," quoth
Elisabeth, "it is the poor sailors who are to be
pitied, and not we who are cosily established here."

I glanced with a slight shrug of my shoulders
at the bare stones of the walls, and gave a little
cough of derision for our "cosiness."

A wild night; a night that would play with
men's lives as with pieces of broken match-wood.
The wind rose louder and louder in sudden
blasts, swift and fierce, sweeping over the phos-
phorescence of the sea, which shone hungrily and
cruelly, eternal power speaking loudly in the
rushing of that awful storm.

Towards four o'clock in the morning, during
one of those uncanny lulls of the tempest, which
seems to sink in order to rise again in deadlier
wrath, there echoed from the infuriated ocean
the piteous signal of some perishing vessel. Before it had been repeated the Empress was at my
bedside, looking like an apparition in her long
white night-robe, which was, however, no whiter
than her tremulous face.

"Come and look!" she exclaimed; "there is a
ship in distress there beyond. O God! what can
we do?"

The day was breaking, and as we reached the

window we could discern, by the lurid, dismal light of the storm-tossed morning sky, a large fishing-boat, with her sails rent away and her masts broken, careening between the monstrous waves, one moment lifted on a foaming crest, the next disappearing into the trough of the sea, like a wounded bird with broken wings, driven at the mercy of the tempest—this fellow-reaper of death which spares neither youth nor age, and hears neither mother's prayers nor childhood's cry!

For a moment we gazed vacantly, stupidly, helplessly at this distressing picture, then in common accord we wrapped about us what garments we first could lay our hands upon, rushed down the long corridors, the wide staircase, and after struggling with the outer door, which well-nigh resisted all our efforts, we found ourselves in the open.

Far from everywhere and everything, from coast-guard men and life-saving station, what could be done to help those unfortunate fellow-creatures in their dire peril? Through the driving spume and falling spray we vaguely saw the blurred forms of some fisher-folk from the hamlet, running along the narrow strip of sand towards us, but of what assistance could even they be in such a stress? Right between us and the drifting, rudderless vessel the jagged teeth of a line of reefs shone black and threatening, parting the waves asunder into yawning gulfs. The pitiless wind was tearing at our clothes and flinging our hair across our eyes, and it was almost impossible for us to keep our footing; yet somehow or other we managed to struggle down the rugged path hewn in the cliff, step by step, clutching to the projections of the live rock to prevent ourselves from being precipitated headlong upon the surf-splashed shingle below.

Where we were going or what we intended to do did not cross our troubled minds; we were rushing to the rescue, although rescue was impossible to achieve! At last we reached the bottom of the sloping wall of stone, and clinging to each other we stopped, breathless and drenched, buffeted by that fearful, howling wind, our eyes fixed upon the doomed boat; and as we looked the end came! One huge wave dashed over her, and flung her with a heart-rending clamor of crushing, splitting, wailing horror against the shining, blackened shoals. We saw some dark forms washed from the wreck into the yawning abyss of the boiling seas, a few human forms that would soon be cast up against the bowlder-strewn shore, mangled, bleeding, and lifeless.

In the green, whirling waters the drowning fishermen struggled among the flotsam and jet-sam of the shattered boat. With a sorrowful cry the Empress slipped from my hold and rushed towards the retreating breakers that were going back in search of their prey. Instinctively I bounded after her, and caught her firmly around the waist. Full of pity as my heart was for the unfortunate beings dying in the voracious bil-lows, yet I was not going to let her fly into danger while under the spell of one of these unhesitating impulses of self-forgetfulness, of which I knew her to be so fully capable. Her face was deadly pale, her eyes shone with excitement, and she put out all her strength to free herself from me. She was a skilled and daring swimmer, and although she must have known that none could swim those seas and live, I saw that she was going to attempt it. I, too, put out my strength, and we struggled for a brief minute, until what between the force of the wind and the shifting sands we stood upon, we fell to our knees just as the outer edge of a colossal volume of water came thundering towards us, and all but carried us both into the murderous waste of the Atlantic.

When we rose the shelving, broken hull of the bark had disappeared, and right at our feet the bodies of a boy and a man had been washed up by the big wave and left there dead, as we at first supposed. Our servants, awakened at last by the deafening roar of the hurricane, had hurried towards us by the longer and safer path which started from behind the castle, and they bore the two sailors away. The young lad was clinging with his stiffened arms to a plank whereon was inscribed in white lettering, *Marie-Stella*, the name of the wrecked vessel.

Our efforts at resuscitation were successful, and we were very happy when, after two hours of continuous toil, we found that we had brought back life to the two poor creatures who, it appears from what they told us later, were the captain and owner of the boat, and his son, who was acting as *mousse*, or ship's boy. Before we left the castle of X—— the Empress had placed in the hands of the amazed and overjoyed *patron* a sufficient sum of money to purchase a new fishing-smack, thus saving him from utter and hopeless ruin.

Elisabeth's passionate love for the sea was not dulled by the awful spectacle she had witnessed on that eventful autumn morning, but it was veiled with sadness forever after. Her fearless nature never dreaded this great destroyer, and she used often to say:

"The waves seem to draw me towards them, as if they knew how I love them!" She never forgot the monstrous Atlantic rollers which dashed themselves against the rugged coasts of Brittany, and they created such an impression upon her that she often, even after years had elapsed, alluded to them.

Long before all this took place, when returning on board her yacht from the island of Madeira, she had encountered just such another terrible storm. Her yacht was tossed like a nutshell upon the mountainous waves, but far from being terrified by this, the Empress insisted, in spite of the captain's remonstrances and fears, on being tied with a rope to the mast, in order that she might watch the fury of the sea, and in the midst of the tumult she laughingly exclaimed:

"How many more times must I declare my principles and ideas about the length of life which is allotted to each of us? We live just as long as God permits, and if I have been intrusted with a mission here below, Providence will protect me from every danger!"

During her short stay in Brittany the Empress literally showered kindnesses upon the families of many poor fishermen, whose thatch-roofed huts clustered so close to the cliffs that they seemed but larger birds'-nests clinging to the rocks for protection from the wind and weather; and although they did not know who their benefactress was, they soon found a befitting name for her, and called her the "Queen of Mercy."

While staying in England at the sea-side resort of Cromer, in July, 1887, she gave one of

EMPEROR FRANZ-JOSEPH IN STATE ROBES
AS KING OF HUNGARY

these proofs of delicacy of heart which are not
easily forgotten among the humbler classes. She
was walking on a stormy morning along the
shore, when she suddenly caught sight of a group
of sailors who were carrying the corpse of a
drowned man. She immediately approached and
inquired about this disaster, and was told that
the victim was a poor employé of the railroad,
called Walter Moules, who had accidentally met
with his death in the tossing waters. Hearing
that the man was married and had several children, without a minute's delay she set off for his
humble dwelling, for she said it was necessary
that somebody should warn the newly made
widow of the terrible misfortune which had befallen her before the sailors brought home their
ghastly burden. The kindness with which she
broke the awful news to the poor woman was a
marvel of delicate tenderness, and she remained
with her until the body of the drowned man had
been carried into the little cottage; then turning
to the bereaved wife she said, softly: "Pray for
the soul of your husband; I shall help you, in so
far as the children are concerned, as much as
I can." And then she rapidly walked away. An
hour later one of her Majesty's servants brought
to the widow a pocket-book containing six
hundred pounds sterling, which there is considered a very large sum indeed.

All these little traits which I now relate were
not known among the public, for the Empress
had an absolute dread of any publicity of that
kind, which generally led to more misinterpreta-
tions of her actions.

While I was at Vienna it was learned one
morning that one of the Empress's maids had

died during the night, and very severe comments were made about the fact that the Empress had been seen riding in the Prater on the very same afternoon. It was not told, however, that the Kaiserin had spent the whole of the previous night, as well as several others which had preceded it, at the dying woman's bedside, nursing her with her own hands up to the moment when she breathed her last, and that it was only when death had stilled her sufferings that Elisabeth, who was in sore need of some fresh air and of some change of scene, had gone in search of both in the less frequented parts of the Prater.

She dried the tears of countless wretches, and brought comfort and consolation with her to many and many a stricken home. During the typhus epidemic which raged in the Hernalser-Mädchen-Institute she insisted upon visiting the stricken girls, and upon personally encouraging and consoling them, quite regardless of the danger which she ran; and when cholera and small-pox made their appearance at Budapesth, she accompanied the Emperor, who was obliged to go there for the opening of the delegations, saying that the moment of danger was just the moment when she should be by the side of her husband.

CHAPTER VIII

Doctor Christomanos, who was for three years Greek reader to the Empress, but whose connection with the Court terminated in 1893, wrote soon after her death the following description of her—a description so pretty and so true that it deserves to be translated word for word in these pages:

"When I was presented for the first time to Empress Elisabeth, it was in the summer of 1890, at Castle Lainz. I was requested to wait for her in the gardens, which were a mass of wonderful blossoms and flowering trees. I had never seen the Empress, and knew her only by her photographs and portraits, and I was, I must confess, filled with emotion at the idea that a long-wished-for privilege was about to become mine. I sat on a bench under a great tulip-tree, my heart beating with nervousness, awaiting her. Suddenly, without a sound having heralded her approach, she stood before me—a slender, black-clad apparition. She held in one hand a white umbrella and in the other a large black fan, and a charming smile of welcome played upon her features. In spite of the fact that her pictures resembled her only as a paste-diamond resembles the

beautiful gem itself, I knew in a flash that it
was indeed the Empress, and I felt that I was
in the presence of the most exquisite and
perfect creature who ever assumed the
human form. I murmured a few sentences
concerning the honor and happiness which
were mine at meeting her—sentences so
clumsy that I blush even now when remembering them; but with wonderful kindness
she helped me over these first few moments
of embarrassment and talked to me as if we
had long been the best of friends, instead of
being, she a great sovereign, and I a poor,
humble, ordinary mortal.

"I have had the good fortune to have
been near the Empress during three years;
I have seen with her eyes the beauty of
nature which she knew so well how to point
out and explain to me. She has revealed to
me a greater source of admiration for the
waves and for the mountains, for the forests
and for the large, undulating plains; she has
made me feel also the natural tie that binds
the truly pure and lofty spirits of some few
privileged beings, the tie of a common love
for flowers and melody, and the glories of
nature in general. Before I knew her I had
never fully comprehended the grand infinity
of the ocean, the deep azure of a summer
sky, the wonderful rhythm of poetry, and
the intense charm of music. It is enough
happiness for one life to have been permitted
to bask in the sunshine of her presence. Her
subjects did not know her and never did her
justice, for when one is as perfect as she
was, one is sure to be misunderstood. Indeed

a throne seems but a lowly footstool to bear such perfect, angelic womanhood! She herself, though, chided me when I thus expressed myself in her presence, and told me that she considered some parts of her duties as a sovereign very dear to her, nay, almost sacred. She proved that this was the case by bending all her efforts upon relieving misery and planning out new ways of helping the poor and the afflicted throughout the vast realms of her consort's empire. She was a queen of grace and of soulful consideration and kindness. Pageant, pomp, and ceremony she did not like, and when she consented to deck herself with the insignia of her lofty rank she was not made any more beautiful by this priceless display of jewels, for the precious stones themselves seemed to gather their magnificence and their dazzling loveliness from their being placed in contact with her. Of a truth, she belonged more to a sphere of angels than to that of the children of men, who live in cities and shun all that is true and pure in unblemished nature. When I used to see her dainty, delicate figure standing on some mountain peak she reminded me of a slender cypress swaying above a cemetery of spirits, and surrounded by the golden radiance of everlasting sunlight! How young she still seemed—she who was already a grandmother! How clear and pure were the great eyes which revealed at times the touching simplicity of a child's soul—those eyes which in the valleys of this sad world of ours have shed so many bitter tears! Wherever she went she aroused

enthusiasm; the peasants of the village of
Gasturi, on Corfu, where she built her magnificent palace dedicated to Achilles, used to
kneel before her in the dust when she
approached, calling aloud in their melodious
language: 'O Queen of Beauty, may God
bless thy every step!' All heads were un-
covered when she passed, and the children,
who watched for her coming, would run
towards her with their hands full of blossoming orange and almond boughs. She
adored everything that was beautiful, and
one day when, in Madeira, a strikingly
handsome peasant girl with amber skin,
coral lips, and raven-black hair presented
her with a cluster of crimson camellias, she
gave her a piece of gold, saying to me afterwards, 'That is a cheap price to pay for
gazing on such perfection of form and face.'

"Her enthusiasm for poetry and for
music was plainly shown by her profound
admiration for great composers and great
poets. She erected a monument to her favorite 'bard,' Heinrich Heine, in the gardens of
Achilleon, and it is there that she used to go
and gaze at the great brilliant stars of the
semi-Oriental sky shining through a network of silvery olive-tree branches.

"She feared not death; once she said to
me: 'When the love of life has forsaken one,
Death has already put his cold hand on
one's shoulder.' Another time, when her
yacht was fighting with the waves which
break on the coast of Algeria, she remarked:
'Are you ready to die, or do you think, like so
many, that death is a heroic action, difficult

to accomplish well? As far as I am concerned, it matters but little to me how and
when I will really close my eyes forever, for
there is in every earthly career a moment
when one inwardly dies, and that need not
be the time when actual death takes place.
What is disagreeable is all this ceremony
which surrounds our parting from our envelope of clay—a ceremony which the ancient
Romans abandoned to their slaves. It is not
pleasant, of course, to watch decrepitude in
its advance upon us. As for myself, I await
death at any moment, and you, who are a
philosopher, ought to do the same.'

"A little while later, however, when I
approached the edge of a precipice towering
above the waves, she laughingly alluded to
our previous conversation, and said, 'It is
not necessary for you to seek a poetical
death, it is enough to inwardly die a fine
death.'

"I could not but admire the extraordinary qualities of this sunny soul, which,
after thus familiarizing itself with the
greatest enemy of mankind, could live on, at
peace, and just as if she were going through
a task which she loved only because she
considered it in the light of a duty!"

The Greek teacher of the Empress, Mr. Rhoussopoulos, who also several times accompanied
the Empress on her travels, although he does not
express himself with the same poetical flow of
language as does Doctor Christomanos, yet gives
some very interesting and touching details about
her Majesty's attitude under a great many different circumstances. He lays great stress on the fact

of Elisabeth's always doing her best to make
those about her happy. That is very true and a
very marked trait of this golden-hearted woman's
character, and one which I cannot tire of mentioning. She could not endure to see any one suffer
even the slightest pain or vexation. He relates
that shortly after the marriage of Marie-Valérie,
she had promised to give him a photograph of
this her favorite daughter, in her wedding-dress.
One morning she brought to the professor ten of
those pictures, which had been taken in various
attitudes, and asked him to select one of them.

"The choice is difficult, your Majesty, for they
are all equally lovely," replied Rhoussopoulos.

"Then you had better keep them all," she
replied, smiling.

In the spring of 1890 the Empress went to
Wiesbaden, accompanied by her Greek teacher,
and during her stay there used to keep the windows of her villa open day and night. This caused
the professor to ask her whether she was as fond
of European landscapes as of Oriental ones, and
whether she liked to travel in Europe.

"Yes," answered the Empress, "but I generally prefer to 'look upon Europe in profile,'"
meaning thereby that she liked to see the European coasts best from the deck of her yacht.

She was extremely fond of Paris, and France
generally, for there she could wander about without the fear of being perpetually annoyed by the
indelicacy of the people, who in other countries
crowded around her to dog her slightest step.
There she also delighted in meeting her sisters,
the Queen of Naples and the late Duchess
d'Alençon. Once during a walk in the Bois de
Boulogne she said to Professor Rhoussopoulos:

"How I used to love my rides through these beautiful paths! I would never have believed then that the time would come when I would walk along them while learning Greek. Still there is always one charm for me in Paris which nothing can efface—namely, the memory of Napoleon I. What a great man he was, and what a pity that his insatiable ambition should have led him to seek an imperial throne."

The political ideas of the Empress, declares the professor, were extremely broad. She said to him on one occasion:

"Everybody seems to think that a Republican form of government is the best, and my teacher, Count Janos Majlath, has written much about this. Poor Count Majlath! I can never think of him without the deepest sorrow, remembering the terrible death he sought, together with his daughter, in this same lake of Starnberg, where my cousin Louis was drowned. But to return to what we were saying: I myself must say that, theoretically speaking, a republic is without a doubt the most reasonable form of government, but in Austria there exist so many different races and populations assembled within one frontier that the dynasty alone can form the link to hold them together. And so with us, monarchy, it seems to me, should always be the most practical plan to follow. By-the-bye," she added, "you seem surprised to hear me talk about such things. What do you think about the book published in London at the end of the fifties, and which is called *Blick auf den Anonymen Rückblick?*"

This was a book which had been strictly proscribed in Austria, and of which only a few copies had been smuggled into the country; it is, therefore, easy to imagine the degree of the professor's amazement upon hearing the Empress mention it.

"Do you possess that book?" she continued.

"It is forbidden in the entire monarchy," he replied.

"That is not what I asked you; my question is, 'Do you possess that book?'"

The professor remained mute, and blushed with embarrassment. The sovereign began to laugh, and having drawn from her pocket a small key, she unlocked a secret drawer of her desk, exclaiming:

"You probably imagine that I have never read anything of the kind, so now see here," and she handed to him half a dozen volumes and pamphlets, among which was *The Fall and Disintegration of Austria,* which was published soon after the Austro-Prussian war, and which created at the time a tremendous sensation, for the author declared therein that the Hapsburg Monarchy could not possibly last any longer, and wrote in a violent and blood-thirsty fashion against the reigning house. It is easy to understand the stupefaction of Professor Rhoussopoulos, especially when her Majesty quietly remarked:

"Do you know who was the author of this book?"

Of course the professor was aware that the name of this writer was Lang, a young man whose father was the devoted servant of Emperor Franz-Joseph; but this was all the more reason why he should refuse to reveal to Elisabeth what she apparently wanted to know.

"Oh, I see!" laughed the Empress. "You don't

know the author, but, surely, you are well acquainted with his father; and so I am glad to be able to tell you that the poor old man has never been and will never be made responsible for the perhaps a little too advanced ideas of his son."

Moritz Jókai, in his beautifully written appreciation of the late Empress, which appeared in print a week after her death, says:

"She was the ideal woman, as wife and mother, as beauty and queen. Especially was she admirable as a patient sufferer, *'mater dolorosa par excellence'* (sorrowful mother par excellence)...

"The woman who suffers in patience is only second to the Divinity. Like her son, the Crown-prince Rudolph, she was a fatalist. She trusted to fate. Fear she never knew—neither fear of man nor of the elements. To what extent the Queen was the guardian angel of Hungary, history alone can show. She conversed in our language with a purity of accent and a choice of expression that no one else could rival....Many distinguished Hungarians might with advantage have taken lessons from her. She was the patroness of Hungarian literature, and I have personally much cause to remember her with passionate gratitude. In 1889 the Queen graciously accepted the dedication of one of my novels.

"The court was at Ofen, and there I presented her with a copy of my work. She talked to me for a long time on the subject of our literature, displaying great penetration and a sound critical faculty of judgment. Just as I was going to take my leave she said:

"'Wait a moment, and I will show you my little daughter.' She opened a side door and beckoned to a nurse who held the small offshoot of royalty on a lace pillow in her arms.

"The baby was Marie-Valérie. The Queen took her from the nurse and pressed the laughing child's cheek against her own. That was the most beautiful reward of my life. And now it is all over—such infinite grace, love, and exalted feeling! All shut away in a coffin, she rests under a burden of wreaths here below, but her soul is floating, untrammelled, in heaven. No longer does the dread shadow pursue her—the shadow which drove her from country to country. At last her great soul has met that other soul which, dreaming or waking, she never could forget. . . . If our beloved Queen had drawn her last breath on a bed of sickness, we should have then covered her with flowers and tears, and blessed her resting-place, and she would have vanished from our midst. But the Queen who has died a martyr's death will never vanish; her spirit will hover near us forever. When storms from without threaten the Fatherland, and our nation is torn asunder by internal feuds, she will show us her bleeding wound, and the mouth of the wound will speak to us, saying: 'Love the Fatherland. Love the King.' Pray God we may!"

The Hungarians are talking of erecting a statue of the Empress at Ofen, representing her on horseback. This would, indeed, be a splendid idea, for not only did she never appear to better advantage than when in the saddle, but also the

Magyars of the Pùsztá saw her so very often riding among them that it is thus that they remember her best. I myself can conjure her up most easily in my dear remembrance of her as the graceful figure beside whom I rode so many and many a mile, our horses almost touching each other, our enraptured eyes scanning together the endless plains or the rich grass and woodland of Hungary.

How well I recall her looks and actions when we rode out alone to witness a Tzigan wedding, late one evening, in a forest near Yémisàr!

The scene which we witnessed that night was solemn and weird in the extreme. It was illuminated by a huge pile of flaming pine-logs, in front of which, with his back towards the fire, stood the Vajda, or chief Zingaro, draped in a long crimson mantle, holding in his hand an ebony staff with a silver knob, as a symbol of his dignity and autocratic power. The authority of this personage over his tribe is supreme, even to life and death. It is he who performs the marriage, birth, and burial ceremonies, according to the true Zingaro rite, for although thousands of the Tzigans have nominally embraced Christianity, yet they still remain at heart as devoted to the worship of fire as their ancestors who dwelt on the slopes of the Indian Himalayas.

Hand in hand the young couple stood before the flames, under the drooping branches of the great dark trees, listening reverently to the solemn words of the Vajda. The bridegroom was only sixteen, and the bride little more than twelve — ages, however, corresponding, both as regards physical and mental development, to about twenty and sixteen in the case of Europeans.

The handsome, stalwart boy, clad in a crimson dolman and dark breeches, high, tasselled boots and small velvet cap with a heron's plume, towered head and shoulders over his tiny, dark-eyed *fiancée*. She was an extremely pretty creature, this graceful girl, and her scarlet skirt and bodice, with the necklace of gold sequins which glittered at her throat and in her dusky braids, set off her strange beauty wonderfully. As soon as the Vajda had concluded his address, an earthen vessel was dashed to pieces on the ground as a symbol that the past of both young people had come to an end, and that a new life was beginning for them, and the bridal couple were sprinkled with a mixture of salt and brandy for the purpose of putting to flight any evil spirits that might be lurking about them. Heavy silver rings were then exchanged, and after the Vajda had placed his hands in token of blessing over their bowed heads, the youthful pair were regarded as duly married, and received the congratulations of their relatives and of the numerous members of their tribe.

Shortly afterwards feasting and dancing began—the latter to the sound of that inthralling music which the Tzigans draw from their violins and cymbals. It is a music that stirs the listener to the utmost limits of terrestrial—nay, one might say almost heavenly enthusiasm. Its exquisite melodies seem to penetrate the very marrow of one's bones, to send a thrill through the entire body, and to raise the soul far above earth. It is heard nowhere save in Hungary, Roumania, and the Balkans. The musicians let all their heart go out in the strains of their perfect instruments, and it seems as if their hearts would break were they to cease these floods of inthralling harmony.

They play as a lark carols—naturally, passionately—bringing one through all the phases of love, of pain, of rapture, until every nerve tingles. Then, suddenly, with one deep, plaintive chord, as if the strings were rent asunder in a last sweet, lingering sigh, they are silent, exhausted by the plenitude of their own power.

Nothing can give an idea of the enthusiasm they arouse. I have seen the great Liszt himself listen to them spellbound, with tears falling down his sunken, pallid cheeks. I have seen spoiled and *blasé* men of the world entranced by the matchless melodies of these artists of nature, and one night, in the Banàt, when the stars were coming out one by one in the clear violet skies, I saw Prince Louis E—— and a party of his guests give the Tzigans, who had been playing for them, not only all the money they had about them, but their watches, chains, studs, rings, etc., the women taking the jewels from their fingers and the flowers from their bosoms to fling them at the feet of the dark-eyed musicians. The most remarkable thing about this is that the Zingari do not know a note of music. They are merely the interpreters of the nightingales, of nature's own sweetest harmonies. They play by tradition, because music is in their souls, and because they cannot help giving utterance to it. The Hungarian bands, styling themselves Tzigans, and hiring themselves out to play in foreign cities, have nothing in common with the Zingari of the Pùsztá. The former are pleasing to hear, well taught and well drilled, but they are only mechanical nightingales who sing for money, very different from the free, fiery, and untutored artists of the great southern plains.

The dancing of the Tzigans also in no way resembles the jerky motion which we are wont to consider the acme of terpsichorean art. It is poetical, graceful, and dignified, and at the same time coquettish and exquisite, especially where the women are concerned. In fact, these dances, as we saw them on many a night in those days, are a mixture of the wild Hungarian Czárdàs, the Hindoo Nautch, and the stately minuet of bygone days. The men in their tight-fitting attilàs, with an embroidered dolman hanging from the left shoulder, clatter the long spurs attached to their boots, and the girls move with that swift grace inherent in their race, making up a beautiful picture as they wind their way in and out of the intricate mazes of this peculiar but charming dance.

Not long after we attended the Tzigan wedding I just described, we became the involuntary witnesses in the same forest glades of another Tzigan ceremony, which may be regarded as a kind of epilogue to the wedding festivities, for it illustrates the sanctity with which the Zingari regard the marriage vows.

One evening the Empress and myself rode to the Czikànà, or camp, belonging to the great Vajda, Ferénzi-János, but found it deserted. The faint sound of wailing voices coming from the pine-woods in the distance, however, attracted our attention, and guiding our horses cautiously over the tangled bracken and osmunda-bushes which covered the ground, we soon came in sight of a scene which I shall never forget.

The moon was shining brightly, lighting up

the spot with fairy-like splendor. All around the
pine-woods stretched the ruddy glow of gypsy
fires, flashing between the dark boughs and
throwing a crimson gleam on a space where the
trees had been cut down. There, bound to a stake
like a prisoner of the redskins, was a woman, her
perfect figure clothed in nothing but her raven
tresses. Her great black eyes had an agonized
look in them, and blood was dropping from four
incisions made with some sharp instrument in
her shapely arms and limbs. Surrounding her
was the entire tribe—men, women, and children—
chanting a kind of sinister invocation, while towering over the victim was the majestic form of the
Vajda, still holding in his clenched hand the
leather thong with which he had been chastising
her mercilessly. With a cry of dismay we both
sprang from our saddles, and scattering the
crowd, rushed towards him.

"What do you mean, János Ferénzi?" cried
her Majesty, clutching his arm. "What has this
unfortunate woman done that you should treat
her thus?"

The noble face of the Vajda, which at first had
expressed nothing but astonishment at our unexpected appearance, now assumed a look of dignity and of sadness which I, for one, had never
seen there before.

"There has been love, and of the love sin,
and of the sin a curse would come upon my tribe
were it not punished," he said, solemnly. "This
woman has betrayed the man to whom she was
in honor bound. I, Ferénzi-János, must avenge
the disgrace inflicted on one of my people. Her
woe was wrought by her own hand, and she must
eat the fruits of her crime."

The words fell slowly and mournfully on the silence of the night, troubled only by the river waves beating, with a dull murmur, against the rocks fifty feet below, and by the soughing of the wind which had arisen. Ferénzi-János was indeed in his own eyes, and in those of his people, a judge and an avenger. In vain did we try to plead and argue in behalf of the woman. He remained immovable, quietly but firmly refusing to grant even an imperial request.

"Nothing can help the culprit," he said. "For twenty-four hours must she remain at the stake, and then she will become a wanderer on the face of the earth. The incisions you see are the signs of her degradation, and no tribe will ever allow her to rest in its midst. Believe me," he added, "we are only just. We warn our women of what awaits them should they sin. It is for them to keep themselves pure. Moreover, you have been our friends and you will not betray us, because in your heart you know that this punishment is well deserved."

What could either of us argue against such reasoning? We exerted ourselves so much in her behalf, nevertheless, that at last the miserable woman was unbound and sent out of the camp that night instead of being left at the stake until the following sundown. This was a great concession on the part of Ferénzi-János, and seemed to fill his people with astonishment. I need hardly add that through the Empress's care the wretched woman found a home on one of the royal estates, where I have reason to believe she remains to the present day. The impression made upon us by this incident was a lasting one, and often did we talk together of the wild, weird scene of the forest of Yémisàr.

One thing which always struck me about my Tzigan friends is the nobility of their demeanor. They all seem to be born aristocrats, so dignified and impressive is their bearing under all circumstances. I think that I can describe them as stanch monarchists, for they are exceedingly loyal to their Vajdas, and to their Queen, wandering majesty though she is, living in canvas tents wherever her fancy may lead her.

The Zingari whom one meets in cities are degenerates, and cannot give any idea of what the free-born child of the Pùsztá is like. To know the latter well, it is necessary to visit their picturesque settlements on the plains, or in the dense pine forests which here and there break the monotony of the boundless grassland of the country of their adoption. It is difficult to win their confidence, or to secure a welcome to their camps, and many savants who in the interests of science have desired to study their mode of life have been discouraged from so doing by the icy barrier of disdain and mistrust which this still half-savage people seem determined to place in their way.

As far as I am personally concerned, I found no trouble in making friends with them, a fact due perhaps to a service which I had been able once to render to the tribe of Ferénzi-János under somewhat singular circumstances. I am sure that I found them, especially after I had taken the pains to acquire some knowledge of the Romany language, firm and reliable friends, ready to stick to one through thick and thin in unswerving allegiance. They showed me complete trust, revealing to me many of their secrets with absolute sincerity and truthfulness.

No one who has seen so much of them as I have can do otherwise than indorse Grellmann's theory concerning the Hindoo origin of this remarkable people. The two languages are very similar; for instance, in Hindustani the word snow is "hima," and the word bearer, "laya," while in Romany the words are "him" and "loya." In both languages "himalaya" means "the bearer of snow." Many other proofs might be given as to the certainty of the fact that the Himalayan slopes were the original home of all the gypsies previous to the year 1417, when they made their first appearance in Europe. The religion has remained almost entirely that of fire-worshippers. The earth, which they call "phno," has, according to them, existed from all eternity, and is the origin of everything that is good, because a raging and undying fire burns in its bowels. Their god is named "Devel," and their devil "Beng." They fear both, and curse both freely when some misfortune reaches them. Their most solemn oath is to swear by the dead, an oath which it is the direst dishonor to break. But in spite of this they do not believe in an after-life. They have no word for paradise and none for heaven, although they sometimes talk of a region inhabited by devils, a "beng-ipe" (demon's home).

It is a great mistake to imagine that the Tzigans pride themselves on the possession of the powers of divination and even witchcraft with which they are popularly credited. On the contrary, they ridicule the belief.

Late one afternoon my imperial friend and I happened to be riding home through a *cikania*, where I often had been alone before. We stopped to talk to a beautiful young Zingaro, with whom

I was acquainted. A wild, handsome girl she looked, with a scarlet hood thrown over her jetty hair, and her glittering eyes gazing into the darkening heavens, where the crescent of the new moon was rising.

"Tell me my fortune, Revicta!" suddenly exclaimed her Majesty, holding out her open hand to her. The glow of the camp-fire was bright enough for her to read the lines of the delicate palm, which she took between her brown and shapely fingers. For a moment she remained silent, looking up with surprise into the lovely face above hers.

"You want me to prophesy for you? You want to hear what Revicta, the daughter of the flames, can say about your future?" half chanted she, in that peculiarly monotonous recitative of the gypsy. "Ah! in the past and in the present lie the seed to bear fruit in the future," continued the girl, speaking now in Czeschen. "Revicta can say only that which she sees. She cannot lie to a friend of her tribe. True Romanies do not believe in fortune-telling. It is good enough for the non-gypsies to do so. To you I cannot tell what I do not know, even for gold."

The words fell gently from her lips. She dropped the Empress's hand, and with a queenly inclination of her proud head she turned away, and walked softly towards her tent, moving noiselessly on the smooth greensward.

As for myself, I never believed much in predictions of any kind, nor in visions either, and I smiled contentedly upon hearing Revicta's assertion; yet, strangely enough, I had once a vision, and about the Empress, too, which came back very vividly to me, and very painfully as well, after her assassination.

The circumstance to which I am now alluding took place during the late autumn of the year when I spent a few days at the old château of X——, on the Breton coast, with her Majesty. It was on a cold November afternoon. I was riding over the heath of Quiberon, in Brittany, where I had remained for some weeks after Elisabeth returned to Vienna. Far below me, at the foot of the cliffs, the waves were dashing against the rocks with a loud, grinding sound of rolling pebbles and shaking bowlders, and the wind was shrieking through the dried stalks of the furze and broom. The melancholy of the scene brought vividly back to my mind tales I had often heard of the terrible carnage which took place on this very spot in 1795. It seemed to me as if I could even see the broad face of the moon throwing a livid light on the deserted battle-field of those days, and dead and dying piled in great heaps, which the furious waves of the rising tide approached in leaps and bounds. I almost fancied I heard the moaning of the wounded, abandoned to their wretched fate, and saw the "Whites" and the "Blues," as the Royalists and Revolutionists were respectively designated, lying side by side in their last moments of agony. So absorbed was I in this retrospective revery, that I suffered my hunter to adopt a snail-like pace, as he also gazed seaward where so many of his kind had found a watery grave in those long gone times. The scene was a desolate one indeed, well in keeping with my thoughts, and the incident which brought me back from the retrospective musings was strange enough to make me think that I was still dreaming with wide-open eyes.

Just as I was about to round the point which discloses the entire panorama of this tempest-tossed stretch of water, called La Mer Sauvage, I saw plainly before me, in spite of the rapidly gathering dusk, a white figure standing on the very edge of the precipice, and seemingly swinging to and fro with a gentle, undulating motion, as if about to clear the bastion-like ramparts formed by the cliff.

I checked my horse so violently that, unused to such rough treatment, the delicately organized thoroughbred reared straight up in the air, and it took me a few moments to soothe his aggrieved feelings. When I had succeeded in doing so, I looked again towards the spot where the figure had stood flutteringly outlined against the evening sky, but it was no longer there. Giving my fretting horse his head, I galloped madly away, unmindful of the grand panorama before me, of the sacred Druidical stones which I passed at lightning speed, although I usually loved to give a lingering look at those weird and terrible monuments of the times of the Gauls.

It was late when I arrived home, just in time to dress and to hurry down to the dining-hall, where our numerous guests had already assembled. I had no time to think of the quaint apparition perceived during my homeward journey, and as dinner was followed by an impromptu dance, it was after midnight when I retired to my room. I was wellnigh tired out, and I dropped into a deep sleep as soon as my head touched the pillow. It did not seem that a long time had elapsed when, suddenly, I awakened, with a start.

The tiny enamelled clock at my bedside rang out thrice its soft, silvery stroke. While the sound was yet dying away I opened my eyes and looked about me with a feeling of oppression and anxiety.

The large, high-ceiled room, lighted by the rosy glow of the night-lamp and by the fitful gleams of the fast-consuming logs on the hearth, looked as peaceful as usual. Not a fold of the heavy draperies on the walls had been disturbed; the tall green fronds of the palms before the windows were unruffled by so much as a breath of air, and a stray moonbeam glided through a parting of the window-curtains and fell aslant the floor, like a sheaf of silver rays.

Wearily my eyelids drooped, and I was about to doze off once more, when a second time I started as if a hand had touched me. The November night was very cold for Brittany, and the wind swept in icy gusts around the castle. Everybody was asleep, and when I at length lay down again there was not a sound in the whole big pile of buildings save the crackling of the logs on the broad hearth.

Lulled by the low moaning of the sea at the foot of the cliffs far below my windows, I tried again to go to sleep; but I was kept from doing so by an incomprehensible feeling of anguish. Cold perspiration stood on my brow, and I experienced great difficulty in breathing. Dazed and surprised, I looked around me, but the fire had now almost completely died out, and the dim, rosy light from the smouldering embers was not strong enough to allow me to distinguish anything clearly. I was trying to reason myself into going to sleep again in spite of all, when a very slight rustle attracted my attention and made me shudder from head to foot. It was so slight that none but ears sharpened by fear could have perceived it, and yet there it was—a soft, silky, gliding, undulating motion of something invisible gradually approaching my bed. I lay there incapable of moving, straining every nerve in my effort to realize what that sound could be, but the beating of my pulses was so loud that I could less and less distinguish whence it came. Suddenly my heart died within me, for the curtains had parted, and from the sheaf of moonbeams, now broadened to a regular flood of scintillating light, the figure I had seen on the cliffs floated towards me. I am no coward, and I may assert that I am not fanciful either; but yet I seemed to become paralyzed by some kind of magnetic power which I had never experienced before. Stir so much as a finger I could not; all my vitality was concentrated in my eyes. Mechanically I heard the clock ticking monotonously; I listened to every sob of the waves against the rocky beach below, and to the fast-rising wind as it shook the deep-embrasured casements, but all these sounds were dull in my ear, as if heard from a far-away grave where I was entombed alive.

The figure reached my bedside and bent over me. I clenched my teeth convulsively to smother a cry of agony, for I could now distinguish every detail plainly, and I saw Elisabeth's features pale as death, her great blue eyes dilated and bent upon me with a heart-rending expression of sadness and of woe, and one slim, emaciated hand pointing to a little wound on her bare breast, and from which two or three drops of blood had oozed upon the white folds of her robe. And then I swooned away, losing all consciousness of that awful picture.

When I regained my senses I could see

through the opening between the heavy tapes-
tried window-hangings that the sun had risen.
The room, with its luxurious furnishings, its
numberless knickknacks and bibelots, was
peaceful and undisturbed, but I could not shake
off the horrible impression of what I persisted in
telling myself was but a ghastly dream. I telegraphed to Elisabeth during the course of the
morning, and she replied immediately that she
was very well, expressing surprise at my, to
her, quite meaningless and anxious inquiry. So I
called myself a fool, and tried to dismiss the
whole affair from my brain.

Of course I never mentioned a word of it to the
Empress, and when I regained Austria we resumed as of yore our rides over hill and dale,
talking often of Brittany, a subject, however, to
which, much to her astonishment, I did not take
very kindly, for it always recalled to me the vision
seen during one of the most trying nights which
I ever spent in my life.

CHAPTER IX

From our long forest rambles Elisabeth would often bring back, tied to the pommel of her saddle, all manner of queer objects—strangely gnarled branches, bright-hued berries, long waving reeds—which she afterwards disposed gracefully and with a quaint, original taste about her apartments.

Very characteristic of her was the originality which she showed in the arrangement of her private apartments. Whether she was staying at one of her own palaces or in a plain suite of rooms at a hotel, her first care was invariably to send for flowers, quantities of them, both potted and cut, and to dispose them herself in all available nooks and corners. Next came her books, well-thumbed volumes, handsomely but soberly bound, and written in the many dead and living languages which she knew. A large square box containing portraits and photographs of those she loved was always included in her luggage, and she took special delight in grouping these souvenirs of home about her.

When she built and furnished the Villa Achilleon she gave proof of what her artistic sense really was.

This imperial abode has been so often described that it seems futile to do so again here,

and yet no pen or even brush wielded by the
cleverest of writers or of painters has ever given
an adequate idea of the chastened magnificence
and truly unique taste displayed throughout this
creation of her imagination, executed in marbles
and mosaics, precious woods and more precious
metals.

Corfu was a fitting place of residence for the
grieving Empress. She followed in her selection
the example of Agrippina, widow of Germanicus,
who, in the year 20 A.D., cast into the depths of
despair by the loss she had sustained, landed
upon the shores of this enchanted island to seek
the consolation usually brought by beautiful
scenery, coupled with perfect rest and estrangement from all social noise and turmoil.

The attention of the Empress had been
directed to the classical spot where the villa now
stands by the late Freiherr von Warsberg, the
great authority on the landscape scenery of the
Odyssey. Within the incredibly short time of little
more than one and a half years the modest villa
Braila, on the Gasturi Hill, in the island of Corfu,
long known for its enchanting position, was replaced, under the direction of the Italian archi-
tect, Rafael Charito, by a palace conceived and
carried out in the spirit of ancient Greece. The
eastern slope of the hill facing towards the sea is
covered with olive plantations, while the opposite
incline has been laid out as a beautiful park, on
wide terraces. The west front rises two stories
high, but the villa leans against the hill, so that
the upper story at the opposite side is level with
the first terrace.

The principal entrance is on the south front,
which, with its projecting porch, its loggias and

balconies, presents an exceedingly picturesque aspect. The vestibule is connected with a large, sumptuously decorated *salon,* upon the ceiling of which Paliotti has represented the four seasons. To the right is the chapel, carried out in pure Byzantine style; to the left the dining-room, Pompeian to the minutest detail. A marble staircase with bronze balustrades leads to the second story, where the apartments of the Empress were situated. The central *salon* opens on the Centaur terrace, and has empire decorations, with frescos of Aurora on the ceiling, painted also by Paliotti. All the various apartments are filled with art treasures of Pompeian and ancient Greek origin which the Empress collected herself.

The arrangements of Elisabeth's private suite of rooms reflected the individual taste of the august chatelaine in all its well-known refinement. One of the most magnificent features of the building is the peristyle into which the Empress's rooms opened. It is supported by twelve marble columns, in front of which are placed marble statues brought from Rome, while the walls are painted by Paliotti and Pastiglione with scenes from ancient Greek mythology and romance as they were described by Homer, Aesop, and many other ancient poets and chroniclers.

The building contains one hundred and twenty-eight rooms, and the stables have accommodations for fifty horses.

From the windows of her Majesty's sleeping apartment and boudoir the view is admirable, reaching far away to where the mountains of Cyprus and Albania tower into the sky. All the rooms are furnished with that exquisite taste ever displayed by the Empress in all interior arrangements.

Almost all the carpets, rugs, tapestries, and lamps were bought by Elisabeth in Morocco and Tunis, while the marvellous frescos with which the walls are decorated are, as I just remarked, the work of the celebrated Italian painters, Scanni, Paliotti, and Pastiglione. This delightful and truly imperial abode cost over forty million florins, not including, of course, the treasures of art which adorn the spacious picture-gallery, etc. The grounds are a dream of extraordinary magnificence, with their ever-blooming thickets of tropical plants and trees, their groves of palms, blue-gum trees, and their sparkling fountains. Behind the villa is a huge field of roses, comprising twenty-five thousand bushes, of all kinds and colors. A trellised walk covered with climbing noisette and nyphetos encloses this unique collection, the flower-laden branches meeting and interlacing overhead, and then drooping in perfumed showers almost to the ground. It would be indeed difficult to give an idea of this vision of loveliness, for the "rose-garden" is so planned that it has the least possible appearance of design. The luxuriant bushes of crimson, yellow, pink, and white roses seem to have chosen their own places, and to have chosen them most happily too.

The stables, saddle and harness rooms, are, one might almost say, the greatest marvel of this superb residence. The Empress ordered everything in this portion of the establishment to be brought from England, down to the wainscoting in light oak which lines the coach-houses and saddle-rooms. The stables are at some distance from the house, and constitute a very charming feature of the landscape, with their many gables, their latticed windows, and their pointed roofs, overrun with creepers and climbing roses. The broad sanded alley leading to them gently ascends through the park, and is bordered on both sides with beds of pink and white geraniums, and groves of blossoming camellias, azaleas, and monster ferns.

The gardens and park descend in sloping terraces to the very edge of the sea, where a flight of steps, made of pink marble, leads to a private harbor. A light-house, also built of marble and provided with an enormous electric lamp, throws its dazzling rays over the water and on the surrounding woods.

The sea-wall of pink marble is crowned with vases of majolica filled with aloe plants, and separates the grounds from the rippling dark-blue waves.

On a slight rocky elevation at the farther side of the garden an exquisite little Greek temple is perched, about which, as well as around its rocky base, a wealth of noisette and multiflora climbing specimens are vying with each other to shed all the perfumes of Arabia on the mellow air. Single climbers wrap the great trees on the border of this Eden, displaying their matchless beauty of blossom in the very wantonness of security, hanging out their brilliant wreaths, fearless of hand or knife, for the Empress loved them and cared for these blossoms of nature more even than for the Golden Rose of Merit sent to her years ago by his Holiness the Pope.

In this Greek temple the Empress used to sit with her dogs at her feet gazing on the deep-blue

sea, which appeared here and there between the
forest of flowers, seeking comfort and consolation
from the pain ever gnawing at her heart.

Unfortunately, even the beauties of Achilleon
failed to attain any such end, and the poor Niobe,
hunted by the restlessness of a pain too great to
be explained in words, decided not very long ago
to abandon her lovely Greek villa.

> "Who shall assuage thy grief,
>   thou tempest tossed,
> And speak of comfort,
>   comfortless to thee?"

The monuments which had been erected in
the gardens to the memory of Crown-prince
Rudolph, and of her Majesty's favorite poet,
Heine, were taken away and sent, together with
most of the art treasures contained in the *salons*
and galleries of Achilleon, to Schloss Lainz, in the
neighborhood of the castle of Schönbrunn, which
then became the favorite retreat of the Kaiserin, a
terra-incognita (land-hidden, unknown) which is
concealed from the public gaze by thousands of
woodland acres.

If Achilleon was a marvel of Greek and Pompeian reconstruction, Lainz seems to be torn out
of the pages of some ancient record of legends or
fairy tales. Surrounded, in spite of the immensity
of the domain, by high, forbidding-looking walls,
it is still further protected from any gaze, save
that of the birds, by a belt of century-old trees of
extreme magnificence, which cast their deep-green
shadows upon the most velvety of emerald swards.
Here again Elisabeth's love for flowers showed
itself, the gardens being as near perfection as
perfection is to be attained here below. The castle
itself is embedded in masses of blossoms which

literally beggar description, the many tropical plants finding during the cold months a refuge in the enormous winter-garden, which opens from the Empress's private suite of rooms.

The building itself is very roomy and decorated in Renaissance style, and the lofty entrance-hall is adorned with many beautiful paintings, including the celebrated "Hunt of Diana," by Makart. A majestic *salon*, the walls of which are inlaid with wonderful mosaics, is called the Marble Room, and there is it that, hidden behind a movable panel, a jewel of an altar stands, of pure Renaissance design, where the Empress's chaplain used to say mass every morning at sunrise. This altar is ensconced in a fretted and carved extension of the Schloss, according to the rules of the Catholic Church, which prohibit anything being built above such places of worship.

Up-stairs are the private apartments of the Emperor and Empress, separated by a large library so filled with palms, ferns, and shrubs in full bloom, emerging from great bronze and silver boxes, that it closely resembles a conservatory.

The Kaiser's bedroom is austerely simple, a camp bed covered with military blue cloth, a *prie-dieu* surmounted by a large crucifix, a superb painting representing the Blessed Virgin, and another of the Empress and her children, being about all it contains. Far more luxurious is Elisabeth's sleeping chamber, but still the dominating note is peculiarly quiet and peaceful. Walls and furniture are of a soft, creamy whiteness—that of the finest of velvets—the floor is covered with white bear-skins, and the windows are shrouded by cream-hued velvets, and

Alençon laces. Opposite the narrow white lac-
quered bed stands a matchless alabaster statue
representing a weeping Niobe. The pedestal of
this exquisite masterpiece is smothered in banks
of delicately foliaged green plants, and was
lighted all night, whether the Empress was there
or not, by tiny opalescent globes containing perfumed candles. During her long attacks of insomnia the poor bereft mother found a sort of comfort
in contemplating this, her counterpart, and used
to lie with her lovely eyes fixed on the white form
so pathetically pure and beautiful.

The bed stood in the middle of the room,
protected at the upper end by a huge screen, the
central leaf of which consisted of an admirably
painted picture of the Blessed Virgin. Between
two of the four tall windows stood a statue also
representing Mary, holding in her outspread
hands a magnificent antique rosary of gems,
which sparkled under the rays of the ever-
burning sanctuary lamp of ruby-tinted crystal
hanging above it.

The Empress's study, which opened into her
sleeping apartment, was filled with *souvenirs;*
little frames, containing her children's and grandchildren's first attempts at drawing, hung above
the great square writing-table; a portrait of the
dead king, Louis II. of Bavaria, was supported by
an easel draped in cloth-of-silver. Everywhere
there was a picturesque litter of casts, sketches,
books, and small and large bronzes. There were
many priceless vases, adorned, of course, with exquisite flowers. The hearth was wide open and
oak logs burned there morning and evening,
shining on the carvings of the high chimney-
piece, excepting in midsummer, when it was all

EMPEROR FRANZ-JOSEPH WITH THE CHILDREN OF HIS
FAVORITE DAUGHTER, ARCHDUCHESS MARIE-VALÉRIE

filled in with flowers and plants. A beautiful marble copy of the Belvedere Mercury stood near by, with great clusters of snowy azaleas and white camellias around it.

The dining-room was in keeping with the rest of the little castle, for there, also, flowers played the predominant rôle. In the corners fountains of marble harbored the most brilliant and also the most delicate specimens of the aquatic flora, which spread their intoxicating fragrance from beneath the prismatic spray of the water-jets.

Here on a *console* stood a remarkable toy, which the Empress took especial delight in winding up for the benefit of her grandchildren. It was a mandolin player dressed in the costume of the Renaissance, and the merry strains of the instrument he held accompanied the little automat's voice, which was extremely good and sounded astoundingly natural. When Archduchess Valérie's children came to Lainz the Empress always had some surprise in reserve for them. Often it took the form of dwarf fruit-trees brought to the table at dessert, and from the diminutive branches of which the little ones gleefully gathered monster cherries, rosy cheeked apples, luscious pears, apricots, plums, or currants.

The Empress, this ardent lover of flowers, has often been compared to the edelweiss—the ice-blossom—which can thrive only in an untainted atmosphere; but this comparison holds good only in so far as her crystal-like purity went, for to be simply and beautifully passionless, in the grosser sense of the word, and far removed from human frailties and sins is not to be made of ice. It is what made her the most poetical, the most lovable figure among the royalty of Europe.

I myself have always thought that the edelweiss was no fit emblem for the absolutely unique type of blameless womanhood represented by Empress Elisabeth. After all, the edelweiss is easily attainable and can be procured from the inhabitants of any Alpine village. A far likelier simile could be drawn between her and the wolfinia-carinthiana, which grows upon the very summit of the Gärntnerkögel, in her Majesty's beloved Carinthian mountains, and nowhere else in the world. Like the wolfinia, the Empress soon drooped in any atmosphere that did not suit her, and her avoidance of just such atmospheres was what caused the ignorant crowd to accuse her of being eccentric, odd, and frozen.

Every evening when at Lainz she retired to her own room punctually at ten, after having spent the previous hour or two in writing to her children and grandchildren, and to her sisters, with whom she kept up a constant correspondence, especially with the ex-Queen of Naples, of whom she was very fond.

She rose at five, and by six was out of doors walking about the gardens, arrayed in one of those short tailor-made silk-lined black serge dresses which she wore so much. She never could bear a dress to trail or even to touch the ground, save at court functions and state balls, and insisted on having all her skirts made very short, as she could not bear the trouble of holding them up, which, she declared, made her awfully nervous. She invariably carried a book with her in her rambles. When there, also, during late years, she wrote a great deal of prose and of poetry, for she said that writing amused her and kept her from thinking. That is rather a strange way of putting it, especially when one knows how full of thought, and beautiful thought, indeed, her literary work was.

As an example, here is a portion of a letter written by her to a friend, and describing a visit which she made to an eccentric old gentleman who lived in the neighborhood of Cairo, and whose great wealth and originality caused much talk there during many years:

"The drive was a long one. It led us at first along the straight white boulevards of Cairo, then through winding, ancient streets, and beneath the splendidly *mosaiqued* arches of old Cairo, where the bizarre and attractive conflict of European and Oriental life spreads its strange panorama. At last we left the town, with its medley of loaded camels, white-bearded sheiks, Bedouins, and red-coated English soldiery far behind us, to enter a broad avenue of century-old sycamores, which followed the green bank of the old river. On we drove, until at a bend of the road we suddenly caught a glimpse of a densely wooded promontory jutting out in the dark-blue waters of the Nile, and surmounted by a feathery bunch of tall palm-trees, the foliage of which seemed pencilled with extraordinary exactitude against the pale green and pink evening sky. The red-hot rays of the sinking sun shed their glory about this matchless picture, which we admired in almost awed silence.

"Rapidly the carriage turned from the main avenue into a private one barred by gigantic iron gates, which, however, were thrown wide open in our honor, while a

boab, or porter, wrapped in the numerous
folds of his snowy *gandurah,* salaamed with
deep obeisance as we whirled past him.

"Truly it seemed as had we entered fairy-
land! All around us were clusters of tama-
risk and orange and glowing pomegranate,
overshadowing parterres filled with deep-
hued flowers and protected by low hedges of
thorny dwarf cactus. Above our heads the
interlaced branches of colossal rose-laurels,
magnolias, and jasmine trees formed a fragrant bower which ended in a sort of glade,
whereon arose the lacelike white marble
minarets and towers of what appeared to be
an enchanted palace. Fountains played on
aquatic blossoms of all descriptions, multicolored birds flitted over the lanceolated
leaves of pink and blue lotuses, and soft-
eyed gazelles scampered over the velvety
lawns, losing themselves under the deepen-
ing shadows of the miniature tropical forest
which backed the half-Moorish, half-Indian
construction. Seen in the waning yet still
brilliant light of the eastern afternoon,
the tableau, such as I have attempted to
describe it for your benefit, was like unto the
evocation of some poet's dream, and I hardly
believed myself to be awake when the carriage drew up before a flower-laden flight of
steps. Ashamed of an astonishment so thoroughly out of place for a hardened traveller
like myself, I alighted and commenced to
walk up the marble steps, where I was met
by an apparition well in keeping with my
surroundings, for I do not remember to have
ever been so much struck by the personal

appearance of any man in my life.

"Our advancing host was a man of considerably over medium stature; the easy grace which marked his movements told of a body in which true proportions of every limb, muscle, and sinew were the most marked characteristics. The face was noble, of a clear sunburned brown inclining to an olive tint, the brow was low and broad, the nose firm in its contour and somewhat aquiline, while the mouth, surrounded by a silvery mustache and flowing beard, was of a generous Greek fulness of lip. The eyes, in marked and startling contrast with this darkish complexion, were of a dark luminous blue, yielding a strange radiance, and overshadowed by black lashes and brows. This majestically moving figure was clad in a loose robe of rich material and wonderfully blended colors, while on the hoary head was wound a turban of white and silver silken stuffs.

"'Welcome to my *Thébaide*,' he said, in a deep, sonorous voice, as he bent over the hand which I extended to him; and retaining it in his, he led me across a mosaic terrace of great beauty to a chamber which I almost despair of describing by means of such poor tools as pen and ink.

"When I first entered it I could not speak, in the extremity of my amazement, for although I believed that I had seen a fair portion of this world's luxury, yet stood I speechless with surprise before this, to my mind, exact reproduction of Aladdin's treasure-chamber! It appeared to me as if both

walls and ceiling were thickly incrusted with
gold and gems of the most magnificent
description, and of a truth such was really
the case, for on the pale-blue velvet serving
as *tentures* hung an unparalleled collection
of jewelled weapons, and other ornaments of
barbaric splendor: scimitars in scabbards
scintillating with sapphires, diamonds, and
rubies, yàtagáns incrusted with emeralds
and pearls, scarfs of cloth-of-gold fantasti-
cally embroidered with precious stones,
while hanging-lamps of solid gold depended
from the ceiling, above great tables of mala-
chite, lapis lazuli, and jade. The entire floor
was covered with azure velvet, and the low
divans running all around this glittering
room were piled with silken cushions of a
deep-tinted amber color. A dainty repast of
fruit, sweetmeats, and drinks, iced to a turn,
lay in readiness on an inlaid table, on each
side of which two servants in turbans of
white and gold stood with folded arms.

"In such company, and amid such surroundings, the hours flew like minutes, and
it was with a feeling of regret that I rose at
last to bid farewell to this extraordinary host
of ours."

This is pretty good English, and pretty good
style for a foreigner who wrote to "prevent herself
from thinking!" I should say.

The only time when the Empress appeared at
any court ceremony since the death of her son
was on the occasion of the visit of the present
Czar and Czarina to Vienna. Her presence excited
then even more interest and curiosity at the state
reception given at the Hofburg than did that of

the young Czarina, although the latter had never
been in Austria before.

The Muscovite imperial couple were received
by Elisabeth at Castle Lainz, which was a great
compliment paid to the visitors, for guests
were never entertained at Lainz, which the good
Viennese called the Empress's "Sacrosanctum."
When the special train steamed into the little
station of Lainz, the Czar and Czarina found,
much to their surprise and gratification, that
the Empress had accompanied her husband, and
that both of them stood waiting on the platform.
The Emperor wore his favorite field-marshal's
uniform and the Russian Order of St. Andrew,
and Elisabeth was draped in the severe folds of a
black-velvet dress and mantle. Her small head,
with its weight of golden-brown braids, was
crowned with a hat covered with black feathers,
and in one slender hand she carried her accustomed black fan, while the other held a gigantic
bunch of violets.

The *déjeuner*, which followed almost
immediately upon the arrival of Nicholas II. and
Alexandra-Féodorovna, was a success from every
point of view, for it was not only a gastronomical
feast, but it was typical of Elisabeth in being also
a feast for the eyes and higher tastes. Flowers,
music, perfumes, beautiful surroundings lent
themselves to make up a positively entrancing
tout-ensemble.

At the court ball the charming impression
received during their visit to Lainz seemed to
dwell upon the minds of the imperial guests.

The old Hofburg had put on its most splendid
appearance for the occasion. Lighted from base-
ment to roof, filled with gorgeous exotics, and

decorated in the most original and wonderful
fashion, it yet preserved its appearance of being
a page torn from the illustrated chronicles of
the Middle Ages. Early in the evening the great
salons and galleries, the throne-room and Rittersaal were crowded with women in dazzling
costumes and men in magnificent court and military uniforms, while a string of carriages kept
unceasingly bringing other distinguished guests
to the palace.

A few minutes after eight o'clock the grand-
master of the ceremonies, Count Kalmàn-
Hunyàdi, announced, by rapidly striking the floor
of the throne-room with his ivory wand of office,
that the court was approaching, and the Emperor, with the Empress of Russia on his arm,
made his appearance, followed by the Czar, led
by Empress Elisabeth, by his brother, Archduke
Karl-Ludwig, with Archduchess Maria-Theresa,
and by other members of the imperial family.

All eyes were immediately turned upon the
lovely Austrian sovereign who, in spite of all the
sorrows and sufferings through which she had
gone, could still be truthfully called the most
beautiful woman in her dominions. Her toilette
was a vision of severe elegance, *chic*, and perfection of taste.

The endless fan-shaped train and bodice
were of softest, most shimmering black velvet,
veiled with black-silk gauze, embroidered with
pearl-hearted black violets. On her proud head
sparkled a diadem of black pearls and black
diamonds, whence fell to the very hem of the
court mantle a transparent veil of black gauze
powdered with jet. Around the shapely marmorean neck hung row after row of softly gleaming

black pearls interspersed with brilliants, and she carried in her hand a sheath of Russian and Neapolitan violets, tied with jet-embroidered black streamers, to which was fastened an enormous black marabout fan adorned with a crown in diamonds. On the left shoulder was attached the Stern-kreuz decoration, also in diamonds. The Czarina wore a court mantle and a skirt of light-blue *moire-nacrée,* entirely veiled with gold-spangled blue tulle, the mantle being secured to the shoulders by epaulets of natural roses, a cluster of which also arose from the coronet of pink pearls, sapphires, and diamonds surmounting the waved hair.

The Empress was in one of her most charming and amiable moods, smiling and conversing graciously with all the ladies of the *corps-diplomatique* in turn, and so youthful did she look that her contemporaries would have easily been taken for her seniors by at least twenty years. At half-past ten their majesties retired to the private council-room, where the presentations of the evening were made.

When these were at an end, tea was served in the Gobelin-room for their majesties and their immediate *entourage,* while the other guests partook of supper in the Mirror and Pietradura rooms, at tables reserved for eight people each. At midnight the reception was over, and the imposing old palace was wrapped once more in darkness.

CHAPTER X

Like all mothers who truly love their children, the
Empress was to a certain extent jealous of any
outside influence which might be brought to bear
upon them, and when the question of the Crown-
prince's marriage was first mooted it became a
very vexatious one to her. Of course she saw its
necessity, not only as it was thought that it would
steady down the rather wild young Prince, but
also on account of providing for the dynasty a
line of direct heirs to the ancient crown which he
was to inherit. There were, at the time of which
I speak, but very few marriageable Catholic princesses, and the one who was finally selected was,
from the outset, by no means a satisfactory
choice to Elisabeth, for she was the daughter of
the King of the Belgians, whom the Empress
could literally not endure, and of Archduchess
Marie-Henrietta-Anne, herself daughter of the late
Archduke Joseph, Palatin of Hungary, a woman
who has always played a rather effaced and
paltry rôle at the court of her tyrannic, unkind,
and unfaithful husband, King Leopold.

Long were the discussions which the Empress
and I had in private about this projected alliance.
We both of us disliked and mistrusted Princess
Stéphanie, who was a strange mixture of a *bigote*
and a flirt, and who already, at her early age—she

was not yet seventeen—showed signs of a stubborn, narrow-minded, and set temper, bordering on mulishness; besides all which she was by no means a pretty girl, very thin and angular, with very light hair, and a delicacy of complexion which betokened rather lack of health than real refinement of appearance. She was ungainly in all her motions, and had none of that grace without which a woman possesses no charm whatsoever.

During the negotiations which took place between the two courts the Empress was singularly despondent, a mood very foreign to her, and her tenderness for Rudolph seemed to become greater every day. He himself did not appear to attach a very serious importance to the step which he was about to take. Light-hearted and somewhat sarcastic, if not a trifle cynical in his way of looking upon women in general, with the sole exception of his mother, whom he absolutely adored, and justly thought to be unequalled both morally and physically by any other member of her sex, Rudi used to come every afternoon at dusk into the oak-panelled library, which was the Empress's favorite retreat—and where, when I had the happiness of being with her, we invariably spent the hour before dinner—laughing, joking, and attempting to put all our prognostications and fears to flight by his merry banter.

"Where is the use of your making yourself miserable, mother mine?" he would say, sitting down on a cushion at her feet, before the brightly burning logs on the hearth, and taking the Empress's slender hands between his own. "You know very well that as long as it is an impossibility for me to find a wife who resembles yourself in

CROWN-PRINCE RUDOLPH—JUST BEFORE HIS DEATH

the very slightest degree, I may as well marry this good little Belgian girl. She is neither homelier nor more uninteresting than the rest of her kind, and as she is very young I may have a chance of moulding her temper the way it should be moulded. So don't you worry, and be quite satisfied that I am not madly in love with her, for in that case I know that you, jealous darling, would be a million times more unhappy yet!"

How well I can recall those oft-repeated little scenes: the dim rosy light of the fire which threw fugitive gleams of color upon the embossed and emblazoned ceiling, and on the porphyry sculptures of the high mantel-piece, in front of which the Empress's two favorite gigantic Danish dogs lay stretched out at full length, while she herself, gowned in one of those exquisitely draped and lovely creations of velvet and fur, which she generally wore when we dined quite by ourselves, sat without speaking much, but with a half smile on her lovely lips, which was, however, belied by the sadness of her deep, changeful blue eyes.

"My poor boy! my poor boy!" she kept repeating, "I am afraid you do not realize what misery such a marriage as that which you are about to make can bring about. The girl may be, as you say, moulded; she is young enough for that, Heaven knows; but such moulding is not an easy or a pleasant process, and you, my dear, are not at all the kind of a man who possesses the perseverance to undertake the moral education of his wife! My love for you shows me very plainly the defects which mar your many good qualities, and I know just as well as if the thing had already happened that you will get tired and annoyed at this rôle of mentor, which you now consider to be so easy a one. Your father wishes you to marry. To be sure, he looks upon your union with Stéphanie more in the light of a necessary political event than anything else, but I am bound to consider the other side of the question, which is your home life, your ultimate happiness—in a word, your entire future. Now, Stéphanie is not, and never will be, the wife for you; she is fond of admiration, of power, and of domination, and what is more, instead of looking upon religion as a means of making our sojourn here below less arduous and painful than it else might be, she closes her eyes to all the true beauty of the Catholic faith, and simply follows its strictest precepts in a spirit of defiance, one would almost think, and just as a child recites a piece of poetry learned by rote, the true sense of which it neither comprehends nor assimilates!"

These conversations took place many and many a time, and the Empress and her son gave vent to their feelings, in the very same fashion, time after time, without any appreciable result on either side, for matters had already gone too far to allow the Crown-prince to be sufficiently influenced by them to retreat from the now fully adopted course; and as to the Empress, although she told me regularly after each of these encounters that she well knew how futile her objections had become, yet she seemed impelled by some inner force to give expression to them. As subsequent events have shown, it would have been far better had her wishes in the matter been treated with more regard. Her keen intuition served her in good stead when she so bitterly opposed this marriage, which brought in its train a succession of catastrophes, miseries, and tragedies, unparalleled in history.

The Emperor and his counsellors had their way, and at last the time for the wedding was fixed, and the parents of the bride, with their daughter, made their entrance into Vienna. During the ceremonies and popular rejoicings which preceded the great day, Elisabeth, although acting her part as mother of the bridegroom and hostess of one of the grandest courts of Europe to perfection, as she did everything else, could not succeed in shaking off the deep and lasting melancholy which seemed to have settled upon her. Her distant, even icy behavior towards her future daughter-in-law, as well as towards King Leopold and Queen Henrietta of Belgium, was so marked that it was noticed by everybody.

The prelude of the wedding entertainments was a popular festival in the Prater, and was certainly one of the most magnificent sights of the kind ever seen. Thousands upon thousands thronged the immense park, which had at that moment just put on all its spring loveliness. The delicate shade of the budding branches, the deep green mosses stretching like velvet under the grand old trees, the azure, sunlit sky, and the millions of blossoming violets, primroses, and narcissus which peeped forth everywhere, made a fitting background for this bridal fête, and the long road from Schönbrunn to the Prater was lined by row upon row of spectators who had come from all parts of the empire to obtain a glimpse of the gorgeous procession, headed by the royalties and consisting of sixty-two court equipages, which wended its way through the much beflagged and oriflammed *allées* (alleys). The luxury displayed on that day can be better imagined than described. The equipages were marvellous, the horses the best and finest contained in the imperial stables, and the gala liveries, as well as the toilettes of the ladies and the glittering uniforms of the men present, made up an unrivalled *coup d'oeil.* In the foremost carriage were Prince de la Tour-et-Taxis, Grand Equerry of the Empire, and Prince Hohenlohe, then Grand Master of the Court. In the second carriage were the Emperor, who wore the uniform of a Belgian colonel, and the King of the Belgians in Austrian uniform. The other carriages were occupied by the Empress, with the Queen of the Belgians; Crown-prince Rudolph, with his bride; Princess Victoria of Prussia—now Dowager Empress Frederick of Germany—with her brother the Prince of Wales; Prince William of Prussia—the present Emperor of Germany—who wore the uniform of an Austrian captain, with Archduchess Gisela; Prince Leopold of Bavaria, with the Countess of Flanders, and the Grand-duchess Alice of Tuscany, etc.

Empress Elisabeth, who wore a dove-gray moiré gown covered with priceless lace and a small bonnet wreathed with pale violets, looked so excessively young and handsome that it was an impossibility to believe her to be the mother of the tall, manly, and athletic Crown-prince. During the long drive she hardly ever spoke to Queen Henrietta, but sat very upright, bowing continuously to right and left in acknowledgment of the cheers and hurrahs of the populace, but with a look bordering on absent-mindedness on her fair features. The acclamations of the multitude became positively deafening as the cortège reached the Prater-stern; the horses of the advance-guard could hardly proceed, for the people in their enthusiasm several times broke through the cordon of police, and serious accidents became so probable that the Emperor stood up in his carriage and requested the crowd to make way, laughing as he did so in his own cheery way, and calling out to them amid the sudden silence which his action had created:

"Aber Kinder, seien Sie doch nicht so dumm, Sie wollen die Hochzeit des Kronprinzen und nicht sein Leichenbegängniss und den Eueren feiren! Geben Sie uns doch Raum zu athmen!" (But, children, don't be so foolish. It is your Crown-prince's marriage which you want to celebrate, and not his funeral as well as your own; don't smother us this way!) Roars of laughter and more hurrahs were the result of this extemporary speech, and the good-natured Viennese gave the example to their still more enthusiastic brethren from Hungary, Poland, Bohemia, Croatia, and elsewhere, in rendering the advance of the file of equipages more possible and less dangerous.

In the evening of that memorable day the entire city was illuminated in the most magnificent fashion. The night was a singularly clear and beautiful one, the stars were sparkling in the clear sapphire skies, and the multitudes which filled all the streets and thoroughfares were still greater than during the day. For many nights and days previously the hum of collecting people and the tramp of many feet had been heard throughout the capital. People of every stock and province had flocked from wild Silesian forests, from remote Bavarian mountains, from Moldavian plains, and from Czechen orchards. Pyramids of gas-jets flared up towards heaven, while trees

made entirely of small, burning, luminous leaves
threw their glare upon the tall buildings, every
window of which was outlined with garlands of
multicolored electric globes.

In front of the numerous palaces which line
the Ringstrasse, brightly tinted fountains excited the admiration of all on-lookers, and the
Volks-Garten, the Stadt-Park, and the Schwart-
zenberg-Platz had been turned into fairy-like
places, upon which the good burghers looked
with open-mouthed admiration.

The wedding ceremony, which took place in
the Hofburg-Kappelle, was also one of the most
splendid events on record. Unfortunately, during
the mass, which was said by the Prince-Cardinal
of Vienna, the Empress's self-control completely
broke down, and she gave way to a violent fit of
weeping. The Crown-prince looked anything but
cheerful, and the Emperor himself was evidently
in the worst of humors. The many lights burning
in gold candelabra, the crimson velvet draperies,
and the masses of blossoming plants which decorated the chapel could not make up for the
impression of sorrow and of loss which seemed to
pervade the august assembly.

Princess Stéphanie was certainly most insig-
nificantly homely and ill at ease, in spite of her
magnificent dress of white brocade thickly
embroidered with silver in a marvellous design of
oak and laurel leaves, myrtle and heather blossoms. The low bodice was covered with silver
filigree lace, and she wore a veil which had been
presented to her by the city of Brussels, and upon
which the arms of Belgium and of Austria were
woven in the most exquisitely delicate manner.

In spite of her sadness the Empress looked

handsomer than ever. She wore a pearl-hued velvet gown with a long square train draped with antique Argentan-lace. Her wonderful hair was braided and coiled about her small patrician head in the fashion so familiar to those who knew her, and was adorned by a pointed diadem of immense diamonds and emeralds. In her hands she held a great cluster of white orchids, white violets, and lilies.

As soon as she could possibly do so, and very shortly after the guests had risen from the elaborate supper, which had concluded the wedding feast, Elisabeth retired to her private apartments, where a few nights before I had had occasion to witness the really terrifying depth of her grief. It was after one of the magnificent fêtes given in honor of the young *fiancés*, and noticing how pale and wan she looked, I followed her to her room, well aware that she stood in sore need of a sympathetic listener.

On that occasion, after having had the weight of her court-train and jewels removed by her women, she closed the door, and without a word began to pace the floor like a caged tigress in her incontrollable agitation. It was very rare that the Empress thus gave way to her emotion, but when she did so the full force of her indomitable nature became apparent, and revealed a depth of feeling which her usually calm and self-contained demeanor gave one no reason whatsoever to believe that she possessed. I knew her well enough not to fall into the error of offering any consolation or even of making any kind of remark, and so I sat quietly before the fire which had been lighted in her sleeping apartment—the nights being still cold—gazing abstractedly into

the leaping flames, and thinking within myself
that the fate of the high and mighty is not often
enviable.

Suddenly Elisabeth, with a swift movement,
came towards me, flung herself upon the floor,
and, burying her proud head upon my knees,
burst into an uncontrollable passion of tears. Like
the goose that I have always been, instead of
attempting to soothe her I was so terrified and
pained by this unusual display of sorrow that
I knew no better than to follow suit, so there we
both sobbed our hearts out in the most undigni-
fied manner, as if we had lost all that made life
worth living for! After a while, and when a little
calm had succeeded the tempest, Elisabeth rose,
and wiping her eyes with her poor little handkerchief, which had by now been reduced to the state
of a wet sponge, she stroked my hair and said,
softly:

"You are a good sympathizer, and perhaps the
only woman on earth who forbears from talking
when words would be but added torture."

"That does not prevent me from doing a deal
of thinking," I replied, smiling faintly through my
own tears, "and also from being ready to curse
very freely all those who bring about anything
that hurts you, who deserve nothing but joy and
happiness."

"All that I can say, if this is the case,"
rejoined the Empress, "is that I do not get my
deserts, for life has not been dealing very kindly
with me, especially lately. Mark my words: this
business will bring untold misery; that girl is no
more fit than a wooden doll to be Rudi's companion. She has no heart; she has not even beauty—a
quality upon which all Hapsburgs set, as you

know, an inordinate amount of value. I am not blinded by my love for my boy—she cannot keep him straight! I do not even say that he will get weary of her, for to state this would be to admit that he has at any moment been in love with her. But, dear me, how her ways and manners—or lack of manners, if you prefer it so—will pall upon him! How soon he will become exasperated by her complaints, her childish exactions, and her monotonous, narrow-minded ideas! Do you think for an instant that he can stand an existence such as she will make for him? She is jealous; I have noticed it myself, and her sister Louise has told me as much. Now what do you suppose is going to happen when she learns, which she will surely do soon, that he does not love her, and, possibly, that he has become interested in some other woman?"

I shook my head; there was indeed nothing to answer to such logic, yet I felt so heartily sorry for the Empress that I tried, perhaps clumsily, to show her the future in less sombre colors.

"He is such a dear boy," I said; "he would not hurt a fly, much less his own wife, and she is not very intelligent, if you will pardon me for saying so, not very clear-sighted either; self-love and self-admiration are difficult armors to pierce, and she possesses both to an extraordinary degree. I am quite sure that the last thing that she will think of is that she is not the central figure of the universe. Her empty little head has been completely turned by becoming the wife of the heir to the throne of Austro-Hungary, and by the time that she awakes from her present dreams she will have, let us hope, gained sufficient knowledge of the world to realize what is due to her rank and position, and to avoid *bourgeois* scenes or public scandals. Trust to her singularly well-developed *sécheresse de coeur* (dryness of heart) to render her perfectly satisfied with being the Crown-princess, instead of fretting herself about the Crown-prince's possible coldness or indifference."

"Nay, nay, you do not show your usual insight into human nature, my dear!" petulantly exclaimed the Empress. "She will, on the contrary, make many serious scenes. She has pride, but not of the best kind; it is a vainglorious kind of a pride, and it will not come to her assistance when she has wounds to conceal. It will all crumble to dust, and cause her to forget entirely that queens and empresses must carry their sorrows within themselves, and not show them forth to a public always eager to see them writhe and smart under the common agonies and every-day sorrows common to all womankind."

There was no denying this! Time has shown that every word pronounced by the Empress on that night was wellnigh prophetic, and that she had, with her extraordinary cleverness, read her daughter-in-law's character to a nicety.

There was one person at the Austrian court who thoroughly understood and appreciated the anxiety displayed by the Empress with regard to the Crown-prince's marriage, and who also thoroughly mistrusted the possibility of his future happiness with Stéphanie. That was old Archduke Albrecht, the uncle of the Emperor, and one of the few persons who always did justice to Elisabeth's merits, intelligence, and loftiness of purpose. There was not a more popular man in the Austro-Hungarian army, nor in the length and

breadth of the dual empire, than the Archduke.
Kind-hearted to a fault, and of a shrewdness
which was coupled with an extraordinary
amount of *finesse* and wit, he was beloved
wherever he went. At the end of the seventies I
had the pleasure of counting the Archduke as one
of my guests during the great Galician military
manoeuvres, and I became then more than ever
imbued with the feeling that he was what can be
truly called *une âme d'élite* (an elite soul). Indeed,
I loved and reverenced him so much that I cannot
resist the temptation of saying a few words especially concerning him, as a kind of homage to his
memory.

Up every morning at half-past four o'clock,
the Generalissimo was on the manoeuvring field
at five, his quick eye taking in at a glance the
strong or the weak points of regiment after regiment. I delighted in accompanying my august
guest on these expeditions, and could not but
wonder at the remarkably diplomatic way in
which he managed, when his interference was
needed, not alone his staff of officers, but also
every man present.

I remember that one day he had reason to be
dissatisfied with the corps of drummers belonging to one of the infantry regiments of General
Count Mensdorf's brigade. Galloping up to where
they stood, drumming away for dear life, the
Archduke brought his charger to a dead stop
right in front of them, and, beckoning to the
tambour-major, said, with a smile: "These men of
yours can't drum, my lad!" The man, with an
awe-stricken face, stood at attention, unable in
the extremity of his confusion to utter a single
word of apology or explanation. The smile

deepened on the usually rather stern face of the
Archduke, and jumping from his horse he seized
hold of the drum held by one of the men nearest
to him, and without further ado executed so
masterly a charge of rat-tat-tats that the very
trees echoed again! After fully five minutes of this
superb performance the old field-marshal stopped
as abruptly as he had begun, and handing the
still quivering instrument to its amazed owner,
once more mounted his horse, exclaiming as he
galloped away: "That is the way one ought to
drum!" From that day the drummer-corps of that
regiment became certainly the best in Austria.

Archduke Albrecht was a passionate student.
He spoke Heaven only knows how many languages, and was so well versed in the manifold
dialects used throughout his nephew's empire
that he was able to converse with Hungarians,
Poles, Slovacks, Czechen, Bosniaks, etc., as glibly
as with Germans. His wealth was almost boundless, but so was his charity, and many were the
good deeds accomplished by him in secret, especially at Vienna.

In 1879 I had undertaken to supervise twice a
week one of the *volksküchen* (people's kitchens),
to which I have referred already in this volume.
One fine morning I noticed a rather seedy-looking
individual who entered the hall, and sitting down
at one end of a small table ordered a "portion" of
soup and beef from one of the ladies in attendance. A twinkle of merriment came into my eyes,
for at one glance I had recognized Archduke
Albrecht, the owner of more millions than he
could well count. Anxious to see the fun out, I
brought the coarse plate and cup myself to the
corner where Emperor Franz-Joseph's uncle sat,

and handed them to him with the utmost impassibility. He seemed somewhat embarrassed, and looked diffidently up at me through his spectacles. Not a muscle of my countenance relaxed, and with a slight nod I walked away, watching, however, from my corner how this poor man's fare would please the archducal palate. I may add that the entire "portion" was consumed without a single sign of distaste being manifested, and that at the end of this frugal repast his imperial and royal highness rubbed his mustache and fingertips on his handkerchief just as unconcernedly as any other *habitué* of the *volksküche*. As for me I went about my duties seemingly unaware of the keen look which he occasionally shot at me from under his bushy white eyebrows. At last he rose and prepared to go, but, as if suddenly altering his mind, he walked up to me, and drawing me to one side, said, gently:

"You have recognized me in spite of my attempt at disguising myself, so I might as well tell you that I sometimes come here in order to see whether the food is what it ought to be." Then he added: "Do you not think that on this cold morning some hot coffee with plenty of milk and sugar would be a pleasant addition to the dinner of all these poor devils?"

I laughed a ready acquiescence, and ten minutes later a small notice placarded at the entrance of the *küche* informed the delighted customers that in consideration of the unusual severity of the weather, hot coffee was to be distributed without extra charge during the entire course of the day.

Poor Archduke Albrecht! In the midst of all his wealth he was yet to be deeply pitied, for he never recovered from the blow inflicted many years ago by the tragic death of his lovely and beloved daughter. The young Archduchess was extremely fond of smoking cigarettes, but her lungs being somewhat delicate her otherwise indulgent father had forbidden her to smoke. One evening she was enjoying on the sly a tiny cigarette, and in order that the smell of the fragrant herb should not betray her, she was leaning out of the window of her boudoir. Suddenly catching sight of her father, who was walking in the palace gardens below, she hid the burning cigarette behind her back, while answering some remark which he addressed to her, quite unconscious of the fact that she had set fire to her vaporous gauze dinner-gown. In a few seconds she was literally wrapped in flames—flames which were rendered more murderously violent by her running from the room in an agony of fear. Burned in the most shocking fashion, the young Princess lingered but a few days in the most horrible bodily torture. The accident having happened at Schönbrunn, she was carried back to Vienna in a bath-tub full of oil, it being her whim to die at her own dear home. The most skilful doctors tried all that could be done to save her, but it was of no avail, and the charming girl, so dear to all, succumbed in her father's arms, entreating him to the very last to forgive her disobedience of his orders.

There was, in spite of this great sorrow, a vein of humor in the Archduke's composition much appreciated by the essentially jovial Austrian people, and like his nephew, the Emperor, he enjoyed a good joke, even when it was at his own expense, quite hugely!

Very fond of hunting and shooting, Archduke Albrecht made a point of spending a couple of months of every summer in one of the numerous villas which he owned in the Tyrol and Upper Austria; and when there he was indefatigable in the pursuit of the fleet-footed chamois. On these occasions he wore the customary *yoppe,* or hunter's uniform, of gray cloth *passepoiled* (braided) with green, the soft felt hat adorned with a chamois-beard, and the tall leathern gaiters of the ordinary Tyrolese mountaineer. Truth forces me, moreover, to state that as a general rule these garments were somewhat the worse for wear, and that there was nothing "dudish" about the appearance of the hero of Custozza.

Viennese society still laughs about a little adventure which occurred to him when returning from a hunting expedition in the mountains above Ischl. Through some extraordinary chance the Archduke had wandered from his party, and losing his way among the narrow wooded paths descending to the valley, he determined to reach the first *yâger* (hunter) hut which he could succeed in finding by himself. Quickening his pace, he hurried on in the gathering gloom, until he reached a steep incline covered with slippery grass. A little ahead of him he soon discerned a dark figure seemingly heavily laden. Wishing to inquire his way home, he hailed the unknown in a stentorian voice, and the figure came to a stop. To his surprise the Archduke found that it was that of a young girl of nineteen or twenty years of age, who, with the usual pluck of the Austrian peasant woman, had burdened herself with a gigantic load of firewood, on top of which was perched a chubby baby about two years old, who

maintained his perilous equilibrium by means of
a long scarf tied by his careful mother around his
fat little body and her own neck.

"What do you want?" cried the girl, scanning
the belated hunter with anything but a friendly
look.

"Can you tell me the shortest road down to
Ischl?" replied the Archduke.

"I am going there—you can follow me," she
retorted, curtly.

Accepting this rather ungracious invitation,
the imperial sportsman resumed his way beside
her, but his sense of courtesy making him feel
annoyed at seeing a woman carrying so exagger-
ated a weight, he said, pleasantly:

"This is far too heavy for you, my good girl.
Give me that child; I will carry him."

"Much you must know about carrying children, you old fool!" politely exclaimed the girl.
"No, you take the firewood and I will keep the
youngster. You may well do that, for had you not
met me you'd have run a good chance of spending
your entire night on the mountains."

Hardly able to repress his amazement, the
Archduke undid the scarf, transferred the little
urchin to his mother's arms and the ponderous
bundle of fagots to his own shoulders, and what
with his gun and his game-bag, he was a pretty
heavily burdened archduke indeed! To add insult
to injury, the girl continued to chaff him unmer-
cifully about the comical appearance he presented, and, as he later on asserted, he soon
became a little tired of his bargain.

For a full hour he trudged wearily along,
wishing himself anywhere but among the high
mountains with a load of wood on his back; but

EMPEROR FRANZ-JOSEPH IN 1893

at last relief arrived in the shape of his party,
which came upon the ill-assorted couple at the
crossing of two paths. No pen could describe, or
pencil portray, the amazement of the hunters at
seeing their august master thus accoutred, and
their exclamations betrayed the Archduke's
identity to the appalled girl. Falling on her knees,
she craved his pardon for the crime of *lèse-
majesté* which she had unwittingly committed,
and tears of shame sprang to her bonny blue eyes
as she watched two of the Prince's hunters
remove the fagots from his bruised shoulders.

"Don't cry, there's a good girl," pleaded
Albrecht, much distressed. "You did quite right,
and I am mighty glad to have met you to show me
the way!" So saying, he lifted the girl from the
ground, and pulling a well-filled purse from his
pocket, he pressed it into the baby's wee hands,
adding, with a kindly smile: "Here is something
to buy your mammy a donkey, for she might not
always find old fools to help her carry her firewood!"

Stéphanie is the only person with whom
I have ever seen him act in a curt and abrupt
manner. He could not endure her, and fled her
presence with an amusing display of energy; and
when matters came to a crisis between her and
Rudi, I know that in his heart he unhesitatingly
sided with his great-nephew.

During the summer which followed her son's
marriage the Empress seemed absolutely unable
to shake off her mélancholy forebodings, and it
was only when she went to Gödöllö that the free
and invigorating country life which she led there
restored in a measure her much-shaken health
and her peace of mind. Her piety, which was

always great, although she spoke as little about it
as about all other of her deepest feelings, became
even greater. Every morning she attended mass
at five o'clock, and then after a very summary
breakfast she mounted her horse and galloped off
through the magnificent park, which is traversed
in every direction by broad, sandy avenues.

A mishap which occurred to one of her favorite hunters at that time took, in her eyes, almost
the proportions of an irretrievable catastrophe.
Her nerves had become so unstrung that she had
no longer the same power of recuperation which
she had possessed for so many years. The accident to which I am about to refer may give the
measure of her softness of heart, even where
animals were concerned.

We were riding alone together over a narrow
path in the glad light of a beautiful autumn
morning. A thunder-storm during the night had
purified and cooled the air, the trees and bushes
were still sparkling with moisture, and the
dew-drops on the flower-filled grass glittered
like countless gems in the sun-rays, while a host
of little birds were twittering and singing in
sweet, abrupt gushes in the branches overhead.
My chestnut mare, "Black Pearl," was close to
Elisabeth's magnificent hunter, "Sir Launcelot."
I noticed with regret that the Empress seemed
singularly dejected, and resolving to arouse her
and dispel her gloomy thoughts, I said, briskly:
"Come, your Majesty, let's have a gallop; it
will do us all the good in the world, and 'Sir
Launcelot' is dying for it."

The Empress, who understood my motives
perfectly, replied with a smile:

"All right, dear, let's go ahead," touching her

hunter slightly with her spur as she spoke. Off we went, "Sir Launcelot" laying his length out in his mighty strides, and my pretty chestnut racing her best by his side. They dashed neck to neck on the damp moss at a rattling pace, breaking straight for the open. Literally we were racing. The pace became tremendous as we reached the short grass of the Pùsztá. Here a high fence towered, there a brook rushed angrily, but we stopped at nothing; and both horses, their mettle roused, needed no touch of stick or spur, and rose in the air with bounds that knew no obstacles.

"Take care!" I cried, suddenly catching sight of a broad, brawling brook running between two steep banks. The Empress only tossed her head; such dangers as that which just lay before her she enjoyed more than anything else, especially when in her present mood. The jump was an awkward one, with a bad take-off, and an ugly mud-bank for a landing; the water was swollen by the recent storm, and the turf was sloppy and soft as a sponge. At that particular place it was risking life and limb to try it, but unhesitatingly she worked her horse up and charged towards it. "Sir Launcelot" was over like a bird, and I landed "Black Pearl" by a beautiful clear spring after him by a couple of lengths. On we rode, tearing across country for a mile and a half; at last we dashed into a field breathless, but having almost forgotten our troubles in the excitement of the moment. Checking her hunter, the Empress sprang to the ground with a merry laugh, while I, with a contented smile, murmured: "That was a ringing run!"

Elisabeth flung her arms around the glossy neck of "Sir Launcelot" and kissed his velvety

nose. "Is he not a beauty!" said she, exultingly,
leaning against the horse's side and patting his
shining mane. He was, indeed, not a very large
horse, but with grace in every line—a small head,
delicately tapered ears, slender legs, and large,
intelligent eyes. The horse now stood alert, every
fibre of his body strung to pleasurable excitement
as the voice he loved best said, fondly:

"You dear old rascal, that was well done!"
They made a lovely picture, horse and rider, thus
together, the beautiful woman, her eyes still
flashing with pleasure, her cheeks suffused with
delicate pink by the rapidity of the pace, and
her lovely figure set off to perfection by her short,
dark habit, leaning against the handsome steeple-
chaser.

A few minutes later we were away again,
racing once more on the slightly undulating
plain, leaping over blackthorn hedges into sloppy
green meadows, over angry little brooks gurgling
amid banks of rushes. Truly we had become
intoxicated with the rapidity of our motion. The
Empress "showed the way." Half an hour had
gone by in that splendid running without a single
check, in a speed like lightning, past clusters of
brown-stemmed bushes and hedges bright with
scarlet berries, while far away before our eyes
stretched the blue haze of limitless distance, and
above our heads a flight of cranes was making for
the south. We had loosened our horses to their
full will and their full speed; we had only to leave
it to the gallant tempers and the generous fires
that were in them to make them hold their own.
All at once water gleamed before us, this time
wider, brown, swollen, and rushing fast. "Black
Pearl" and "Sir Launcelot" scented it from afar,

and went on with ears pointed and greyhound strides, gathering up all their force for the leap that was before them. Perhaps in our enthusiasm we had become oblivious of the fact that the pace had been too rapid a one, even for perfect hunters, and instinctively, as I noticed the alarming breadth of the "yawner," I checked my horse slightly. "Sir Launcelot," however, rose blindly to the jump and missed the slippery bank. With a reel and a crash, to my horror, the Empress was hurled out into the brook, and the magnificent hunter lay there with his breast and forelegs resting on the ground, his hind quarters in the water, and his back broken. His race was run!

It is needless to say that I was off my horse in a second and helping the Empress, who was drenched with water and mud, up the bank. Her face was startlingly pale, but she seemed physically unhurt. She staggered to where the horse that she loved so well was undergoing the throes of a last agony, and kneeling down, regardless of the water which swirled about her, she threw her arms over his neck and leaned her own head down upon his, so that her face was entirely hidden. She knelt so long, thus motionless, that a fear of her having fainted began to creep into my heart, and I touched her on the shoulder. She did not move for a little while longer, and when she at last raised her face the silken mane of the horse was wet with great, slow tears that had forced themselves through her closed eyelids; then she laid her lips on "Sir Launcelot's" forehead just as if he had been a human being, and with a backward gesture of her hand to me she walked off rapidly.

Surely there have been many idols less pure

and true than the brave and loyal-hearted beast
to which she had just said an eternal good-bye.
Dragging "Black Pearl," who was quivering and
shaking all over, by her bridle, I followed
Elisabeth, entreating her to mount my horse so
that she might get back quicker to the castle,
where she would be able to change her sodden
clothes. A shake of the head was all the answer
that she gave me, and seeing that to urge my plea
would be but to hurt her more, I continued to
walk by her side without saying another word. Of
our long tramp back to the imperial residence I
will say but little, although it has remained in my
mind as one of the most painful moments of my
none too agreeable existence.

This new sorrow seemed to cast a deeper
gloom upon the Empress, and we departed from
Hungary a few days later to spend some weeks at
Ischl, where we all hoped that the pure mountain
air, which she loved so much, would help her to
shake off her persistent despondency.

Ischl is one of the prettiest and sweetest
places in this world. It is calm, sedate, and
simple; its mornings are radiant, and so are its
evenings, when the moon climbs over the heights
of the pine-clad mountains and shines delightfully on the green ripples of the rapid little river
Traun.

The sadness which had overtaken Elisabeth
was not of a kind from which her *entourage* had
to suffer. She was too considerate, too truly kind
to cast her own sorrows upon others, and her
sweet, patient smile was always given to those
whom she loved. Her indomitable courage, both
moral and physical, was really a thing to be
marvelled at; for it never flinched. This has been

well proved by the fact that at the last she could walk aboard the steamer at Geneva without betraying to any one the fact that her poor weary heart had just been pierced by the foul weapon of an assassin. The press reports argued at the time that she herself was not conscious of this, but I knew her better than that, and I realized fully that her inveterate hatred of any fuss, or of attracting attention upon herself, alone held her upright then, until she fell to rise no more.

So strong was that feeling with her that it made her consider being pitied as almost akin to being shamed.

During the sojourn which we made at Ischl that year, an incident took place which is an excellent illustration of the Empress's powers of endurance, and which to this day I verily believe is known to nobody. It still stands out as clearly in my memory as if it had occurred yesterday.

Always an intrepid mountaineer, the Empress delighted in climbing wellnigh inaccessible heights. Her slender, fair limbs, as strong as steel in a velvet sheath, would carry her upward to peaks where the *yägers* themselves found it troublesome to go, but where she maintained that the only air fit to be inhaled in this wide world of ours was to be found.

Although not quite as passionately fond as she herself was of these dizzy excursions, nevertheless I loved her too dearly not to accompany her, had the road been even far more arduous; and often we would stay overnight in these wild regions in some chalet perched on a ledge of rock at a great altitude.

On the occasion to which I refer, we somehow or other lost our way on the high mountain range

which towers above the quaint little town of Ischl.
We had climbed very high up, and night was
falling, bringing with it an extremely low
temperature. So cold, indeed, was it that
although we were barely in autumn, snow-flakes
began to drop like great feathery tufts from the
darkening sky. On and on we struggled, pausing
from time to time to peer into the gathering gloom
for the sight of some light, or at least of some
familiar landmark. Finally, just as we were
despairing of getting out of this predicament, the
Empress pointed with her alpenstock to a reddish
glow shining through the increasing curtain of
snow, and with renewed vigor we quickened our
steps towards what we knew to be the beacon-
light of a mountain refuge.

We were not disappointed, and in a few minutes we had obtained admittance into the incom-
modious but to us perfectly delightful seclusion of
the narrow, stuffy, closed shed, where we were
glad enough to take shelter from the now raging
storm. In the most democratic fashion we took
our places with some *yâgers* and cowherds
around the brightly blazing stove, awaiting with
what patience we could muster the moment when
we would be able to turn our faces towards Ischl.

Towards nine o'clock, the wind having
chased away the snow-laden clouds, the moon
shone forth in a purified sky, and engaging the
services of one of the *yâgers* as a guide, we
commenced our perilous descent, risking much to
avoid causing anxiety at the imperial villa, where
her Majesty was expected. Cautiously we advanced on the slippery rocks, holding on at times
to bowlders in order to maintain our equilibrium
on the treacherous path. First went the *yâger*, an

EMPEROR FRANZ-JOSEPH IN HUNTING-DRESS

old Tyrolese, as sure-footed as a goat, followed closely by the Empress, behind whom I stepped as briskly as circumstances permitted. Suddenly I saw a jagged bit of rock detach itself from the precipitous slope we were skirting and, thundering past the Empress, roll with a deep thud into the darkness beyond. A short exclamation from the imperial lady made me inquire if she were hurt, but receiving no answer, and seeing that she did not slacken her pace, I took no more heed of the affair, having more than enough to do in making my own progress.

The night was far advanced when we at last reached the Kaiser villa, and we went straight to our apartments to remove our damp, soil-begrimed clothes before taking some refreshments, and then some sleep, of both which commodities we were sorely in need. As the light from the swinging-lamp in the upper hall fell on Elisabeth's face I was struck by its extreme pallor, and also by the fact that her left hand was hidden in the breast of her gray cloth *yoppe*, or hunting-jacket. My immediate inquiry brought out a reluctant avowal to the effect that the loose stone had fallen directly upon the hand, with which she had been clinging to the rocky wall for support, but I was peremptorily asked "not to make a fuss, and not to speak of the matter to a living soul." Between the two of us we bandaged the sadly crushed, delicately tapering fingers, which must have caused excruciating torture to their plucky owner during that long tramp down the mountain-side, but which could neither bring her to wince or to complain, nor prevent her through it all from being the leading spirit in our small party. On the morrow the Empress appeared wearing, as she often did in the house, a pair of long *suede* gloves, and no one was ever allowed to notice what effort it cost her to use those poor maimed fingers.

CHAPTER XI

In the mean time the matrimonial relations of
Rudolph and Stéphanie were not by any means
satisfactory. Already the prognostications of the
Empress were fulfilled, in a measure, for dissensions and continual misunderstandings were
gradually becoming more frequent between them,
and the Crown-prince showed a moodiness which
he had never displayed before. Very talented,
the young man, who had always been interested
greatly in literature, began to wield his pen
to some purpose, and wrote several remarkable
works, including, later on, a volume of *Travels
Through the Orient,* of which he was not only the
author but also the illustrator.

Stéphanie's worldliness had now completely
outweighed her much-boasted religious feelings.
A true butterfly of fashion, she cast herself into
the whirl of society with an energy and passion
which nothing could subdue. Her personal appearance had not improved very greatly, but she
was always admirably dressed, and knew how to
make the most of the scanty amount of looks
which she possessed. That Rudolph was thoroughly dissatisfied with his new mode of existence could not long remain a secret at court, and
once more two *partis* formed themselves, the
one in favor of the winning young Archduke, the

other—and I am glad to say the weaker of the
two—took part for the Princess, who began
already to be called by this faction, "Die Arme
Stéphanie" (The Poor Stéphanie).

A little over two years after her marriage the
Crown-princess gave birth to a little daughter,
who was named after the Empress, but even this
family event did not serve to unite the hearts of
the young parents. The Crown-prince, like his
mother, sought comfort and forgetfulness in
devoting much of his time to sports of all descriptions, and became more than ever a devoted
follower of Nimrod. He had always loved both the
hunt and the chase, but now he threw himself
into all bodily exercise with untiring eagerness.
This, of course, was a new cause of grievance for
the Crown-princess, who immediately adopted
the pose of a neglected and abandoned wife, and
heaped reproaches upon her luckless husband's
head. Scenes which were indeed of the most
bourgeois kind became more and more frequent. Stéphanie raved, cried, and vituperated to
such an extent that what is in German called
"Gemühtlichkeit" (the comfortability of home)
fled from their home. Rudi, thoroughly out of
patience, entered upon a course which, if not
entirely commendable, at least was excusable, for
he absented himself as much as possible from an
environment which had become even to him,
easy-going as he was, a perfect hell upon earth.

One dark autumn afternoon I was sitting at
home dreaming before a roaring blaze of cedar-
logs, when the door of my boudoir was suddenly
flung open and, without any of the ceremonious
announcements which invariably herald a royal
visit, the Crown-prince rushed into the room,

dressed in plain clothes, and with a face so wild and haggard that I was nearly frightened out of my wits.

"What on earth is the matter?" I exclaimed, jumping to my feet.

"Everything is the matter!" he replied, casting himself into a low chair, from which, however, he immediately rose again to take a few furious strides about the apartment.

"Cannot you be a little more precise, and stop terrifying me in this fashion?" I said, somewhat peevishly, for his violent entry had considerably startled me.

"I beg your pardon," he said, with more composure. "I know that I am becoming a nuisance to others as well as to myself, but truly, I must speak to somebody or else explode. My poor mother is not at present strong enough to be troubled by my sorrows, which she predicted, I am bound to acknowledge, so I came here to unburden my heart. We have always been awful chums," he added, relapsing into his habitual familiar slang, "and you have been very good to me, stanch and true and as thoroughly reliable as any man friend could have been."

"Thank you," I laughed, "that is a great compliment; but really, Rudi, won't you please sit down and tell me what has occurred? I know that you haven't been feeling very happy of late, but still, surely matters cannot be bad enough to make you act in this fashion!"

"Oh yes they are; my wife is simply unbearable; in fact, sometimes I think that she cannot be altogether in her right mind. She is so jealous that if I merely look at another woman, if I dance with one, or pay any of these small little compliments without which no conversation can be carried on, as you know very well yourself, with any members of the fair sex, she treats me like a dog, and rampages about for hours together."

"Well, that is all very nice," I said, impatiently, "but we warned you how it would be; and besides which, you cannot deny, Master Rudi, that you are a sad flirt, and that she may not be entirely wrong when she objects to the many hearts that you break."

"Oh, stop that—do! I would have been a right enough kind of a husband if she had known how to behave herself, but I cannot bear to be watched, and followed, and tracked, and questioned, and annoyed, as she persists in doing. I tell you what I'll do if this goes on much longer. I will give her something serious to cry for! Until now, Heaven knows, I have nothing to reproach myself with, and I can look her straight in the eye without a tremor; but when it comes to my having to give her an account of every minute of my days and nights, and to finding out that my private letters are being opened, my body-servant cross-questioned, and my pockets searched, I draw a line; and so would you if you were in my place."

"My dear boy, be so kind as to ring the bell for tea, and while we are drinking this beverage which our English friends claim to be so powerful a restorative, I will take the liberty of reading you a lecture."

He looked puzzled; then the quick, merry, winning smile, which reminded one so much of his mother's, flitted over his drawn features, and, pressing the electric button of the bell, he sat down more like a reasonable being and, lighting a cigarette, gazed abstractedly out of the window,

watching the snow-flakes as they began to fall
upon the now completely denuded trees of the
Ringstrasse.

A few minutes later, as we sipped the comfort-
ing cup, which had been brought in at his sum-
mons, I renewed the subject, and pointed out to
him what a disastrous effect any outbreak on his
part would have upon the Empress. This was the
best way to take him, and he softened at once;
but still I knew him well enough to see that his
exasperation had almost reached its last limits,
and that sooner or later some scandal or other
would come to add its bitterness to my beloved
Kaiserin's already full cup of misery.

When he left me that afternoon he was somewhat pacified, but I shuddered as I thought of all
that was to come.

Disliking the Crown-princess from the very
first, I could not look very charitably upon the
rôle which she was now playing, and her heartlessness infuriated me absolutely. What a different man Rudolph would have been but for the
baneful influence which his wife exercised over
him. In all truth, he was one of the most chivalrous, kind-hearted young men I have ever met,
and to-day I am convinced that the change in his
whole being which led to the tragedy of Mayerling
can justly be laid at the door of the sour-
tempered, overbearing, narrow-minded woman
whom he was so unfortunate as to marry.

Matters went from bad to worse, and Rudi,
rendered thoroughly wild by being always falsely
accused, ended by carrying his flirtations further
than he ought to have done. This alteration in
his principles—which, in spite of all that has
been said to the contrary, were good, high, and

noble—was brought about by Stéphanie herself
in the following manner:

Rudolph, who, as he said himself, did not
know what to do with his evenings when there
was no official occasion which he was forced to
grace with his presence, and who dreaded a
tête-à-tête with his irascible wife, went one night
to visit a well-known actress who had been
presented to him by one of his friends, a young
officer with whom the lady in question was on the
best of terms. The Crown-prince drove to her
house in an ordinary *fiacre* (carriage), which he
left at the door waiting for him. Meanwhile
Crown-princess Stéphanie, finding out by means
best known to herself where her husband was
about to spend the evening, followed him in one
of the court equipages. Upon arriving at the
above-mentioned lady's house she alighted, and
bidding her coachman wait for the Crown-prince,
she got into his hired conveyance and peremptorily ordered the amazed jehu to drive her back
to the Hofburg. Recognizing the Crown-princess,
the man did not dare to disobey; and as for the
imperial coachman, he sat transfixed with astonishment and horror upon his box, not knowing
what was best for him to do. Half an hour later,
upon leaving the house, Rudolph had the
decidedly agreeable surprise of being confronted
by his wife's carriage, coachman, and beplumed
chasseur (footman). No wonder that this incident
capped the climax of his already only too just
exasperation, and that night the apartments of
the heir apparent echoed with the resounding
noise of reproaches and sobs. Shortly afterwards
the Crown-prince purchased the hunting-lodge of
Mayerling, the spot where he was to breathe his

last under such tragical circumstances.

His taste for natural studies, which won for him the reputation of being one of the foremost zoologists and ornithologists of Europe, had full play during his more and more frequent sojourns at Mayerling. He took an extreme pleasure in decorating this picturesque residence with his trophies of the chase, and often he would spend hours together in what he was pleased to call his "workshop," preparing with his own hands for stuffing the birds he had shot, and labelling curious specimens of rocks and stones and other minerals which he found in his endless rambles through the surrounding hills and woods.

His apartments resembled more a museum, or the rooms of a professor of natural history, than those of a high and mighty prince. One of the *salons* was arranged so as to represent a forest, with grottos of rock, trees and shrubs planted in enormous boxes concealed under moss and trailing ivy, and was decorated with magnificently disposed and lifelike animals. A huge bear, the first which the Crown-prince had shot when staying at Munkács, seemingly clung to a pine-trunk, and several superb eagles looked as if they were about to swoop down from their elevated positions near the ceiling. Owls, lynxes, pheasants, foxes—nay, even deer and stags—were all to be found in this wonderful room.

One of the most cherished possessions of the Crown-prince was contained in a large glass-case, and was nothing less than the carcass of a horse in the act of being devoured by vultures, hawks, and ravens, the whole group being wonderfully prepared and executed, and giving one an exact idea of the gruesome thing itself. These birds were shot by Rudolph during his trip of "fifteen days on the Danube" which he described in one of his books, and also in Spain, in Egypt, and on the island of Plâwnik, in the Quarnero.

The Prince's study at Mayerling was decorated with wonderful specimens of foreign and domestic arms—guns, carbines, pistols, matchlocks, swords, kandjars, and yataghans inlaid with gold, silver, and mother-of-pearl. These rested on the antlers of the many deer which Rudi had shot or forced. The magnificent snow-white *Edelhirsche* (noble deer) which he shot in Bohemia were perhaps the most remarkable items of this beautiful collection.

He might still have been happy with his scientific and literary pursuits, his hunts and chases and his long-distance rides through hill and dale, for besides all this he was a wonderful musician, a painter, and a draughtsman of no mean talent, and passionately fond of study and of reading, all these qualities being inherited from his mother, but, unfortunately, Crown-princess Stéphanie objected to his stays at Mayerling, or to any travel or occupation which she was not allowed to share. At first, to be sure, had she been so minded, he would have been glad to make her his companion even on his expeditions after fur and feathers; but, to her, brilliantly lighted *salons* filled with well-dressed women chattering about fashion and folly, and with a bevy of young men ready to flirt and to talk nonsense, were far more agreeable than long tramps and rides under forest boughs or on mountain peaks, and her scorn for her husband's favorite pastimes was so well defined, her sneers so marked, that he let her take her own way and stopped asking her to join him. To be sure, after his wretched death she gave it out to the world that she was occupied in compiling and editing his last book, the one in fact which he was engaged in writing when he took his last trip to Mayerling, but like many other things which were at that time bruited among the public, there was but little truth in this *post-mortem* and singularly sudden devotion.

Of course the Empress, who had not been long in finding out what her son's matrimonial life really was, felt altogether broken-hearted about it, and when she spoke or wrote to him, she attempted by all means within her power to console and soothe him. It was at that time that she wrote several singularly touching little poems in the Hungarian language, which betrayed her state of mind.

It was then, also, that she wrote a little poem about the famous legend which connects every misfortune happening to the House of Hapsburg with the appearance upon the scene of a raven, little thinking that some few years later her own death would be thus heralded.

Everybody has heard of the flight of ravens which swept across the little town of Olmütz during the minutes when Emperor Franz-Joseph accepted the crown of Austria, and with it a weight of sorrows such as seldom has been carried by a monarch. When Maximilian was about to start on his ill-fated journey to Mexico in order to assume his duties as sovereign, a raven was seen by him and his wife Charlotte during a last walk which they took in the grounds of their castle of Miramar. The bird persistently followed them, and when they sat down upon a bench under a clump of sycamores it flew, or rather

hopped, towards them and settled itself on one
leg upon the sweeping folds of the future
Empress's train. Again, when Archduchess
Maria-Christina was about to enter the carriage
which was to drive her to the railway station,
whence she departed for her future kingdom of
Spain—a land where she suffered all that a
woman can suffer in her affections, her pride, and
her health—an enormous raven kept hovering
over the horses' heads and actually kept up with
them during the whole drive.

On the afternoon which preceded the Empress's assassination at Geneva, she wandered
for several hours in the mountains about Territet
with her reader, Mr. Barker. The latter had
brought with him a basket of fine fruit, the
Empress being in the habit of partaking of some
every day in lieu of five-o'clock tea. Seated upon
some moss-grown rocks, the imperial lady, while
listening to Mr. Barker, who was then reading to
her Marion Crawford's celebrated novel *Corleone*,
drew the little basket towards her and began to
peel a magnificent peach, of which she offered
half to her reader. Just as she was in the act of
handing him his share, a huge raven flew down
from a tall pine-tree whose dusky branches were
casting a deep shade upon the pair, and touching
Elisabeth's forehead with the tip of its sombre
wing, actually knocked the peach out of her
hand. Remembering the dread legend of the
Hapsburg ravens, Mr. Barker jumped up with an
exclamation of fear, but the Empress began to
laugh, and said to her startled attendant:

"Don't be alarmed! I am not superstitious,
and if something is to happen to me soon, it is
not that poor bird which will have caused it.

Anyhow, you know my ideas about death: I am not afraid of it. When one's heart and soul are dead it matters but very little when the earthly envelope follows suit. My heart and soul have been dead for the past ten years!" she added, with a sad smile.

"Nevertheless, your Majesty," replied Mr. Barker, "I am not easy in my mind. I had a horrible dream last night about my mother, and I know that something terrible is going to happen."

The Empress gazed at him for a moment in astonishment, and then, with a shrug of her shapely shoulders, she rejoined:

"My dear Mr. Barker, I hope that you are too sensible to let evil dreams gain any influence over you. I thought that, like myself, you were a fatalist. Our time comes when it is appointed to come, and nothing that we can fear or fancy will ever alter our fate. Many years ago I had an awful dream myself. It was at the time when my cousin, Louis of Bavaria, died, and this sinister vision of mine came true; but, perhaps just because of this fact, I have schooled myself ever since then not to let such wanderings of my mind when I am asleep create too great an impression upon me when awake. Life is not happy enough for us to spoil what few joys we have by worrying about such prognostications and ill-omened signs from the land of dreams. Follow my example, my dear Mr. Barker; it is a duty which we owe to ourselves and others as well."

But to return to the Crown-prince and his wife, from whose dissensions I have wandered. I am forced to state that shortly after the purchase by Rudolph of Schloss Mayerling, Stéphanie committed another of those dreadful mistakes

which alienated the heart of her husband so
completely from her. He had left Vienna to go and
spend two or three days at his hunting-lodge,
when, on the second evening after his arrival at
Mayerling, an ordinary cab drew up before the
gates of the little castle, and a heavily veiled lady
asked for admittance. According to the rules in
use at all royal and imperial residences, this
could not take place without the visitor's revealing his or her identity, and as the lady refused to
do this, the Crown-prince's valet, Loschek, was
called. When he appeared on the scene, the lady
drew back her veil and revealed the features of
Crown-princess Stéphanie herself. Of course Loschek could but bow low, and make way for his
mistress to enter the premises. Shortly afterwards
the voices of husband and wife, raised in tones of
anger, were heard distinctly by the attendants;
and, unfortunately, the violence of their emotions
rendered them so careless that the following
words were plainly heard by two or three servants, who, of course, did not fail to repeat them
to their own friends and boon companions, thus
spreading among the public a lamentably true
version of what the relations of Rudolph and
Stéphanie were.

"I know that you betray me!" shrieked the
Princess, shrilly. "You come here to receive your
fair friends, and I won't have it. Do you understand?"

Hoarse with fury, Rudolph exclaimed in
return:

"What you say is untrue. There is not a
solitary woman here; you will drive me crazy if
you go on like this, and were it not for the sorrow
that it would cause my parents, I would leave

you this minute forever."

A few minutes afterwards the ill-assorted couple left Mayerling and drove back to Vienna; and when this drive was at an end practically all hope of peace or reconciliation was lost, for so embittered did the Crown-prince now become that he seldom if ever saw his wife alone.

One fine day the latter, beside herself with ever-increasing anger at the powerlessness of her efforts to chain down the unfortunate Rudi, telegraphed to her father telling him that she had decided to return to Belgium. The old King, who was far too wily and shrewd a man not to do everything possible to prevent such a scandal, replied, also by telegraph, in the following fashion:

"Stéphanie: C'est votre devoir de rester à côté de votre mari, le Prince Héritier."

(Stéphanie: It is your duty to remain at the side of your husband, the Crown-prince.)

In 1888 Rudolph was asked by his father to put in an appearance at the Polish ball, which is one of the most brilliant social events of the Viennese Fasching, or carnival. The Crown-prince, in obedience to his father's wishes, drove to the ball in a very despondent mood, for on that very afternoon he had had another violent scene with his amiable wife. But, with the mobility of his pleasure-loving nature, as soon as he entered the dazzlingly lighted and flower-filled *salons* he cast his cares off and gave himself up to the enjoyment of the moment.

The Polish ball is, as I remarked before, a very beautiful function, for all the great Polish nobles who have taken up their residence in the capital make a point of being present, wearing their

national costumes, which are a marvellous combination of gold-embroidered velvets, costly furs,
and costlier jewels.

Under a group of palms and gigantic ferns sat
a young girl of such a remarkable personal charm
that the Crown-prince immediately inquired who
she was. He was informed that she was the
daughter of Baron Vetsera, and of the sister of
those celebrated and enthusiastic sportsmen
known in Austria as the "Little Baltazzis." The
Baltazzis are Greeks, but thanks to their immense
wealth and their passion for horse-flesh, they
implanted themselves many years ago in Viennese society; not in court circles, to be sure, for in
order to be presented at court it is necessary, to
begin with, to be able to prove the regulation
sixteen quarterings on both sides, and the Greek
bankers in question would have possibly been
much embarrassed to prove any quarterings at
all. However, both Hector and Aristides Baltazzi
had been presented to the Emperor, as well as
to the Empress and to other members of the
imperial family, in the hunting-field, and as
one of their sisters had married an Austrian
nobleman of the name of Baron Vetsera, another
the equally noble Austrian Baron Stockau, and
one of the brothers the lovely Countess Ugarte,
the family could be said to hover on the edge of a
very aristocratic set. Moreover, so whispered the
chronique scandaleuse (gossip column; lit.,
"scandalous chronicle"), when Baroness Vetsera
made her début in society after her marriage, the
Emperor had been an ardent admirer of her dark
Oriental beauty, his attentions having caused a
great amount of talk at the time.

Marie Vetsera, the Baroness's daughter, had

spent most of her girlhood abroad, and thus it was that until the ill-fated night of that particular Polish ball no member of the imperial family had as yet set eyes upon her. She was then nineteen years old, and in the bloom of her extraordinary loveliness. Tall, slender, with magnificent dark eyes, shaded by incredibly long and silky lashes, she possessed a charm and a piquancy which, even at Vienna, where beautiful women are the rule and not the exception, produced a distinct sensation. Her perfect figure displayed to admirable advantage by a simple but exquisitely draped gown of white crêpe, which had no other ornament than some clusters of white violets and white heather, she reclined under the green shadow cast by some tall plants, playing listlessly with her fan of white feathers. She seemed quite unconscious of the sweet picture which she made, her small, well-shaped head leaning against a pile of cushions, and a crescent of diamonds—her sole jewel—sparkling in the masses of her dark wavy hair.

There was something so attractive, so delightfully pure and refined and out of the ordinary in her appearance that the Crown-prince asked to have her introduced to him, and was soon sitting by her side, talking gayly about the ever-changing pageant before their eyes. Before long he asked her to dance.

The Austrians are proverbially the best waltzers on earth, and to waltz with Rudi, who had mastered that difficult art with his usual capacity for doing exceedingly well everything that he did at all, was a revelation to Marie. The Crown-prince was not what is commonly called a good-looking man, but he was worse than good-looking, for when he chose to make an effort he became absolutely and irresistibly *séduisant* (seductive).

It is supposed that in novels only does one encounter the famous *coup de foudre* (love at first sight; lit., "bolt of lightning"), but real life has given many proofs that such a thing exists, and we stand face to face with just such an instance when speaking of this first meeting between the heir of Austro-Hungary's crown and the heiress of the Baltazzi millions and of the peculiar style of beauty of the Baltazzi women. Marie, who had been much courted from the very outset of her career in Austrian society, had from that moment no thought excepting for the stalwart prince whose eyes—the finest feature which he possessed—had known so well how to make her understand at once that the time had come for him to lose his heart for good and all. This was no budding flirtation, no little drawing-room intrigue which serves to while away the hours and give a little zest to the insipid existence of most society men and women, but the genuine bona fide passion which has been pictured by the poets from time immemorial.

In Montenegro the mountaineers call this sudden rush of feeling "having met one's fate," and this expresses such an event well indeed, for rare as such instances may be they have pretty nearly always a fateful end—nay, even a tragical one.

Rudolph had in his nature a vein of what in German is called *schwärmerei* (adulation)—a hidden source of poetical ideality—and he was a most likely victim for a love which pertained rather to the soul than to the senses. A great deal of nonsense, and shameful nonsense at that, has been spoken and written about the immense and absorbing tenderness which united Rudolph and Marie from the very first. Slander of the foulest and blackest kind has not been spared to them, and even after their death the slimy tide of misinterpretation and calumny has kept rising about their graves, and has blurred their memory in its muddy ooze.

The truth of the matter is, that love such as they felt for each other is too uncommon a thing not to arouse the ill-feeling and envy of the public, and that almost of necessity revenge is swift, and generally takes the shape of a wave of villanous inventions, of false reports, and of cruel lies, which it is impossible to refute because in such cases proof of the victim's innocence can seldom be given.

The person who was, perhaps, most to blame in the whole lamentable course of this sorry affair was Countess George Larisch. She was the niece of Empress Elisabeth, whose elder brother had morganatically married an actress of the name of Henriette Mendel. The Countess, the only child of this union, was born in 1858, and when she had reached maidenhood, Elisabeth, touched by her beauty, and especially attracted by her perfect horsewomanship, took her up, and introduced her at the Viennese court under the name which had been granted to her mother upon the latter's marriage—namely, that of Baroness Wallersee. Her aunt conferred upon her the title of Lady-of-the-Palace, and in 1879 married her to Count George Larisch, who was then a good-natured, easy-going, young cavalry officer, not very bright but intensely kind-hearted, who belonged to an old family, and was endowed with more than a fair portion of this world's goods. The marriage took place at Gödöllö, and it was the Empress herself who gave the bride away.

This very pretty and elegant woman was wont to designate herself as Rudi's favorite cousin, and I think, as many others have done, too, that she at first harbored hopes of marrying him, although she was fully cognizant of the fact that being of non-royal birth, and for the matter of that the issue of a morganatic alliance, she had not the slightest chance of ever being allowed to wed the heir to the crown. Nevertheless she relied upon her imperial aunt's affection, and also upon the headstrong temper of Rudi, who she well knew would have been difficult to dissuade from accomplishing any plan which had once entered his head. To that purpose she left no stone unturned in order to make herself as agreeable as possible to the Emperor, Empress, Crown-prince; and the two young Archduchesses whom she would have so much liked to call by the name of sisters. Rudolph's marriage being one day freely discussed in her presence, she put out a few feelers, and old Archduke Albrecht, who was present, discovering with his usual sagacity the quarter from which the wind blew, stated to her in clear and definite language that the Crown-prince of Austria would never be permitted by his family nor by the imperial and royal constitution to marry any other than a royal or an imperial princess. The young Baroness realized that the aged Archduke was speaking the absolute truth, and, subsequently, in a moment of pique, she accepted the hand of Count Larisch and became one of the gayest *mondaines* (society women) of the gayest court of Europe.

When some three years later Rudolph married

Stéphanie, the Crown-princess became Countess
Larisch's *bête noire,* and the Countess's behavior
towards her cousin's bride in public, and the
sarcasms and ridicule with which she covered
her in private, were not of a nature to make
Rudolph look upon his consort with a very indulgent gaze. Instead of trying to palliate the wrongs
done to him by his wife, Countess Larisch kept
pouring oil on the flames, and was continually on
the lookout for an occasion to revenge herself
upon the woman who certainly offered reason
enough for dislike, but whose only crime against
her was, after all, in having married the man
whom she herself loved, or pretended to love—
which, as far as the ultimate result is concerned,
comes absolutely to the same thing. Quick as a
flash of lightning the Countess, who unluckily
happened to be also present at the Polish ball
where Rudolph made the acquaintance of Marie
Vetsera, noticed what an impression the girl's
beauty and wit had made upon Rudolph's sad-
dened and weary heart. Seeing at last within her
grasp the means of paying off old scores, she at
once made up her mind to throw the two young
people together as much as possible. She lost no
time in making the acquaintance of Baroness
Vetsera, and from that day on she managed with
extreme cleverness to bring it about that every
time that Rudolph called upon her he should
encounter at her house the girl whom he was
learning to love more and more passionately
every day.

That the moral principles of Countess Larisch
were not of the highest order has been since
then unquestionably proved by the fact that
a few years ago she abandoned her kind and

long-suffering husband, as well as her beautiful little children, for the sake of an opera-singer of the name of Bruck, whom she proceeded to marry as soon as the Count had obtained a divorce from her, and with whom she is now living somewhere in Germany.

The love of Rudolph and Marie might possibly have remained a secret from Stéphanie, for they never met in private, and he was very careful that not a breath of scandal should have any reason to touch the girl he worshipped, had it not been for the Countess, who never rested until she had by her many hints and innuendoes made it clear to the Crown-princess that Rudolph had at last fallen in love in good earnest, and designated to her kind notice the possessor of her husband's heart. This took place shortly before Queen Victoria's jubilee festivities in 1887, festivities at which the Crown-prince and Crown-princess of Austria were to represent Emperor Franz-Joseph and Empress Elisabeth.

Two or three weeks before the date appointed for the departure of Rudolph and Stéphanie for London, Marie Vetsera was called to England, where her sister lay ill. This was a mere coincidence, but presented to the Crown-princess by the cruelly sarcastic tongue of Countess Larisch, the fact took the proportions of a purposely made appointment, arranged by the lovers, with a view of being able to meet on a foreign soil with an ease which was not to be found within the limits of the Austrian empire. Upon hearing of this the Crown-princess at the very last moment stubbornly refused to accompany her husband, wounding the feelings of the aged British Queen almost beyond pardon by her curt denial, and offending almost as much the Emperor and Empress, not to speak of her own father and mother, King Leopold and Queen Henrietta of Belgium, who were among the Jubilee guests.

It is useless to record here the really atrocious scene which took place between Rudolph and Stéphanie on that occasion. The Crown-princess forgot herself so far as to use when speaking of Marie Vetsera some epithets which befitted neither her sex nor her exalted rank, and which, when applied to the woman he loved, Rudolph could not let pass without resenting in the angriest fashion possible. He then and there declared to his consort that he was through with her, and that he would never forgive what she had said. With this declaration of war he took his departure for England, while Stéphanie, for once frightened wellnigh out of her wits, left Vienna to spend the time of his absence away from all observing eyes.

That Rudolph met Marie Vetsera and her mother in London, and called upon them several times, is quite certain, but what plans were decided upon by the two young people it is impossible to state. Let it suffice to say that some time after his return to Austria the Crown-prince sent a private and confidential letter to our Holy Father, the Pope, entreating him to dissolve his marriage, and to use his influence with the Emperor to obtain the latter's sanction to Rudolph's renouncing all his rights of succession to the throne, and retreating altogether from the public gaze. This letter was sent to Rome by a special and trusty messenger, who was to bring back his Holiness's answer thereto. Almost immediately upon the reception of this document

Leo XIII. despatched one of his own confidential couriers to Emperor Franz-Joseph, enclosing in a letter of his own to the Emperor the one which the Crown-prince had written.

It is impossible to depict the horror and amazement of the unhappy father when he received this quite unexpected blow, for although he was aware that the relations between his son and his daughter-in-law were much strained, yet he had no idea that this state of affairs had gone so far as to bring about such a decision on Rudolph's part; moreover, he knew Rudolph too well not to realize that some really terrible thing must have happened to cause him to take such a step without even mentioning it to him.

He at once summoned Archduke Albrecht, his uncle, his brother, Archduke Charles-Louis, and the Prince-Archbishop of Vienna, wishing to communicate to Rudolph the Holy Father's letter in their presence.

The interview which followed is wellnigh indescribable. Rudolph, much moved by the deep grief of his father, to whom he was extremely attached, fell at his feet and craved his pardon for being its cause, but at the same time refused to give any explanation of his conduct in the presence of witnesses, and it was only later on, when the Emperor had retired to his private apartments for the night, that the Crown-prince was induced by him to make a clean breast of the whole matter.

Here we reach a point in this terrible affair which is of so delicate a nature that one positively recoils before the almost impossible task of explaining it. There are in this world some terrible fatalities, and many instances in which the

ARCHDUKE KARL-LUDWIG, BROTHER OF THE EMPEROR

words of the Scripture, which say that "the sins of the fathers will be visited upon the children," come true in a really ghastly fashion. The stormy conversation which took place between the Emperor and his only and much-beloved son was witnessed by none, and yet there exist to-day several people who know how awful was the discovery made by both of them on that never-to-be-forgotten night, when Rudolph confessed to his father his love for Marie Vetsera, and his intention of giving up his entire future, his lofty rank, and his unequalled position in order to marry her!

When at dawn the Crown-prince staggered out from his father's presence, his face was gray and drawn and haggard, like that of a corpse, and in his eyes, which glittered with the burning light of fever, there was a look of harsh resolve which betrayed not only the fact that he was a desperate man, but also that he had left behind him all hope of the realization of his most ardent desires.

As to the Emperor, when his valet entered his room at the usual hour he found his imperial master bowing low over his desk, with his head pillowed upon his folded arms. The Emperor was fully dressed in the uniform which he had worn on the previous evening, and the servant, thinking that perchance his master had fallen asleep while writing, permitted himself to touch him lightly on the shoulder. What was his fright and amazement when he discovered that Franz-Joseph, this man of iron, who never knew a day's sickness, was in a dead faint! Realizing with the quick intuition of a thoroughly loyal servitor that the Emperor would wish his condition kept secret if possible, the valet forbore from summoning help, but applied restoratives himself, and when the Emperor had recovered consciousness tactfully avoided betraying by look or sign his own curiosity as to what might have brought about so curious and unparalleled an incident.

During the course of the morning the Emperor sent for his son, but was informed that his imperial highness the Crown-prince had started early for Mayerling accompanied only by his body-servant Loschek, and that he had left word to the effect that he intended to spend two or three days there, in the company of his brother-in-law, Prince Phillip von Coburg, and of Count Joseph Hoyòs, who were as a rule his favorite hunting companions.

On the 30th of January, 1889, Europe was startled and terrified through its length and breadth by the news, flashed over the wires from Vienna, that Crown-prince Rudolph had died suddenly from the rupture of an aneurism of the heart, at his hunting-lodge of Mayerling. The official Viennese organ, *Die Offizielle Wiener Zeitung*, of January the 31st, contained on its first page, surrounded by a deep black border, the following announcement:

"Seine Kaiserliche und Königliche Hoheit der Durchlauchtiste Kronprinz-Erzherzog Rudolf ist gestern am 30 Januar in Seinen Jagdschlosse in Mayerling, bei Baden, am Herzschlag plötzlich verschieden."

(His Royal and Imperial Highness, Crown-prince Archduke Rudolph, died yesterday, January 30th, at his hunting-lodge of Mayerling, near Baden, from the rupture of an aneurism of the heart.)

It would have been truer if the paper had contented itself with declaring that Rudolph had died of a broken heart, for a broken heart it was which led to his violent and untimely death.

Later on, during the course of the day, the most contradictory reports appeared in print. Some of these declared that the Crown-prince had succumbed to the effects of a shooting accident, others that he had died of congestion of the lungs; others again hinted in a very guarded but still fully understandable fashion that he had fallen in a duel.

On the following day nothing at all was printed save a simple statement emanating from the highest quarters and declaring that the heir apparent had died suddenly at his castle of Mayerling, and giving out the usual regulations for court mourning.

A great many foreign journalists, requested by their newspapers to find out all that they could about this disastrous event, drove immediately to Mayerling, but found it impossible to penetrate farther than the outer gates of the park surrounding the *schloss* (castle).

The neighborhood is known as "The Pearl of the Wiener-Wald." It is exceedingly romantic, dotted with the picturesque ruins of ancient castles, of churches, of monasteries, and of convents. The most remarkable and interesting monastery in the region is Heiligenkreutz, which is one of the oldest in Austria. It was founded in 1336 by Margrave Leopold, and in the chapter-house is the vault of the Babenbergs. The building is beautiful, and exquisitely carved in a lacelike pattern of pinkish-gray granite; and an old well, which is always shown to visitors, is of so curious a workmanship that it is said not to have its like in the entire world. The treasure-chamber and library—containing over twenty thousand volumes—are also great attractions, and so are the superb stained-glass windows of the chapel. In a word, Heiligenkreutz is indeed very justly celebrated, for it is one of the most perfect relics left of the poetical times of long ago.

It was the Crown-prince's delight to spend hours there, poring over the black-letter records and rolls of quaint old parchments in the Archive Hall, fingering with a feeling akin to awe the handiwork of the learned monks, whose bones have been crumbling away for centuries under the stone pavement of the cross-shaped cloisters.

The surrounding forest is, if one is to believe the oldest inhabitants, as well as the written statements left by preceding generations, haunted by a wild huntsman and a white lady who are, it appears, in the habit of galloping at night on shadowy horses under the interlaced branches of the magnificent trees. A narrow road overhung with evergreens leads towards the Castle of Mayerling, which also was once a monastery belonging to the monks of Heiligenkreutz.

On January the 30th, this beautiful place became transformed into the saddest and most melancholy spot upon earth. Snow was falling heavily, and throwing a cloak of blinding whiteness upon the entire landscape. The sky, of a gray copper hue, seemed to touch the summits of the trees, and no noise was anywhere to be heard save the dismal croaking of those eternally ill-omened ravens; no figure was to be seen excepting the cordon of gendarmes which surrounded the entire extent of the park, and stood motionless, carbine in hand, to prevent any intruder from penetrating within the circle of the private grounds. The shutters were closed throughout the entire castle, and at the door stood an officer of police with his sword drawn.

On January 31st, just as the gray, bleak, cold day was coming to an end, the door opened, and the gleam of many blessed candles cast a red glow upon the snow without. Presently some servants, clad in deepest black and holding torches in their hands, stepped out, preceding the Prince of Coburg and Count Hoyòs, who stood for a few moments on the steps until a perfectly plain, black-painted *fourgon*, drawn by two black horses, drew up before the portal.

All present were bareheaded, and shivered in the freezing wind which moaned among the snow-laden trees. After a minute or so, six huntsmen belonging to the Crown-prince's service appeared, carrying between them the long, narrow black coffin, absolutely unornamented, which contained the last remains of the man— young, athletic, strong, and buoyant—who but a few hours previously was the hope and the joy of one of the greatest empires of this earth.

Not a voice was raised, the necessary orders were given in whispers, the coffin was placed in the terrible *fourgon*, and the horses at last started at a foot-pace, while the Prince, the Count, and two or three officials sent by the Emperor, seated themselves in the three carriages which completed the dismal procession, and followed the *fourgon* out of the gates and into the darkness which had now gathered, and which made the narrow mountain-roads very dangerous to traverse. Suddenly the Prince of Coburg opened the

window of his carriage, and called out to the man
who drove the *fourgon:*

"For God's sake trot, for we shall all go crazy
together if we don't soon get away from this!"

On they rolled into the night at a quicker
pace, until they had left behind them the dense
woods and had reached the high-road which
leads to Baden. Once there, occasionally a cart
driven by some peasant met them, and little
thinking that this funeral cortège was that of
Austria's Crown-prince, the driver called out in
the peculiar drawl of the yokel: *"Is' wer g'stor-
ben?"* (Is somebody dead?) Finally the small town
of Baden was reached, and the coffin with its
escort was transferred to a special train which
was awaiting their arrival.

The night was almost over when the body of
the Crown-prince was borne into his private
apartments at the Hofburg. The temporary coffin
was opened and the corpse laid on the bed, and
then it was that the Emperor and Empress were
brought face to face with the full horrors of the
awful death of their only son.

There are but few who know how the ill-fated
Prince really met with his end. So much has been
written and said about it that was thoroughly
untrue, and so much kept back, rather impru-
dently, which it would have been better to state
frankly, that justice has never been done to the
motives which led this plucky, courageous, hon-
orable, and also sincerely religious young man to
give himself to death. It was rumored at the time,
and it also has been declared since, that before
committing an act so severely condemned by the
Catholic Church he had actually killed with his
own hand the woman whom he loved better than

life. *This is thoroughly and shamefully untrue.* Marie Vetsera died during the night of the 29th to the 30th of January, 1889, and she did die in the arms of the Crown-prince, but it was not he, as everybody persists in believing, who killed her. It has been authentically proved that it was she herself who cut short her fair and beautiful existence while Rudi had absented himself for a moment from the *salon* where they had been talking together.

Early in the morning of January 29th, Marie Vetsera received a letter. She was at that moment sitting in her dressing-room, and putting the finishing touches to her toilet. Her maid and her sister, who were present, noticed that as she perused the contents of the letter, which had been brought by a special messenger, she turned ghastly pale and shook like a leaf, but when asked what was the cause of her emotion, she refused to give any explanation, and tearing the letter into small pieces she threw them into the open fire, and watched them until they had been completely reduced to ashes. Shortly afterwards she complained of a headache, and said that she would go for a short walk in order to see whether fresh air would not do her good. Dressed in a simple, dark serge skirt, a jacket, cap, and muff of sombre fur, and with a small bunch of violets fastened at her breast, she left her mother's house and walked down the Ringstrasse until she reached a celebrated florist's shop, which she habitually patronized. There she purchased another and much larger bunch of violets, and on leaving the shop stepped into an *unumerierter*— one of those private cabs which a great many of the Viennese aristocrats use for their morning drives—which had stopped in front of the florist's as soon as she entered the shop. The horses trotted off at a sharp pace, and the shopwoman who had waited upon Marie, and had accompanied her to the door, said, as she returned to her counter:

"Well, that's funny! If I am not mistaken, the baroness has driven off in Crown-prince Rudolph's private cab, driven by Bratfisch himself."

Bratfisch, the Crown-prince's *fiacre*, was a well-known character in Vienna. He was the typical personification of those children of the Kaiser-stadt (Emperor-city), who are perhaps the most entertaining and thoroughly original beings in existence. He was absolutely devoted to his imperial master, who used to laugh very heartily at his extraordinary antics, as well as at the stories which he knew how to relate with amazing gusto about the people whom he had driven during the course of his life—stories that Rudolph, in his genial, careless manner, often caused him to tell.

Bratfisch had received orders to await a lady carrying a bunch of violets in her hand before the above-mentioned florist's, and then to drive her as rapidly as possible to Mayerling. When she arrived at the hunting-lodge she was met on the steps by Rudolph, who, taking her hand in his, drew her into the *salon,* into which his private apartments opened, and carefully closed the door.

Count Hoyòs and the Prince of Coburg were out shooting in the woods, whither the Crown-prince had refused to accompany them, pleading that he had a bad cold. Just before the arrival of Marie the Crown-prince had sent off a telegram, written in Hungarian, to his father at the Hofburg, telling him that he was not feeling well enough to be present at the family dinner which was to be given that evening in honor of Archduchess Marie-Valérie and her fiancé, Archduke Francis-Salvator. The telegram ran as follows:

"*To His Majesty the Emperor, in Vienna:*

"Forgive my not appearing, as I am not feeling well; it is nothing serious, however. Love to my mother and to all.   "RUDOLPH."

(*Engedelmet kyrek, ha lem gyùvek. Keveset beteg vagyòk. Tisztelema foeherzepne*, etc.)

Whatever the conversation may have been between the two unfortunate young people on that dark and dismal afternoon in the little *salon* of Schloss-Mayerling can better be imagined than described. The awful disclosure which the young man made to her was truly of a nature to unbalance the steadiest brain, and Loschek, the valet, said later on that he had heard, when passing the door, on different occasions, the muffled sound of violent sobbing.

During the preceding few weeks Marie had been excessively melancholy, and had several times alluded, in the presence of her family and friends, to her wish to die young if she could not obtain her heart's most ardent desires, but what those were she did not say! Indeed, a gentleman who had known her from a child, and who was a constant visitor at the Vetsera mansion, remembered that on one occasion she had told him half-laughingly that, thanks to the strain of Oriental blood which flowed in her veins, she had no fear whatsoever of death, even if self-inflicted, and that she was always provided with the means of putting a swift and painless end to her existence, if ever it became too distasteful to her. The gentleman in question, taking this in the spirit of a spoiled child's *boutade* (whim), gave it but scant attention, until subsequent events forced him to recall to mind the conversation which he had had with her on the subject.

When Count Hoyòs and Prince von Coburg returned to the castle for dinner, they found that the Crown-prince had already retired, leaving a message to the effect that he felt too ill to appear at the evening meal, from which he begged to be excused. There was no sign of Bratfisch, nor, of course, of Marie Vetsera, and Loschek having been the only one to witness her arrival, the two noblemen were not informed that a lady had come to Mayerling on that day. They sat for a while over their wine and cigars, and then, thoroughly tired out by their day's sport, they went to bed, and absolute silence reigned over the entire building.

At five o'clock in the morning the huntsmen began to move about in the yard; the grooms opened the stable doors and started upon their day's work, casting an occasional glance upon the shuttered windows of the castle, for they knew well that, like his father, the Crown-prince was an early riser, and that, therefore, he would probably soon appear at one of the casements, as was his wont, to call out some orders to them.

Loschek also was up and preparing his imperial master's bath in the dressing-room adjoining the Crown-prince's sleeping-apartment. Several times he approached the door, expecting to hear himself called, but the silence remained untroubled, and as hour after hour slowly passed the man began to feel sorely worried. He had been sent by Rudolph on the previous evening on an errand to Baden, and did not know if, or when, the Baroness Vetsera had left Mayerling. Finally, anxious beyond endurance, he tried to turn the knob of the door, but much to his astonishment found that it was fastened on the inside, this being entirely against the Archduke's usual custom. For a few moments he stood motionless and then knocked twice rapidly on the oaken panel. Receiving no answer he fled down to the dining-room, where the Prince of Coburg and Count Hoyòs were waiting for their breakfast. Trembling in every limb, Loschek confusedly tried to explain to them that something must have happened to the Crown-prince, intermixing his incoherent statements with allusions to the visit of Marie Vetsera, which were, of course, absolutely unintelligible to his amazed hearers. Gathering, however, from what he said that something very much out of the ordinary had occurred, the Prince and the Count, followed by the terrified Loschek, ran upstairs three steps at a time, and in their turn began an assault upon the door, which, when they obtained no sign of life from within, ended in their bursting it open.

The scene which met their gaze was of a nature to strike the most self-contained person with horror. On the lounge near the window lay the body of Marie Vetsera, still dressed in her dark serge gown, but with all the violets of her two bouquets scattered about her. Her white face, outlined against the crimson silk of the cushion upon which her head was resting, seemed cut out

of marble. Half leaning against her shoulder, half
upon the floor, lay the Crown-prince, his hunting-
suit drenched with blood, and his lifeless hand
still grasping a heavy cavalry revolver. Crazed
with grief and amazement, the three men bent
over Rudolph to see whether life was really quite
extinct. One look at the shattered skull, however,
sufficed to show them that all hope had fled.
Prince von Coburg, stepping back with an exclamation of dismay, trod upon something which he
mechanically picked up. It was a small empty
bottle of brown crystal, which was labelled
"strychnia." Mechanically also he placed it on a
neighboring table, and with the help of his two
companions lifted the form of the Crown-prince
from the ground and laid it upon the bed. Then
they all hurried from the room, and closing the
door after them, walked down-stairs, feeling as
numb and unnerved as if they were just awakening from some dreadful nightmare.

When they had had sufficient time to recover
their senses to some extent, Prince Phillip ordered
the entire household to be brought before him,
and making them take, each separately, an oath
of absolute secrecy, he gave directions that the
entrance to the castle and to the castle grounds
should be denied to everybody without distinc-
tion of sex or rank.

Before starting for Vienna, where the Prince
was sending him to carry the terrible news to the
unfortunate parents of the dead man, Count
Hoyòs decided that it would be best to enter the
death-room once more in order to make certain
that the Crown-prince had not left behind him
some letter or writing of some kind which would
throw light upon the situation. This second

examination of the premises brought about the discovery of four letters lying upon the table which stood at the head of the bed, addressed respectively to the Emperor, the Empress, Divisional Superintendent Szoegyenyi, and the Duke of Braganza, a very dear friend of Rudolph's, beside which lay a crumpled piece of paper, whereon were written, in Marie Vetsera's hand, the following words:

"DEAR MOTHER,—I am going to die for Rudolph; we love each other too deeply to endure existence apart from each other, and a cruel fate which *nothing can alter* has made it *impossible* that we should ever belong to each other. He has had to give his father his word of honor that he would never see me again. There are circumstances which prevent our union, circumstances which I can discuss least of all with *you*. I am happier to die than to live. Forgive me.

"Your unhappy MARIE."

This note, written with a pencil and evidently in a great hurry, was blistered with tears. The letter addressed by Rudolph to the Duke of Braganza, unlike those addressed to the Emperor and Empress, was unsealed, and contained these few words:

"DEAR FRIEND,—*I must die. In honor I can do nothing else.* Good-bye. The blessing of God be with you.

RUDOLPH."

To Divisional Superintendent Szoegyenyi, the Crown-prince wrote:

"DEAR SZOEGYENYI,—You will find herein enclosed a codicil act in accordance with

my last will and testament made two years
ago. You will find in my study at the Hofburg most of my papers, and I leave it to
your discretion to decide which of them seem
fit for publication. These papers are locked
up in the drawer of the table which stands
near the sofa, and so I also enclose the little
golden key wherewith to open it. When you
receive these few lines I shall be no more.
I must die. Give my most affectionate
remembrance to all my friends. *May God
bless our beloved country.*   RUDOLPH."

The Count, putting all these various docu-
ments in his pocket-book, drove furiously to the
station at Baden, where he jumped into the first
train he could catch for Vienna, and before mid-
day he had reached the Hofburg, where his appearance in hunting-dress, and with a face perfectly
death-like in its awful pallor, struck with amazement all those who met him during his rapid progress to the door of the Empress's apartments.

General-Adjutant Count Paar, who was on
duty at that moment, undertook to lead the Count
immediately to the Empress.

She was sitting at her writing-table, which
was surmounted by a large portrait of the Crown-
prince in hunting-suit—just such a costume as
that in which he was clad when his stiffening
corpse had been found that very morning by the
man who now stood shaking from head to foot
and hardly able to control the violence of his
emotions before this poor mother, as yet ignorant
of the crushing blow which had befallen her.

The Empress, at this sudden and incomprehensible intrusion into her privacy, and after a

quick glance at the convulsed features of both gentlemen, started to her feet and, pressing her hand to her side, exclaimed, in a short, peremptory fashion not habitual to her:

"What is it? What has happened? Something is the matter with Rudi. Tell me at once!"

Her features had all at once become drawn and as colorless as the white morning-gown which she wore. Count Hoyòs, who would have given all he possessed to be miles away, was forced to relate as best he could the main points of the tragedy which he had come to reveal.

Standing upright before him, her blue eyes frightfully dilated by a fixed expression of indescribable horror, Elisabeth swayed for a second as if she were going to fall; then straightening herself again, without a tear, but with a kind of dry, gasping sob choking her utterance, she murmured:

"The Emperor—don't tell him; it must be I who break it to him. Wait for me here; do not say a word to any one; I will be back!" and swiftly, almost running, she left her room and rushed towards her husband's study, where she knew that he would then be at work upon the affairs of the State. As she opened the door and entered the spacious apartment where the Sovereign was employed in signing papers, handed to him one by one by his aides-de-camp, she said, shortly:

"Franz, I must speak to you alone."

With a wave of the hand the Emperor dismissed his aides, and the imperial couple were left alone together.

Half an hour later, Count Paar and Count Hoyòs, who were discussing in an awed whisper the dreadful drama of Mayerling, saw Franz-

Joseph enter the room, his eyes swollen with
weeping, and his whole countenance quivering
with distress. With him was the Empress, just as
pale, just as calm, and just as self-possessed as
she had been when she left them. She drew a
chair forward for the Emperor and gently
motioned him towards it, taking hold of his hand
and mutely caressing it, while he sat down upon
the proffered seat with a broken exclamation of:

"So it is true—really true!"

Again the stalwart man broke down, and
sobbed convulsively, the Empress bending over
him and soothing and consoling him as if he were
a child in pain.

Ah yes! he might well send his celebrated
message to the people of Vienna a few days later,
when thanking them for the sympathy which
they had shown to him in his troubles—a message which ran as follows:

"Tell my people that it is thanks to the
courage and devotion of that noble woman,
the Empress, that I have not given way to
absolute despair."

Meanwhile Crown-princess Stéphanie was sitting at her piano playing some new melodies
which had been sent to her that morning. She
wore a pink crepon peignoir, much adorned with
lace, and on her light hair a coquettish little
combination of ribbons and lace. So loud was her
playing that she did not hear the door open, and
was very much startled when, without any warning, her husband's father and mother stood
before her. She was not used to such visits, for
especially during the last few days she had
clearly noticed how distasteful her society seemed
to be to both the Emperor and Empress. Realizing

that something extraordinary had happened, and not being very easy in her own conscience, she turned to her father-in-law and said, breathlessly, as if she had just been running hard: "Is Rudolph really ill? Have you bad news?"

The Emperor replied, in a trembling voice: "Yes, we have bad news. Very bad news."

The Crown-princess recoiled a few steps, and with an awful scream, which rang throughout that entire wing of the palace, she fell headlong at the Empress's feet, her face touching the carpet, shrieking out in a wild, almost unearthly fashion: "He is dead, and it is I who have killed him!"

She became so violently hysterical that it was only with the greatest trouble that the Emperor and Empress could hold her down upon the sofa whereon they had laid her. At last her moans and sobs subsided, and she asked for explanations, declaring that she would start at once for Mayerling.

"It is impossible that you should go there," said the Empress, sternly. "You are not in a fit condition to undertake anything of the kind. I will send for your physicians, and you will go and lie down until you have somewhat recovered your strength." Then turning to her husband, Elisabeth said, softly:

"Leave her with me, Franz; you have gone through too much already. All this additional agitation is very bad for you."

"And you—what about you?" he answered, clasping her hands in a passionate grasp.

"It will be time for me to give way later," she replied, drawing him towards the door and out of the room. "I have other things to think of just now."

Indeed, when she did "find time to think of herself" she fell into a fainting fit, which resembled death so closely that two hours elapsed before the physicians in attendance upon her were able to pronounce as to whether she would ever recover consciousness or not.

The impression caused at Vienna and throughout the entire Austro-Hungarian Empire by the astounding news of the Crown-prince's death is quite indescribable. The streets were filled to overflowing with crowds of sobbing people, and the newspaper offices were on the point of being taken by storm by the populace when it was found that no details about the heir apparent's death were to be published. Thanks to the sagacious intervention of Duchess Ludovica in Bavaria, Empress Elisabeth's mother, the Emperor was brought to understand that it was absolute folly to try to conceal any longer from the public the fact that Rudolph had committed suicide. Duchess Ludovica was, as I have had occasion to say ere this, a very remarkable woman, and the Emperor, who is no mean judge of character, had the highest opinion of his mother-in-law's acumen, and was only too glad to lean upon her and to take her advice in this as in many other matters at that critical period of his existence.

Special editions of the official newspaper appeared therefore heavily bordered with black, and stating that in a moment of temporary aberration Crown-prince Archduke Rudolph of Austro-Hungary had taken his own life. There was also a manifesto, which was signed by the Emperor, printed beneath this announcement, and couched in the following words:

"To my People:

"Deeply moved by a sorrow too profound for words, I humbly bow before the inscrutable decrees of a Providence which has chosen to afflict myself and my people, and I pray Almighty God to grant to us all the courage to bear the load of our irreparable loss," etc.

A special train was sent on the 30th of January to Baden, conveying the doctors and surgeons who were intrusted with the autopsy of the Crown-prince. Among these were Doctors Widerhofer, Hoffman, and Kundrat. The protocol of this autopsy states that Crown-prince Rudolph's death "was caused by a fracture of the frontal bone produced by the bullet of a large-calibre revolver, discharged at short range, the projectile penetrating the brain and passing out of the skull at the base of the cerebrum."

While this was taking place, and while so many were thinking, to the exclusion of everything else, about the dead Prince, what had become of the young girl whose self-inflicted death had determined him to kill himself while she was still near to him? By the care of Count Bombelles, the Crown-prince's tutor and best friend, who had been sent immediately by the Emperor to take charge of everything at Mayerling, the fair body of Marie Vetsera was concealed in a room which Count Bombelles himself locked with his own hands.

On the night of the 31st of January a small postern-door in the northern wing of the castle was stealthily opened, and another black, unadorned coffin was carried by four trustworthy attendants into the depths of the woods, where another *fourgon* awaited it. It was conveyed as

secretly as possible to the chapel of Heiligenkreutz, and from there, twenty-four hours later,
to a distant railway station, where it was
embarked for Trieste, and taken thence to Venice.
It was only then that "Baronin" Vetsera, the
mother of Marie, and the Baltazzi family
announced publicly the death of the young girl,
and had her remains formally brought from
Venice to Pardubitz, where the family vault is
situated.

Of course it goes without saying that the
secret was not absolutely preserved, and that
soon a loud rumor arose to the effect that Marie
Vetsera had not died in Venice, but at Mayerling,
and that she had been shot by the Crown-prince.
This has been more than disproved by the autopsy performed upon Marie, which revealed the
fact that she had died from strychnine poisoning,
and that her death had preceded that of the
Crown-prince by more than two hours.

Could anything have been more dreadful
than the despair of the unfortunate young man
when, after having disclosed to his beloved the
true reason which made it *impossible* for him to
fulfil his promise of marrying her as soon as he
had succeeded in obtaining the dissolution of his
union, he found that she had swallowed the
deadly drug which she had brought with her?
When, a few minutes later, she breathed her last
in his arms, no wonder indeed that, seeing his
honor jeopardized, his hopes dashed to the earth,
and his entire existence ruined, he should have
decided to end his own career without any further
delay!

The crumpled letter which Marie had written
to her mother was not the only one of the sort

found, for when her dress was removed another sheet of paper, evidently torn out of a book, was discovered secreted in the corsage. It was intended for her sister, and I give here a copy of it:

"He has told me *all. I cannot tell you what he did tell me.* I can never be his now. I am alone for a moment, while he has gone down to send away Bratfisch. I knew that something dreadful would happen to prevent our being happy, so I brought the poison with me, and I am going to drink it. When he returns it will be too late to save me, and I will die in his arms, happy to be with him till the last. Forgive me and love me, pray for me, and take care of our poor mother. She will feel this *more than you can think or know.*"

The Vetsera family left on February 3d for Italy, while the court, immediately after the Crown-prince's funeral, abandoned Vienna for Budapesth.

Before leaving his Austrian capital the Emperor took all necessary steps to insure the absence from Austria of all those who had been directly concerned with this fearful affair. Countess Larisch, in high disgrace, went to travel abroad; Count Hoyòs and the Prince of Coburg both left the country; and as to Bratfisch and Loschek, who had been provided with the means to live in idleness for the rest of their days if so they chose, they disappeared completely from view.

It was a long time before the Emperor could forgive or forget the unguarded words pronounced by Prince Phillip of Coburg, who when speaking to several eager auditors said:

"Do not ask me how this awful catastrophe happened. We are forced to draw a veil over such doings. It is sad enough that it should have happened! For Heaven's sake, do not ask why it did."

CHAPTER XII

The first anniversary of the Crown-prince's death was celebrated with much solemnity throughout Austria and Hungary by the people. But the clergy in quite a number of places created a painful impression by refusing to perform the *Seelen-Messe,* or *Bout de l'An* mass,* in consequence of the circumstances connected with the Prince's death. The most glaring instance of this utter absence of charity was at Botzen, in the Tyrol, where the widowed Crown-princess was staying. Having sent to request the dean of the cathedral to celebrate the customary mass for the repose of her husband's soul, he curtly declined either to perform it himself or to permit it to take place in the cathedral. The ceremony, therefore, was performed in the parish church of Gries, a little village in the neighborhood of Botzen.

Much disagreeable comment was caused by the failure of Stéphanie to return to Vienna upon the sad anniversary, in order that she might accompany the Emperor, the Empress, and Archduchess Valérie to Mayerling for the purpose of being present with them at the ceremony of the consecration of the chapel erected on the spot where her husband met his death. It was positively expected that she would have made a point of

(lit., "Soul-Mass," or "End of the Year" mass celebrated one year after death)

spending the day with her little daughter, and
that she would have followed their majesties'
example in passing a few moments in prayer at
the Archduke's tomb in the vaults of the Capuchin church at Vienna. But she very unwisely
absented herself, an act which gave great pain to
all those who so dearly loved the dead Prince.

The visit of the Emperor and Empress with
Archduchess Valérie to Mayerling on the 30th of
January, just a year after the frightful death of
poor Rudi, was marked by several exceedingly
pathetic incidents. The scene at the railway ter-
minus, when starting on their pilgrimage to the
fatal spot, was pitiful in the extreme. The Emperor
had offered his right arm to his consort, and with
his left hand he was gently stroking the small
black-gloved hand that rested upon his sleeve, as
he bent slightly towards her, murmuring words of
consolation. Archduchess Valérie followed close
behind. The two ladies were attired in the deepest
mourning, and were weeping bitterly. On reaching the chapel which had been erected on the
scene of the tragedy, a mass was performed by
the abbot, Baron von Grimmenstein, assisted by
Court Chaplain Monsignor Meyer, the priest
kneeling at an altar of exquisitely carved Istrian
marble, placed on the very spot where the bed
had stood on which the Archduke was laid out by
Prince von Coburg and Count Hoyòs, after the
discovery of the suicide by these two gentlemen.
The chapel is built in antique Gothic style, and is
entered by a portal supported by four pillars of
Swedish granite. Statues of St. Joseph and St.
Theresa guard the portico, above which there is a
magnificently painted window.

The only persons present besides the imperial

mourners and their immediate attendants were the Carmelite nuns, who have taken possession of the former shooting-lodge. Their Superior, to whom the Emperor addressed a few gracious words at the conclusion of the service, is a French noblewoman, the young Princess Jeanne Bibesco, whose mother was a Princess d'Elchingen, and a member of the family of the famous Marshal Ney.

It goes, of course, without saying that Stéphanie has never forgotten and never will forget the decision taken by her husband several years before his death, to the effect that his only child, Archduchess Elisabeth, should be intrusted absolutely, without any restriction whatsoever, to the *sole and complete* guardianship of Emperor Franz-Joseph and Empress Elisabeth of Austria, and that moreover she should not be allowed to pass the frontiers of Austro-Hungary before she had attained her majority. This token of Rudolph's *post-mortem* dislike and lack of confidence was hard enough to bear without there having been added to it the wide-spread public rumors which it aroused.

Archduchess Elisabeth was, when a child, one of the most interesting little ladies possible. She has inherited all her father's sweetness of temper, and bids fair, when she is quite grown up, to resemble her beautiful grandmother, Empress Elisabeth. Her grandfather dotes on her, and seems to have transferred to her all the love he bore his only son. The idol of the Viennese people, who call her *die kleine frau* (the little woman), she never drives out without receiving a perfect ovation, and many eyes fill with tears of pity when gazing on the tiny princess, so early and so tragically deprived of a father's love.

A few years ago an incident occurred which is so characteristic of the little Archduchess that it is worthy of being placed on record. There is a well-known young ladies' school at Dresden, where a great many Viennese girls are sent, when they reach the age of ten, to finish their education under the care of the celebrated Madame F——, the owner of the school in question, and an Austrian by birth. Until the autumn of the time to which I refer, the little girls were in the habit of receiving from home, once a month, small boxes containing some of the delicious confectionery for which Vienna is renowned. Unfortunately, several cases of sickness among the pupils having been caused, according to the house physician, by too many bonbons, Madame F—— gathered the young people around her one morning and declared to them, solemnly, that she absolutely forbade any more indulgences of this nature, and that she would moreover address a circular to the children's parents requesting them not to send sweetmeats or any other toothsome dainties to them during their stay at her school.

The edict caused terrible consternation among the little *gourmandes* (gluttons; those excessively fond of eating and drinking). There came very near being an open revolt against so arbitrary a measure, and matters were looking very black indeed when, suddenly, a dark-eyed, fair-haired little beauty of eleven summers climbed on a table, and silencing her noisy troop of comrades, harangued them as follows:

"Children," she exclaimed, in vibrating accents, "we must be revenged! We cannot allow such injustice; we will not submit to an undeserved punishment which robs us of our only pleasure. Madame is an Austrian, and as such, she must submit to anything done by our imperial family. Do you know what? We will send a round-robin to our little Archduchess, imploring her to forbid madame to treat us so cruelly."

"What little Archduchess? Who is she? Where does she live?" cried such of her excited listeners as were not Austrians.

With a smile of pity for so much ignorance, the speaker explained to her now delighted audience that Archduchess Elisabeth, the Emperor's granddaughter, was powerful at the court of Vienna, and that should she consider their prayer favorably, the whole imperial family would come forward, if necessary, to crush madame's decree against the importation of sweets.

The truth of this statement was so patent that without further delay the little girls set to work in great glee to draw up their petition—a document which cost them much pain to compose, and which ran thus:

"DEAR ARCHDUCHESS ELISABETH,—We love you and your grandpapa very much, and we are here in Dresden at school, where we are generally pretty well satisfied. To-day, however, something awful has happened. Madame has forbidden our dear parents to send us any more bonbons for ever so many years; no more sugar-plums, no more chocolates, no more cakes, nor anything sweet and good. So we want to ask you to help us out of our trouble, dear Archduchess! *Please, please* tell your dear grandpapa to send word to madame that she is to let us have bonbons again as before. With this ardent prayer we close our letter.

Our best love to your dear grandpapa and
grandmamma. We all kiss your little hands,
and remain your true and respectful little
compatriots."

When the long list of names had been signed
to this remarkable epistle, it was carefully put in
an envelope and addressed to *"Die Kleine Frau
Ezherzogin Elisabeth, p. Ad. Ihrem Grossvater,
den Kaiser von Oësterreich, Wien."* (The little
madame, Archduchess Elisabeth, care of her
grandpapa, the Emperor of Austria, Vienna.) And
with many misgivings and heart-beatings it was
duly mailed.

A week later, Madame F—— was much surprised to receive a huge box addressed to "The
pupils of the F—— Institute, Dresden." It came
from Vienna, and was stamped on the lid with the
imperial coat-of-arms. She immediately summoned all the children, and as soon as they caught
sight of the gigantic package, the little Austrian
conspirators huddled together, whispering to one
another, with glowing faces and glistening eyes.

On the top of the box lay a pink and silver
card, on which was written, in a round, childish
hand: "From Archduchess Elisabeth, to her dear
little compatriots in Dresden."

Under the card was a letter sealed with the
imperial crest, which Madame F—— opened and
read with boundless amazement. It was written
by Countess Coudenhove, the lady-in-waiting to
the little Archduchess, who said that as a rule no
notice was taken of such petitions as had been
sent by Madame F——'s little Austrian pupils,
but that in this instance the little Archduchess
had begged so hard to be permitted to grant it
that their Majesties had allowed her to choose

and send the contents of the box to her dear little compatriots, with the wish that they might be allowed to enjoy them to their hearts' content.

With shouts of joy the children, now almost beside themselves with delight, crowded round the box to examine its sweet and fragrant contents. Nothing can give an idea of their enthusiasm when, one after another, boxes of exquisite bonbons of all descriptions were brought to light—boxes made of daintily tinted silks with the imperial arms and crown stamped in gold on each of them; bags of silver tissue tied with azure ribbons and filled with chocolate pralines, each of which was wrapped in multicolored tissue-paper, with devices and mottoes; marvellous bars of Viennese nougatine enclosed in satin wrappers, on which the pictures of the Emperor and Empress were painted in water-colors; tiny crystal bonbonnières containing sugared petals of roses and violets and orange blossoms, certainly prepared by fairies for the special delectation of good little Austrian subjects of his royal and imperial majesty, the Emperor Franz-Joseph! The shouts almost deafened poor Madame F——, who, not so very black at heart after all, could only end by forgiving her pupils, to whom she suggested that in return for the kindness and favor just received, they would do well to embroider a handsome bedquilt for their little benefactress. This piece of work was duly brought to completion, and it was superb, all the little ladies having labored at it with a will, while they nibbled now and again some of the Archduchess's exquisite bonbons, loyal little Austrian monarchists forever! The quilt was presented to her imperial highness upon her birthday, and gave her much pleasure.

CHAPTER XIII

IN MEMORIAM

"Of all the crimes of anarchy—
  a catalogue accurst—
This latest act of infamy
  must be adjudged the worst;
Never has base assassin
  struck a fouler, blacker blow
Than that with which this callous fiend
  has laid the Empress low.

"The world stands startled and aghast;
  the brain of Europe reels;
Her tongue can scarcely speak as yet
  the sympathy she feels;
But where is there a heart to-day
  not thrilled by pity deep
For her who died, and for the man
  who lives her loss to weep?"

In December, 1897, Elisabeth's health seemed to begin to fail completely. She was at the time staying in Biarritz, and suffered from neuritis to such an extent that the gravest doubts were entertained as to the possibility of her enduring, even courageous as she was, for any great length of time, the bodily torture which she was undergoing. Finally she made up her mind to go to Paris in order to place herself in the hands of Dr. Metzger, who is a specialist of world-wide renown in all nervous troubles. Dr. Metzger is an original, and refuses squarely to call upon any patients whatever their rank or wealth may be, the consequence of this rule, which is as adamantine as the laws of the Medes and Persians, being that his reception-rooms are every day crowded with an extraordinary number of aristocratic patients, who in order to benefit by his treatment, which is chiefly one of massage, submit to long hours of wretchedness while waiting for him.

With her dislike for appearing in public, the Empress would not consent to go to the doctor's at his usual consultation hours, and made a point of arriving at his house early in the morning, and before the rooms in which the massage was performed had had sufficient time to become thoroughly heated. This resulted in the treatment doing her more harm than good, and, thoroughly discouraged, she abandoned it, and started for San Remo, where she consulted the celebrated Dr. Nothnagel. He was perfectly astounded at the courage which the Empress displayed, for as he described it himself, the pain which she suffered throughout the whole network of her nervous system must have resembled that which is caused by the exposed nerve of a tooth when it is touched by some sharp instrument.

She hardly ever slept, and ate scarcely anything, but in spite of all this, her admirable, almost supernatural, fortitude never left her, and her patience and continual kindness to her *entourage* were something simply wonderful. She busied herself as usual with her books, her music, and her drawings, took long walks along the sunny, palm-bordered roads which surround San Remo on three sides, and her love for flowers seemed to increase, for she maintained that they were now her dearest companions. Her rooms were simply filled with blossoming plants, palms, and ferns, for all of which she had a great predilection. When during her wanderings about the country she happened upon some peculiarly choice blossom, she used to bring it home with her, place it herself in a vase, and carry it at night into her bedroom, where she placed it beside her couch, so that she might during her long insomnia gaze at its beauty and refresh her tired eyes by admiring the loveliness of petals and foliage.

During a short stay which she made at Villefranche, on the Riviera, she happened to notice growing in the garden of the mayor of that little city some truly magnificent carnations, the official in question being a passionate collector of these fragrant flowers, who spared neither trouble nor expense to secure the finest specimens which it was possible for him to get for love or money. Indeed he looked upon this collection with the tender jealousy of a fond mother towards her offspring, and woe to the sacrilegious hand ever extended to touch one of the enormous satiny blossoms.

The Empress gazed longingly at the luxuriant rows of multicolored carnations, and finally, quite unable to conquer her desire to gather a few of them, she rang the gate bell, and in her simple, winning way begged very sweetly for one or two of the coveted flowers. The gardener, trembling in his boots lest his master should arrive at this inopportune moment, nevertheless was not proof against the request which the imperial lady so charmingly proffered, and, wonder of wonders!

allowed her to pluck two carnations—a gigantic creamy one all flecked with soft pink and a monstrous crimson one—which she preciously and victoriously bore away, her eyes gleaming with pleasure.

On her way home she was met on the road by the mayor himself, who recognized both his property and the Empress, and who hurried into his beloved garden and called his guilty gardener to account in the following manner:

"So you give away my flowers, and some of the finest of them, too, you miscreant!" he exclaimed, with assumed wrath.

"Oh, monsieur!" quoth the old man, "the lady who asked for them was not one to whom one could refuse anything; monsieur would have given them to her himself had he been here."

"Of course I would, you dunderhead!" replied *monsieur le maire,* bursting out laughing. "Why, it was the Empress of Austria herself who was here a minute ago, and she can have all the carnations she wants, for there are not many such angels promenading here below. Come, now, with me and we will gather a bouquet for her such as not even all her imperial greenhouses can furnish her!"

Suiting the action to the words, the worthy mayor descended upon his *parterres* (flower-beds) and sacked them with such an unsparing hand that he had soon a sheaf of long-stemmed carnations which were truly worthy an Empress's acceptance! The gardener, following him dutifully, almost dropped dead in the extremity of his astonishment at the spectacle of so unprecedented a raid upon the priceless collections, and he had by no means recovered from his stupefaction

when he was despatched post-haste to carry this
exquisite gift to the Empress. The latter was just
on the point of leaving Villefranche when the old
fellow, quite breathless with hurry and excitement, presented himself before her. Deeply
touched by the mayor's sacrifice, for she fully
realized what it must have cost him to thus ruth-
lessly *saccager* (completely ruin) his beloved
flower-beds, the Empress hastily drew from her
pocket-case a visiting-card, upon which was simply engraved "Elisabeth," beneath an imperial
crown, and wrote on the back of it, *"Merci de tout
mon coeur pour votre délicieuse et charmante
attention, qui m'a rendue très heureuse."*
("Thank you with all my heart for your 'delicious'
and charming attention, which made me very
happy.")

I dare say that the Mayor of Villefranche now
looks upon this little card as one of his most
precious possessions and preserves it as he would
a relic.

The first steps taken by Dr. Nothnagel were to
urge Elisabeth to adopt a more strengthening
diet, for the Empress, who was a remarkably
small eater, was, as a rule, satisfied with eating
fruit and drinking milk, of which she was very
fond.

To be sure, when in her own palaces she gave
much attention to the *menus* which were presented to her every morning by the chief of her
kitchens, and which she altered according to her
own ideas in the matter. No table in the whole
world was served more daintily or artistically
than that of the Austrian court. Elisabeth used to
say that when one was forced to sit down at
meals perfect ease, vast space, and soft, shadowy

distances were absolutely necessary to preserve some sort of illusion. Her exquisitely refined taste prevented her from appreciating even the most delicate of food when not served in a thoroughly *recherché* (elaborate) manner, and all that priceless porcelain, unique crystal, and mousseline glasses, as well as antique gold and silver plate, could do to etherealize a repast was done at Vienna, Budapesth, Gödöllö, Ischl, Lainz, Achilleon, or wherever else the fair sovereign of Austro-Hungary graced her imperial abodes with her presence.

The damask was so fine that it looked like satin, and for lunch or afternoon tea was replaced by daintily hued cloths and napkins of silk-cambric, edged with lace and adorned with the imperial crests in raised gold embroidery, a transparency of heavy silk of the same tint as the batiste shimmering through this delicate material. So prettily were the viands prepared and dished up that it seemed almost a pity to break up and eat them. The fairies themselves might have feasted upon the tempting *pièces-montées* (decorative cone-shaped "mountain" of cream puffs and fruit preserves; lit., "mounted pieces") prepared by the great artist who for so many years presided over the imperial kitchens. Mr. Kienberger—for such was the name of this official—held his office for over forty years, and his ambition consisted in making each *déjeuner* or dinner which he supervised the most successful thing of the kind in the world. Like a general on the eve of battle, he never left the kitchens and still-rooms of the palace during the last twenty-four hours before any great entertainment took place. He personally superintended every detail, and, as he was a culinary genius himself, often concocted some particularly toothsome delicacy which he alone could make. He also was a great advocate of serving things artistically, and he told me one day very gravely, nay, almost solemnly, that he thought a pigeon served on a gold dish a far more appetizing and pleasing viand than an ortolan sent in on a common china plate.

The imperial kitchens were kept with almost military precision. Every imaginable dainty was prepared at the Palace, and the Empress herself came down every Monday morning to stroll through the kitchens in order to see that everything was going on as it should.

When the Empress was absent, however, matters were not always quite so satisfactory; for the Emperor, who is a most abstemious man, does not, as a rule, care much about what is placed before him, is contented with the plainest kind of food, and rarely makes any remarks on the subject. Once, however, when the luncheon-tray was brought in, he said to his aide-de-camp, who had been working with him in his study during the whole morning:

"You lucky fellow! you'll be able to get something good to eat at a restaurant later on, but I, when her Majesty is away, am condemned to such unpalatable fare as you observe there," and he pointed with a melancholy shake of his head to the rather unappetizing lukewarm viands which lay upon the tray.

The Emperor is a pious Catholic, who keeps as strictly to his fasts as he does to his early rising. At such times he objures all meat, and contents himself with fish—a dish that is rather of a rarity in Vienna—and various kinds of omelets. His Majesty takes his fish preferably with buttered potatoes.

The Hofburg *cuisine* was, when deprived of Elisabeth's supervision, peculiarly Viennese; it was only when she was there that the French *menu* had any chance! Viennese cooking is closely allied to the German in the simplicity and want of variety of its dishes, and in the "done-to-death" character of the meats, but yet it is decidedly more tasty and inventive, *Kaiser-schmarn* and the dumpling-like *knödel* having a world-wide reputation.

In the summer the Emperor's so-called second breakfast is omitted, and he contents himself with a five-o'clock breakfast, consisting of a cup of coffee and a little *kalte-auflage* (sliced cold sausage, ham, etc.). His Majesty sticks to his desk for the next seven hours with scarcely an interruption. At noon comes the lunch, or *gabel-frühstück*, consisting of a soup and a slice of roast. At half-past four is a dinner of six courses, comprising soup, fish, two roasts, pudding, and desserts, washed down with Pilsener beer and claret. Liqueurs are also served, but Franz-Joseph never touches them. When he has risen from the table, the Kaiser has finished his eating for the day and touches nothing more, even when in the evening he is forced to stay up late. Ordinarily he is in bed by nine o'clock, and to his regular, moderate life he owes undoubtedly his longevity and his splendid health. This is how the Emperor lives winter and summer, but the arrangements necessarily undergo great alterations on every occasion when a state function takes place.

EMPEROR FRANZ-JOSEPH IN 1898

Then the splendor and lavishness of the imperial table know no limits. All the royal fruit and vegetables are grown in the country, except when the time of the year absolutely compels their purchase abroad. The wines are mostly Austrian or Hungarian, but also include Burgundies, Moselles, and Rhine wines, as well as Champagne. The Emperor's Tokay wine, grown in his own vineyards—which with those belonging to Prince Windishgrätz are the only two spots on this earth where real genuine Tokay grows—enjoys a world-wide reputation. One tiny glass of it perfumes a whole room with its unequalled "bouquet," and it is considered so precious that all the world was agog when Franz-Joseph sent as a jubilee present to Queen Victoria a case of this priceless sunshiny liquid. At the court of Vienna it is only served on the grandest possible occasions, and is otherwise reserved for cases of sickness.

I particularly remember a dinner given in honor of the King and Queen of Italy, at the Hofburg, some years ago, as the culminating point of luxury combined with the most refined and exquisite taste. The tablecloth was strewn with forced violets, nestling so closely together that they formed a perfect bank of fragrant blossoms, leaving only room for the plates of semi-transparent Sèvres, of the famille-rose, each of which was surrounded with a thick garland of marguerites. Marguerite is the Christian name of the Queen of Italy, and her little namesakes had been used with great profusion in the decoration of the festive board. Before the plate of each woman present a slender, tulip-shaped vase of Venetian glass, mounted in finely wrought gold,

contained a bouquet of marguerites and violets
powdered with gold-dust. The *menus* were
engraved on thin sheets of hammered gold, with
the Austrian eagle embossed on the corner.
Everything was served on gold dishes, and the
dessert-plates were a marvel of beauty worthy of
Benvenuto-Cellini. When the sorbets were placed
before the distinguished guests a faint murmur of
admiration was audible, for even the *blasé* eyes
of people satiated with every form of luxury were
charmed with the little double-headed eagles
made of delicately spun sugar perched on a pale
mauve glass ball containing a tiny electric light.
On the back of each diminutive bird was a large
daisy, also made of spun sugar, wherein the
sorbets were served. The gold plates on which the
whole rested were garlanded with Parma violets.
The dinner was really what one may describe
without exaggeration as being the apotheosis of
gastronomy. The dining-hall—scented as with
dreamy incenses and lighted with mellow wax
candles, the soft brilliancy of which would have
entranced even Lucullus, had he been throned
there on his ivory chair—was a sight to be remembered.

Even during such banquets the Empress
would often partake of nothing but a few slices of
wheat-bread, a cup of bouillon, and some fruit.
She only drank wine when the doctors absolutely
insisted upon her doing so, for she had a horror
for all spirituous liquors, and her favorite tipple,
as she used laughingly to term it, was the juice of
many oranges poured on some cracked ice and
served in her own particular goblet, which was of
the thinnest possible crystal, and iridescent like a
soap-bubble.

One can therefore imagine how much she was annoyed when Dr. Nothnagel prescribed for her rare steaks and chops, as well as concentrated essence of meat. Nevertheless, she submitted to these medical orders, and was much benefited by them, so much so indeed that from the moment when she thus changed her diet she began to mend rapidly, and when, in the spring of 1898, she arrived at Bath Nauheim she had completely recovered her strength. Her sojourn in Nauheim was, however, rendered very disagreeable to her by the extraordinarily rude behavior of the other visitors there. There were a great many Germans, a nationality which Elisabeth could scarcely endure. A striking proof of this is that she implored the instructors and tutors of her children to "make them as little German as possible."

Every time the sovereign went out of her hotel she found herself confronted by crowds who were lying in wait for her, and who positively went so far as wellnigh to prevent her progress. To such lengths did these ill-bred people go in order to satisfy their curiosity, that the gentlemen of the Empress's suite had to interfere bodily lest the Empress should be absolutely smothered! The Empress, who disliked beyond all things to be stared at, felt perfectly wretched in Nauheim, and consequently began to discuss with her *entourage* the possibility of going to a place where she could spend a few weeks unobserved and in peace. This finally led to her selecting Switzerland once more, although she had no sympathy for the Swiss nation, and knew well that Switzerland is a very hotbed of anarchism, a land where every being inoculated with nihilism or any other kind of revolutionary tendencies seeks refuge.

Never afraid about herself, she told those who pointed this out again to her, as they had done each time she went to Switzerland before, that there was no reason for alarm, as she would travel incognito under the name of Countess von Hohenembs, and added:

"It is the Emperor that I always think of, with regard to the crimes daily committed by anarchists, and for him alone that I fear them. I myself am too unimportant a personage to attract their malevolence; for it is so well known that I have never meddled in politics, or in any of the affairs of the State, and that I will never do so, that I hardly count in anybody's eyes as a sovereign at all!"

Shortly after this conversation took place the Empress established herself at Mount de Caux, and it must be acknowledged she enjoyed such quiet as she had been seeking. Indeed, she wrote several times to the Emperor telling him how much he himself would be benefited by the absolute peace which she had found there, and asking him to join her as speedily as possible. There was something singular in this earnest endeavor on the part of Elisabeth to decide her husband to hasten his departure from Vienna. One might almost think that it was a sort of presentiment which overmastered her usual reluctance to express any personal wish; for, moreover, she knew that there was at that time a serious ministerial crisis at Vienna, and that therefore it would be very difficult for Franz-Joseph to leave his capital.

Singularly unfortunate is it that he was unable to do so, and he must now feel very bitterly the weight of this refusal of his to spend with his consort the last days which she had to live on this earth.

Elisabeth took a special delight in walking in the fragrant pine-woods, which reminded her, with their needle-carpeted moss, of her dear forests in Upper Austria. She came back from these long strolls with her hands full of mountain flowers, and sent some in the letters which she wrote daily to those whom she loved.

How the idea came into her head to make the unfortunate excursion to Geneva, which ended so tragically for her, is only to be explained by yet one more of those kind and considerate actions by which her entire life was marked.

Baroness Adolph Rothschild, whose beautiful villa of Pregny is one of the most exquisite spots on the banks of the lake of Geneva, had once been very kind to the Empress's favorite sister, the ex-Queen of Naples, and that at the time when this unfortunate sovereign, whom the French writer, Alphonse Daudet, chose as the heroine of his celebrated book, *Les Rois en Exil* (Kings in Exile), had just lost her crown and was leading a miserable existence in Paris. Elisabeth never forgot this, and when she found herself so close to Pregny she decided to go and call upon Baroness Rothschild, promising herself a great deal of pleasure, not only in paying this little debt of gratitude, but also in visiting the magnificent collection of orchids which is one of the most charming fads of the Baroness. General-Adjutant Baron von Berzeviczy, who was in attendance upon the Empress at the time, entreated her not to go to Geneva, or at least, if she did persist in undertaking the trip, not to stay there over night.

"What an old martinet you are becoming, my
dear Berzeviczy," laughed the Empress. "Really,
if I am not careful you will end by making me
come 'to orders' every morning, and by treating
me with quite military tyranny! Nevertheless, I
am going to risk being put under arrest by you for
disobedience, as I am going to Geneva in spite of
all that you may say to the contrary; and what is
more, in order to punish you, you shall remain
here with the remainder of my suite to grumble
to your heart's content, while I and Countess
Sztaray, together with my secretary, Dr. Kromar,
will make our little *fugue!* I am starting in an
hour, and will be back to-morrow evening."

The fears entertained by the Empress's *entourage* were nothing extraordinary, for there were
few who did not recall to mind the gross outrage
to which she was subjected on the Italian shore of
the Lago di Garda a few years before. She was
making a tour of this lake on board a steam-
launch. Having landed with the ladies and gentlemen of her suite at a small Italian town on the
southern extremity of the lake, she was greeted
by the inhabitants with hisses and hideous
howls. So menacing indeed did the attitude of the
mob become, and so vile and outrageous were the
insulting epithets addressed to the imperial lady,
that she was forced to beat a hasty retreat with
her party to the boat. As the latter steamed away
from the landing, volleys of stones were hurled
after it by the people on the shore. The two or
three revenue officers who were the only repre-
sentatives of the Italian government present at
the time maintained throughout the entire scene
a perfectly passive attitude, not making the
slightest attempt to protect the Kaiserin from the

jeers and insults of the populace.

This attack was all the more shameful as the Empress was wearing deep mourning for Rudi, and was in so delicate a state of health that, thoroughly upset by the unfortunate incident, she was confined to her apartments for two weeks from the effect it had had upon her nerves.

Once before also the Empress had run the risk of being assassinated by an Italian. It was at the opening of the exhibition at Trieste, in the early eighties, when an Italian Irredentist threw a bomb into the citadel, by which several persons were wounded. The Emperor and Empress, with the Crown-prince, were to visit the exhibition a fortnight later, and as further outrages were apprehended the Emperor and the Crown-prince tried to dissuade the Empress from going. The Crown-prince related at the time that the Empress would not listen to this suggestion, saying:

"If you fear an outrage, that is a good reason why I should accompany you, for in such an event my place is by your side." Her Majesty, accordingly, went with her husband and son to Trieste, where, as was proved later by Oberdank's revelations, an Italian miscreant was actually watching for an opportunity to murder the imperial couple. That man was afterwards hanged at Udine, and Oberdank and his companions at Trieste.

Elisabeth's love for incognito voyages brought about a great many queer incidents, some of them dangerous, others extremely amusing. For instance, she had quite a little adventure while at Seville. One day during her stay there she started out unattended, save by a

lady-in-waiting, to call on the widowed Duchess
of Montpensier, who was confined to her bed by
rheumatic fever. On reaching the palace of Castil-
leja the porter absolutely refused to admit the two
ladies, and, on their persisting in their attempt to
enter, called upon the police in the street to remove
the trespassers, informing the guardians of the
peace that he was convinced that the women were
filled with the most sinister intentions.

Fortunately, one of the old servants of the
Duchess was attracted to the scene by the noise,
and, being a Frenchman, was able to understand
the purpose of their visit and their identity, which
the porter and the police, by reason of their
ignorance of any language but their own—which,
strange to relate, the Empress did not speak—had
been unable to do. This, of course, put an entirely
different aspect on the affair, the porter and the
police withdrawing with most profound apologies,
cursing, no doubt, their stupidity, while the old
French groom-of-the-chambers conducted the
Empress to the Duchess, with whom her Majesty
spent over half an hour in friendly conversation.

Owing to the Empress's reluctance to appear
in public, especially during the latter portion of
her life, her features were not generally known to
the Austrian public. Indeed, she was the least
easily recognized of any member of the imperial
family. This led to many absurd *contretemps*
(mishaps), all the more so as she was fond of
going about on foot, unattended save by her
Greek professor and a servant not in livery.

One day, when taking the train at Mödling,
whither she had gone on foot, she sent her
servant to order the station-master to have the
train stopped at the Hotsendorf station, near her

palace at Lainz. Seeing that the train was about to start while the man was still talking to the station-master, she called to the conductor: "Tell that man in a black coat to hurry up!" Whereupon the officer merely turned around and bawled out: "Here, hurry up you, or else your good woman will start without you!" evidently taking the Empress for the simply horrified servant's wife. This is but one of many similar adventures which happened to the Empress.

Dr. Kromar preceded the Empress to Geneva in order to have all proper preparations made for her reception at the Hotel Beaurivage, but in accordance with her wishes he concealed the identity of the august visitor who was to be expected. As, however, her Majesty had occupied, some few months previously, the very self-same suite of rooms which he now bespoke for her, the proprietor of the hotel was, in spite of all this secrecy, well aware whom he would have the honor of harboring under his roof. The apartment selected was composed of five rooms, one of which was a *salon;* another, the Empress's sleeping-room, opened into a parlor, which was hastily transformed into a bath-room, for Elisabeth was a great believer in hydrotherapy; and the two remaining ones were to be occupied by Countess Sztaray. The valet and maids were to be quartered on the floor above. As soon as the necessary arrangements had been made, Dr. Kromar left for Territet, whither he had received permission to go and receive some personal friends of his who were to arrive from Austria upon that very day.

The incognito which the Empress was so anxious to preserve was by no means kept, for the *hôtelier* (innkeeper), very proud of seeing his hotel selected by the sovereign, said to somebody who was remarking to him that it was rather a pity to nail down oilcloth upon the brand-new carpet of the parlor, which was being quickly transformed into a spacious and commodious bath-room:

"Oh, I don't mind it at all; it's no matter about the carpet, for, let me tell you, quite between ourselves, these rooms are for the Empress of Austria, and I will be well indemnified, I assure you."

Moreover, preparations were made of such a nature as to attract the attention of almost all the people then staying at the Beaurivage.

Elisabeth arrived at six o'clock on the Friday, and was much pleased with the arrangement of her apartment. Masses of asters, mauve and white in color, had been grouped everywhere, as they were pretty nearly the only flowers that, owing to the lateness of the season, could be furnished by the florist upon such short notice.

"Die sind sehr hübsch," said the Empress, looking at them with the peculiar softening of her entire countenance which manifested itself when admiring blossoms of any kind, *"aber es sind ya todtenblumen."* (They are very pretty, but they are death-flowers.)

In Austria asters are principally used for the decoration of the cemeteries on All Soul's Day, an occasion always observed with scrupulous care by all the subjects of Franz-Joseph, and that is the explanation of the Empress's allusion to the flowers found in her room on that, the eve of her death.

Before leaving Geneva, after the awful catas-trophe, Countess Sztaray divided those asters among all the members of the Empress's suite in remembrance of her.

The Empress was on that evening in a remarkably merry mood. She had been delighted with her visit to Pregny, where she declared that she had tasted the best fruit to be obtained in the length and breadth of Europe, and had left the beautiful villa carrying with her own hands an enormous bunch of the choicest kind of orchids, which Baroness Rothschild had gathered for her, and which, during her trip from Pregny to Geneva, she continued to admire and praise, caressing with the tips of her slender, ungloved fingers the strange, velvety, many-hued petals which bore the shape of some strangely formed butterflies. Her first care when she arrived at the hotel in Geneva was to put her dear orchids into a large bowlful of cold water, attending to this even before she thought of removing her travelling-cloak and hat.

Both she and her lady-in-waiting were covered with dust, and the latter proposed to the Empress that she should step out on the balcony in order to have some of it brushed off before changing her dress. The Empress, however, refused to do so, for fear that it should soil her hair, and preferred to remove her clothes at once and change them for others.

She was very proud of her hair; in fact, the only trait of vanity which I ever noticed in her was the pride she took in those magnificent chestnut tresses which fell down to her ankles. She used to have them brushed for hours every day when I was at Vienna, I remember well, while her reader, Mademoiselle Ferenzy, read to her from English, French, or Hungarian books. Her

Majesty was particularly anxious that the dresser
who brushed her long braids should avoid
pulling out a single hair. This, of course, was an
impossibility, and the unfortunate maid concealed carefully in the pocket of her apron any
hair which became entangled in the brush. One
day the Empress, happening to glance into the
looking-glass before which she sat, caught sight
of the maid concealing a small roll of hair in the
above-described fashion. Jumping up from her
rocking-chair, her Majesty grasped her attendant's hand, exclaiming:

"I have caught you at last! You are ruining
my hair!"

With a presence of mind which would have
done honor to an expert diplomat, the maid
replied, unhesitatingly:

"I implore your Majesty to forgive me; it never
happened before. I only wished to have some of
my sovereign's hair to put in the locket which my
little girl wears around her neck as a talisman."

Whether the Empress believed this clever
invention or not, I do not know, but shrugging
her shapely shoulders she resumed her seat,
laughing heartily, and the next day she presented
her maid with a locket enriched with diamonds,
saying, with a mischievous twinkle in her eyes:

"I think this is the kind of talisman your
little daughter deserves for having such a clever
mother!"

After having changed her dress on the day of
her fateful arrival in Geneva, the Empress drank
a glass of milk, and prepared to go for a little
stroll on the quay which borders the lake. Upon
returning to the hotel she wrote a few letters and
went to bed. On the next morning—that of her

death—she woke up in a charming mood, and
after taking her bath and getting dressed, she
went out with Countess Sztaray to do a little
shopping, stopping several times during her walk
to look into the windows of the florists', jewellers',
and *souvenir-de-la-Suisse* shops which abound
in Geneva.

Soon after her return to the hotel she dismissed her women, who departed by railroad for
Territet, and who, as they passed along the street
on their way to the station, failed to observe a
young man who was sitting upon a bench right in
front of the Beaurivage, intently watching all that
was going on there.

That there was such a young man has been
later on asserted by many people who used their
eyes to better purpose than did the Empress's
small suite.

This man was Luccheni, the assassin, and he
seemed to be taking note of every bit of luggage
which was being made ready in front of the hotel
for transportation to the steamer *Geneva.* He, of
course, saw the Empress's servants leave, and a
little later noticed the *valet de chambre,* who was
to accompany his imperial mistress on her trip
across the lake, make his way towards the wharf,
carrying on his arm the Empress's long black
cloak and in his hand her travelling-case. He was
dressed in plain clothes, and soon disappeared
from view on the gang-plank that united the
waiting ship to the quay. Shortly afterwards
two ladies, both robed in black, left the Hotel
Beaurivage, walking rapidly towards the steamer,
for the clanging of a bell was announcing that it
was on the point of starting. Countess Sztaray
walked a little ahead of the Empress, signalling

with her hand to the men who were in the act of
withdrawing the gang-plank to stop doing so.

At this moment Luccheni bounded across the
street, and roughly brushing past the Countess,
threw himself upon the Empress.

Not a cry escaped her as she fell on her knees
to the ground, and almost instantly she was on
her feet again, while Countess Sztaray screamed
at the top of her voice, to prevent the murderer
from being allowed to escape into the Rue des
Alpes; at the time, however, she believed that he
was merely a thief who had attempted to steal the
Empress's watch.

She threw her arm around the Empress's
waist to support her, but Elisabeth, although
ghastly pale, refused her help, and upon being
asked whether she was hurt replied, with almost
her habitual calmness:

"No, I do not think so—not much at least;"
and turning to a passer-by who was attempting to
brush off some of the dust with which her fall had
covered her, she said, smiling sweetly: "It is not
worth the trouble, thanks very much" (Ce n'est
pas la peine, merci bien).

With a firm step she walked towards the
steamer, crossed the gang-plank, and then fell
fainting to the deck. She was immediately carried
to the upper deck of the Geneva, although all
those who surrounded her continued stupidly to
imagine that she had been merely startled and
was not seriously hurt, and there she was laid
upon some red velvet cushions hastily brought
from the captain's room. In spite of the immediate
use of smelling-salts, cold water, and vinegar,
the Empress did not recover consciousness, and
so terribly white and drawn did her beautiful

features become that Countess Sztaray, who stood by wringing her hands helplessly, finally made up her mind to unfasten the imperial lady's corsage. Upon doing so she gave a terrible scream, for she found that it had been pierced by some sharp instrument above the left breast, and that a few drops of blood were slowly oozing from a very small triangular wound which showed like a deep purple mark upon the tender white flesh.

Meanwhile the steamer had put out from the shore, and was rapidly gliding over the unruffled blue waters of the lake. There was no doctor on board, and the lady-in-waiting, almost beside herself with the sense of her crushing responsibility, demanded that the boat should immediately return to Geneva.

She was obeyed, and a stretcher was hurriedly put together with the help of rugs and cushions upon some oars. Those who were bending over her Majesty at that moment noticed that a faint tremor passed over her face, her wonderful dark-blue eyes opened for the last time, and she stretched her hands out with an infinite longing towards the azure skies above. One fleeting glance upward, then, her hands still stretched out as if in prayer, she murmured *"Merci,"* and with the dauntless heroism of her soft, sad smile lingering about her lips, she gave a tired little sigh like that of a child sinking to sleep, and lay motionless on her crimson pillows.

As soon as the steamer touched the pier, Captain Roux, of the *Geneva,* and his officers carried the stretcher to which the Empress had been transferred out of the vessel and up to her room at the Beaurivage, that room which she had

left, but a short time before, full of life and
energy.

She was tenderly laid upon the bed, and a
priest who had been sent for, and who had
arrived on the spot even before the sorrowful little
procession, administered to her the last sacra-
ments. The physicians summoned to her bedside
did all that lay within their power to revive
the Empress; artificial respiration, friction, and
even bleeding were all vainly attempted, and, at
three o'clock, with another weary little sigh,
Elisabeth's pure and noble soul took flight.

The despair of her *entourage* cannot be
described. Sobs and moans were heard on all
sides, and the Empress's old *valet de chambre*
was taken so violently ill that his condition
required immediate medical attention. Countess
Sztaray telegraphed at once to the Emperor, and
to Count Paar, chief aide-in-camp of his Majesty,
and then took steps to have the Empress's *salon*
transformed into a mortuary chapel.

This room, so filled with sunshine, which
shone through the broad balconies overlooking
the lake shore, was draped completely—floor,
ceiling, walls, and doors, as well as windows—
with black velvet hangings, flecked with silver.
The coffin, lined with white satin and white
velvet, was placed beneath the middle window,
and with her head reposing on a lace pillow the
dead Empress lay therein, clad in a long white
satin robe, her hands crossed over a rosary and
an ivory crucifix, and surrounded by a glorious
garland of snowy, golden-hearted roses. A large
veil of lace half-covered her and fell to the floor,
where, at the foot of the coffin, a cushion made
of white roses bore the inscription, *"Repose*

en Paix" ("Rest in Peace"). Myriads of blessed candles shed a soft radiance over the countless wreaths and bouquets which were sent from every quarter, and nuns and priests knelt continually on *prie-dieus*, reciting the prayers for the dead.

Nothing can describe the loveliness of the expression overspreading the marmorean features of the dead Empress; such absolute, contented peace and restfulness belong only to angels. Although during the moments which had preceded her death there had been a sort of convulsed, suffering look upon her face, yet immediately afterwards the brow became smooth, the lips parted in a heavenly smile, disclosing the pearly teeth, and the only shadow noticeable on her countenance was that which was thrown by the deep fringe of her dark lashes upon her velvety cheeks.

There is but little more to say, for this work should treat only of Elisabeth's earthly career, not of the magnificent pageant by which her people attempted to make up in funeral display for their previous lack of appreciation and of loyalty towards their Empress. I will therefore give but a short description of it.

The mourning-train, with its sorrowful company of sable-clad officials, passing slowly through Switzerland and Austria amid the tolling of muffled bells; the arrival at Vienna—sorrowful and gloomy Vienna—so unlike the gay, brilliant city we all know so well; the superb procession following the coffin to and from the Burg; all this has been described by the press of many countries. The numberless poor, who came from far and wide to catch a glimpse of the casket

containing the remains of Elisabeth of Austria,
constituted the most touching element of the long
journey and of the funeral ceremony.

The pilgrimage of mourners from the suburbs
to the vicinity of the Hofburg commenced at three
o'clock in the morning on the day of the funeral.
By four o'clock there was already a dense crowd
in the Albrecht Platz, opposite the Jockey Club,
and at five, when the troops began to line the
streets, those who desired to see the body lying in
state found that it was almost too late, as
immense crowds had already congregated to wait
for the funeral in the afternoon. The Albrecht
Platz offered an excellent coign of vantage, and
particularly the Albrecht Rampe, an elevated
roadway leading to the late Archduke Albrecht's
palace, and people took up their post there at a
very early hour. The difficulty of keeping order in
the vast crowd was indeed enormous, owing to
the restricted area intersected by narrow streets
into which had congregated a town population of
one and a half millions, with another half million
of country people and strangers. There were two
streams of visitors. One consisted mostly of
women who wished to see their Empress as she
lay in state between eight and twelve o'clock; the
other was waiting for the carriages, the foreign
sovereigns, the deputations, clergy, and military,
and, finally, for the funeral itself. These two
streams in the end united to form a compact mass
of human beings, unable to move backward or
forward, and filling not only the immediate neighborhood of the Hofburg, but also the Graben, the
Kärntner-Strasse, and the Herrengasse.

When the hour of the funeral arrived, some of
the people managed to climb the steeples of the

churches of St. Michael and St. Augustin; and the two rooms of the fire-watch on the tower of St. Stephen's, to which there are three hundred and forty-three steps, were filled with spectators unable to pay for access to windows or balconies on the route to the Neuer-Markt, in which the Capuchin church is situated.

The atmosphere of gloom which spread over the capital bore sure witness to the genuineness of the sorrow which the people felt—sorrow tempered with profoundest sympathy for the old Emperor her death had left so lonely. In this his year of jubilee, Franz-Joseph stood among the rulers of Europe a heart-broken and solitary figure—pathetic to the last degree, bereaved by violence of his only son, and now by violence also of his consort, and with a weight of sorrow gnawing at his soul of which but few can measure the enormity, or know the many hidden springs.

There was from the moment when the Empress's remains were brought to Vienna a universal desire to occupy one's self exclusively with her tragic fate, and this was best observed in the streets, where everything spoke of her. The pavements and roadways were thronged with a dense crowd, in which women dressed in black were a prominent feature. Maids, for instance, wore black frocks and snow-white aprons, a mourning costume characteristic of Viennese women, and walked to the chapel in this dress. Along the street that leads from Schönbrunn to the gates of the Burg-Palace no walking was possible, and the people stood in rows so dense that they formed a kind of additional black pall covering the broad thoroughfare.

The scene within the Church of the

Capuchins was extraordinarily imposing, and at
the same time touching beyond description. The
cardinals, bishops, and other clergy stood on the
right side of the altar; on the left was the heavily
curtained door by which the court had entered.
The Capuchin church, though it was decorated
with black draperies throughout, including ves-
try and corridors, though every wall was covered
with black velvet and every doorway hung with
heavy black curtains, still retained the character
of poverty suited to the order whose convent
adjoins it. The high altar was marked only by a
large cross in cloth of gold. Gold candelabra, with
wax candles, and countless other blessed candles
in sconces, lighted the church, but they burned
dimly in the oppressive heat. The ground was
entirely covered with black cloth, the steps to the
altar and the platform reserved for the court
being marked by white strips of ribbon. On the
walls hung the Empress's escutcheons. They had
to be changed in the night preceding the funeral,
for they merely bore the inscription, *"Elisabetha
Imperatrix Austriae,"* and when the Hungarian
deputations came they remarked this immediately, and protested the moment they left the
chapel. The court officials immediately took down
those hatchments, replacing them by others on
which *"Regina Hungariae"* stood written in letters as big as *"Imperatrix Austriae."*

At the foot of the coffin were placed, on
cushions, the orders and decorations of the dead
Empress, and also the large black fan which
she invariably carried, together with a pair of
long white suède gloves. Her crowns as Empress
of Austria, Queen of Hungary, and Princess in
Bavaria sparkled at the head of the coffin.

The display of flowers was so great and so magnificent that even she, who never had enough of them about her, would have been satisfied, I think.

Queen Victoria's wreath was composed of pale pink chrysanthemums, tuberoses, violets, lilies, and palm-leaves, and the wreath from the Princess of Wales was formed of Maréchal-Niel roses, violets, and silver palms. The former bore the following inscription in German, received from her Majesty in a cipher telegram:

"Ein Zeichen der innigsten Freundschaft und Verehrung von ihrer getreuen Schwester.—VICTORIA R. I."

(A token of the deepest friendship and veneration from her faithful sister. —VICTORIA R. I.)

The latter wreath was inscribed, "From the Prince and Princess of Wales," and bore on a white satin ribbon the following words:

"Sister thou art gone before us,
   And thy saintly soul is flown
Where tears are wiped from every eye,
   And sorrow is unknown."

The inane reports to the effect that the Empress and Queen Victoria had been on bad terms were utterly untrue. Very much to the contrary, the aged ruler of Great Britain admired and loved Elisabeth greatly.

The Empress wrote in the most touching terms to Queen Victoria after the death of the Prince-consort, and that message was the beginning of a most interesting correspondence, which never ceased to be frequent and affectionate in the extreme. The deceased Empress also wrote in

an equally feeling manner to the Empress
Eugénie when Napoleon III. died, and more
recently to the Empress Frederick when she lost
her husband. Indeed she allowed no occasion to
pass without displaying her kindness towards
those in affliction, whatever their rank, and all
those to whom she had thus shown sympathy in
their trouble remembered it when death claimed
her too.

High and low brought or sent their floral
offerings; kings and queens, emperors and
empresses, princes, dukes, counts, bourgeois,
beggars even, managed to convey a vast and
splendid or a small and humble fragrant token of
their reverence to be placed about the coffin.

Dr. Christomanos, the Empress's Greek
instructor, laid with his own hands a cluster of
tuberoses on the steps of the dais upholding the
catafalque, beside the garland of snowy blossoms, four yards wide, sent by the Emperor of
Russia, and touching on the other side a sheaf of
forest flowers and branches, brought by a sobbing Tyrolese peasant early that morning. Those
who read the Empress aright know how much
more highly she would have prized the humble
offering of the peasant than the costly wreath of
the great and powerful sovereign.

The perfume from all these glorious blooms
was almost more than one could bear, however,
and floated heavily on the atmosphere, mingled
with the spicy odor of the incense and that of the
burning waxen tapers.

Sobs echoed ceaselessly under the vaults of
the sacred edifice, and came not only from the
seats reserved for the royal ladies present,
but from the entire assistance, while the poor

Emperor wiped the tears which continually rolled down his pale cheeks.

The Prince-Cardinal also, when giving the last benediction, finished in a voice broken by sobs, and there was not a dry eye when the coffin was lifted by its bearers and borne to the entrance of the narrow stone staircase leading down to the crypt. All the emperors, kings, and princes, all the archdukes and archduchesses, bowed low as it passed. It was their last salute to the dead Empress, and they all remained standing or kneeling in prayer till the Emperor, his two sons-in-law, and the two brothers of the late Empress had returned from the vault, which was after a space of about fifteen minutes. Capuchin friars, with lighted tapers, stood at the top of the staircase and went down with the coffin to its foot, preceded by Prince-Cardinal Gruscha and the assistant clergy, and followed by the Lord Chamberlain, the Emperor, and the princes already mentioned. The coffin was placed upon a bier draped with cloth of gold. A *prie-dieu* near by was reserved for the Emperor, and his Majesty knelt down, covering his face with his hands, and leaning his head on the edge of the prayer-stool.

In that posture he remained during the short ceremony of once more blessing the remains. But that office was not yet finished when the monarch's entire body began to tremble and deep sobs shook him, so that everybody present, including the clergy and even the monks who had seen so many funerals there, were unable to refrain from tears. The unfortunate Emperor rose, knelt again before the coffin, and let his head fall upon the lid, where it remained for several seconds. Kissing repeatedly the wooden

shell which contained all that was left of his
consort, he at last rose, forced himself into an
erect position, and without turning, mounted
the staircase. The Emperor was followed by the
princes, and as he reappeared in the church his
eyes were still filled with tears.

The ceremony of identifying the body and the
handing over of the keys to the custody of the
monks were performed in his absence. After the
Emperor had left the crypt, the monks opened a
small slab of wood at the head of the coffin,
revealing under plate glass the face of the
Empress, and the Father Guardian of the crypt
was formally interrogated by the Lord Chamberlain as to whether he could identify the features
as being those of the late Empress Elisabeth. On
a reply being given in the affirmative, the coffin
was again closed and committed to the care of the
monks, who received one of the keys, the second
one being handed to the Lord Chamberlain.

A copy of the medical reports made by the
doctors who performed the autopsy is also in the
hands of the Lord Chamberlain. The document
runs as follows:

"The weapon employed by the assassin
was of steel, pointed, three-cornered, and
exceedingly sharp. It entered the body
through the fourth rib, which was broken by
the blow. After following the rib for a short
distance it passed inward through the interior border of the lung, entered the pericardium, and penetrated the left ventricle of the
heart. Passing from above downward, it traversed the left ventricle and passed out
through the heart wall. The wound was two
and a half millimetres in circumference and

eight and a half centimetres in length. It had ragged edges, having been inflicted with a sharp but rough weapon. Death resulted from hemorrhage into the pericardium.

"The reason why the Empress was able to walk eighty paces after the heart had been completely punctured is explained by the fact that the flow of blood into the pericardium was very slow, owing to the small size of the wound. Had the weapon not been withdrawn she would have lived longer, for it was by the gradual infiltration of blood into the pericardium that life was destroyed.

"In the case of the Duke of Berry, who received a similar wound, the weapon was left in place, and he lived four hours. It nevertheless required undaunted courage and extraordinary energy on the part of the Empress to have accomplished what she did."

Strangely enough, for a long time previous to the assassination of Elisabeth, forebodings of an impending catastrophe prevailed in the imperial family, and so strong were these that the Emperor was heard several times to exclaim: "Oh, how I wish this jubilee year were over!"

On April 24th—that is, just a little over five months before the catastrophe—the sentinel posted in a corridor or hall leading to the chapel at the Hofburg was startled almost out of his senses by seeing the form of a white-clad woman approaching him soon after one o'clock in the morning. He at once challenged her, whereupon the figure turned around and passed back into the chapel, where the soldier observed a light shining. Hastily summoning assistance, a strict search was instituted and the chapel was explored, without, however, any result.

The sentinel in question was a stolid, rather dull-minded Styrian peasant, who was possessed of little power of imagination, and who probably was entirely ignorant, therefore, of the traditions according to which a woman arrayed in white makes her appearance by night in the imperial palace, either in the chapel or in the adjoining corridors and halls, whenever any misfortune is about to overtake the imperial house of Hapsburg.

On such occasions this spectral visit to the sentinel on duty has been described in the report of the officer of the guard on the following morning and is, therefore, a matter of official record. The previous visitations of the white lady had taken place on the eve of the shocking tragedy of Mayerling, a few weeks before the shooting of Emperor Maximilian of Mexico, and just before the burning to death of the daughter of old Archduke Albrecht, at Schönbrunn. The tradition is so deeply rooted that the same supernatural appearance at the time when Archduke John vanished from all ken was enough to convince the imperial family that he is no longer in the land of the living, as so many believe, but that he really perished at sea, while on his way around Cape Horn from La Plata to Valparaiso.

The guests leaving the Burg after the funeral were much struck by the peculiarly impressive appearance of the city. All the street lamps which had been lighted were swathed in crape, and the flame shimmering through this veil had a peculiarly lugubrious look. The streets were filled with black draperies and black flags, and even from the roofs depended great sable-hued banners which shivered sadly in the breeze. The accursed name of the assassin, Luccheni, was on every lip, and the thought of his awful deed in every heart.

The Hungarian magnates, in their gorgeous mourning trappings, the Polish nobles, the hussars and haiduks in attendance, the princes of the church, the peers of the realm, as well as the small tradesmen, the peasants, and the court servants, all discussed with like energy and equal wrath the possibilities of Luccheni's extradition, and expressed regret and lament about there not having been a single hand lifted in defence of the Empress nor a single breast placed as a shield between her and the weapon of her assassin. Indeed, general indignation was great, and poor old Koloman Tiszä, the aged ex-Minister of Hungary, who was walking with Moritz Jókai, the poet-deputy of the Magyars, wrung his hands and shed tears as they talked about this hideous crime, which finds no parallel in the history of the world. The name of Luccheni was heard again and again like a knell, from one end to the other of the crowd descending the steps of the Capuchin church.

CHAPTER XIV

In spite of all that has been said to the contrary, the murderer of the Empress of Austria knew well what he was about when he committed his foul and villanous crime within the frontiers of a country where the death penalty has been abolished. It is all very well to say that anarchists are possessed with courage of a quality quite out of the ordinary; this is by no means the case, and although among the ranks of Russian Nihilists there have been some instances of lives being sacrificed lightly, cheerfully, and with a singular, if ill-applied, sort of heroism in the interest of the cause, both by men and women, yet none of these unbalanced or demented creatures who seek to attain an impossible bourne by blood-shedding and treachery can ever be called heroes, or even courageous people.

In most cases they seek notoriety, and whether they belong to the lower classes of society or to a higher status, were they certain that the aureole of martyrdom would eventually be denied to them, and that their trial by jury would not be public, nor their ultimate punishment witnessed and discussed by the people at large, there would of a certainty be a large decrease in the number of those abominable crimes which have inspired all decent persons with horror and disgust.

The anarchist movement has made enormous progress since the time, when just thirty years ago it may be said to have been founded by the Russian ex-convict, Baron Bakounine, at Geneva, for it is only since that time that the so-called sect of anarchists has become known; still the spirit of defiance against superiority of any kind wherein anarchy has found its birth existed long previous to that date.

Revolution was not invented by Bakounine. He did not inspire the terrible deeds which took place in France during the Reign of Terror, nor did his theories urge on the Indian thugs. The same spirit which filled the brandy-soaked brains of the assassins of Louis XVI. and of Marie Antoinette is the breath of revolution in its ugliest shape, and it is to be traced from one end of this planet to the other, wherever there exist—and that is everywhere—conditions begetting moral, social, or financial superiority of one class over another.

Luccheni is, like a large number of such criminals, an Italian, and although he pretends he was nothing but a poor and uneducated creature, it has been proved that he on the contrary has more than a smattering of knowledge, which is perhaps the most dangerous condition for a man of his tendencies. His career was checkered by many changes, for he was at different times a soldier, a laborer, a student, and also, during some months, the servant of the Prince and Princess of Arazona. He read a quantity of trash about anarchism and nihilism which he was quite unable to comprehend or to digest, but which aroused in him a violent hatred for those whom he considered to be more fortunate than himself. In him one can find a new and terrible example of the erroneous ideas concerning the so-called philanthropic efforts which tend more and more to educate the masses after a fashion, yet altogether inadequately.

The denials of Luccheni with regard to his having been affiliated with one or more secret societies are absolutely futile, for, on the contrary, it was because he had been accused of being too lukewarm in his principles, and too behindhand in the services which he could have rendered to the cause, that he suddenly made up his mind to disprove these accusations and to alarm the world by an act so gruesome that it would remain absolutely without parallel in history.

This goes far to prove that the man was by no means an illiterate or an ignorant person, for he certainly selected his victim with a care which betokened his anxiety to make his crime a subject of world-wide comment. It is true that he alleged that at first his intention was to kill the Duke of Orleans and not the Empress; but this is probably false, for, long before he committed the murder he had cast his choice upon the Empress of Austria, whom he had seen and watched previously at Budapesth—so at least he himself declared when hard pressed by the examining magistrate. The assassination of the Duke of Orleans, regrettable as it would have been, would have by no means created so terrible a sensation as the one finally perpetrated, the Duke not being a sufficiently important personage to be missed and mourned as was the one faultless and absolutely perfect figure of Europe's sovereignty.

Moreover, Luccheni had accomplices who preceded him to Switzerland. Two of the affiliated—

namely, Pozzio and Barbotti, as well as Pozzio's mistress, a girl of the name of Lina Zahler—were arrested after the crime. It was this girl who purchased in Lausanne a sharp, murderous-looking knife for the sum of twelve francs, which, as she remarked when handing it to Luccheni, "was a good deal of money to pay for an instrument which would serve but once!" So regretful did the girl seem to be about this sum having been spent that Pozzio took possession of the knife, and exclaimed that he would take it back to the shop and recover the twelve francs, while Luccheni contented himself with purchasing a long and slender file, which he sharpened like a stiletto and provided with a commodious wooden handle.

It is very evident that Luccheni attempted, from the very moment of his arrest, to pose as a cynic of the most pronounced description. His declaration to the men who captured him as he was trying to fly in the Rue des Alpes after the perpetration of his shameful deed is sufficient proof of this, for he called out at the top of his voice: "I hit her well, bravo! Long live anarchy! All the other sovereigns will follow, and all the wealthy folks as well. Long live the Social Revolution!" Indeed, he assumed a joyful and smiling attitude, which would have rendered excusable the most atrocious form of lynching, and it is very lucky for him, as he seems to care so much for his life, that he should have fallen into the hands of thick-headed, slow-blooded Swiss, instead of into those of Americans, French, or Austrians, who have not so much mastery over their indignation, and who would have made an end of him there and then.

His letter addressed to the Swiss Federal

Council requesting to be judged in Lucerne, where capital punishment is still in force, is but another incident of the comedy of cynicism which he played throughout.

"I am a soft-hearted, glorious anarchist," wrote Luccheni. "It has been for a long time past my most cherished ideal to strike society in one of its summits. I have now attained this ideal, and I am the happiest man in the world. I am no coward, and do not fear death. In fact, I long to be beheaded and to add my name to the glorious list of martyrs who have fallen while working for our sacred cause."

He is not a coward, so he says; and still what is a man to be called who murders in cold blood a defenceless woman—a woman who never did him or anybody else an injury? And what can it be save braggadocio which inspired his reply to the examining judge when the latter asked him:

"Were you not impressed by hearing the funeral knell ring for your victim? Did it not make you sad and remorseful to know that you had plunged so many human creatures into despair?"

"No," replied Luccheni, with a sneer. "When I heard those bells I considered them to be the funeral knell of the bourgeoisie, whom I detest. Until the world swims in blood there will be no peace and no comfort for us working-people, who outnumber so greatly the useless, wealthy, and privileged beings that have tyrannized over us for centuries."

It is a wonder, still remaining unexplained, that the Austrian authorities should not have taken steps to obtain this wretch's extradition, and it has aroused the indignation of almost everybody to think that he is being treated exactly in the same manner as an ordinary criminal condemned for life. Surely a lesson was needed, and an example should have been made of Luccheni, but there are and will remain some very mysterious points about the sad circumstances surrounding the Empress's assassination, which are better allowed to pass from the minds of those who were truly and deeply fond of her, lest their feelings should become too hopelessly embittered.

During his trial, Luis Luccheni kept up his defiant and self-satisfied attitude. He remained cynical and indifferent, manifested no regret for his act, and coolly stated that if he had the opportunity again he would grasp it once more. Of course the court-room was crowded, every seat being occupied immediately after the doors were opened.

Luccheni was brought to the scene of the trial at an early hour from the prison St.-Antoine, which is in close proximity to the Palais de Justice, only a garden intervening. Although closely guarded by gendarmes in full uniform, he awaited the opening of the proceedings in a small room adjoining the court quite peacefully, conversing with his keepers and smoking innumerable cigarettes just as if he had come there to witness a pleasant spectacle instead of being the central figure of an appalling tragedy.

At nine o'clock the judges took their seats upon the bench. The tribunal was composed of M. Bourgy, President of the Court of Justice, and of MM. Schutsle and Racine, Judge Accessors. To the right of the raised platform upon which they took their places was the seat assigned to the public prosecutor, M. Navazza, while on the left were the clerk of the court, M. Rougnieux, and the members of the jury, a small space being reserved between the jury box and the body of the court for the witnesses in the case.

The prisoner upon being brought into court was placed beside the Advocate, Maître Moriaud, who in absence of counsel for the defence had been appointed to act on his behalf. The seats reserved for the press were occupied by about fifty journalists of various nationalities. Among others present in the body of the court were M. Bremmerd, Federal Councillor; M. Scherb, Procureur General of the Confederation, and Baron Giskra, Secretary of the Austro-Hungarian Legislation and Representative of his Majesty the Emperor of Austria.

Luccheni was smoothly shaved, his mustache was curled with extraordinary care, and he bestowed upon the court a graceful bow, which was a masterpiece of vulgar impudence and reckless impertinence. On a table near by were placed the so-called *pièces de conviction*, consisting of the loathsome file, a military-certificate found in the assassin's pocket, a photograph representing him in his uniform of the Italian cavalry regiment of Monteferrato, and wearing the war medal of the Abyssinian campaign, etc.

This last examination of Luccheni, undertaken by the president of the court, brought to light several facts which until then had remained unpublished. From it was gathered that Luccheni, during the time when he was serving his country, had given satisfaction to his superior officers, and had shown no sign of harboring the anarchistic theories which he displayed later on. In fact, he was so well thought of in his regiment that his

captain took him into his house as servant,
and had at the time no reason whatsoever for
repenting having done so. During his stay in
his captain's house he was known to be
intent upon reading everything he could obtain
about the Dreyfus case, and also about M.
André's polar voyage; he also, when his evening
off duty came around, used to go and hear
conferences on singularly abstruse matters. In
one word, he gave his employers the impression
that he was much above the ordinary run of
common soldiers. Strange to say, three days
before killing the Empress, Luccheni wrote a
letter to his former captain's wife, whom he had
heard was spending a short time in Paris. This
letter, which was communicated to the authorities, was well written, well spelled, and ran as
follows:

"*Madame la Princesse:*

"Having heard that you are in Paris, I
would have been glad to come and pay my
respects there, to yourself, and to your
family, but circumstances over which I have
no control force me to remain in Switzerland
for a little while longer. I have, however,
already bought my ticket for the capital of
France, but perhaps before I arrive there
you will have found out the reason which
prevented me from coming sooner. I am
in excellent health, and hope that yourself
and your honored family are in the same
condition. I expect to leave Geneva on Sun-
day. In the meanwhile I remain, *Madame la
Princesse,*

"Your humble servant,
"L. LUCCHENI."

It may seem passing strange that an anarchist so embittered against the aristocracy should have written thus to Princesse Dolorès di Véra d'Arazona, and when on the Saturday following the day upon which she received this epistle Madame d'Arazona read of the assassination by Luccheni of the Empress of Austria, her amazement and disgust may be better imagined than described.

The questions of the president of the court elicited also the facts that Luccheni was born in Paris on the 2d of April, 1873, and that on the 9th of August, 1874, he was placed in the poor-house of Parma, where he was given the number of 29,239. He was born in the second Arrondissement of Paris, and his *état-civil* designates him as "Luis Luccheni, father unknown; mother, Luigia Luccheni, daughter of John Luccheni and of Marie Macelli (of Albaceto), unmarried, laundress."

The first witness called was M. St. Martin, electrician, who deposed that he saw the prisoner strike the Empress, but was unable to say at the moment whether his object was to rob or to kill her Majesty. He stated that when the prisoner at the bar attempted to escape he pursued him and arrested him with the assistance of the boatman, Rouget; that Luccheni did not offer much resistance, but declared loudly at first that he had done nothing blamable. Here the witness was interrupted by a violent protest on the part of Luccheni, who called out:

"I did not say that. I have never been ashamed of my deed. I told you, on the contrary, that I had just killed the Austrian Empress."

When silence had been re-established, the boatman Rouget was called in, and repeated very nearly the same story as had been told by St. Martin. He was followed on the witness-stand by Veuillemain, a coachman, who was stationed in front of the Brunswick monument when the crime was committed, and who said that he had noticed Luccheni lounging against a railing some minutes before his attack upon the Empress's person; and added that he heard with his own ears Luccheni exclaim immediately after his arrest:

"I hope that I did not miss her! Next will come the King of Italy, but now, unfortunately, I will be prevented from having the pleasure of doing for him myself."

The doctors who attended the dying Empress were next heard, and after explaining the nature of the wound inflicted and reading the reports which they had made ready, they declared, on their soul and conscience, as did also the medical experts attached to the tribunal, "that the Lombroso theories could not be applied to Luccheni, who is perfectly sound of mind, eats and sleeps well, and has not the slightest trace of melancholy, remorse, or regret even, in his composition."

Another witness, M. Sartoris, who is a painter, deposed that Luccheni told him once that he would kill some person of mark in order to at last be able to see his name printed in a newspaper, but that he had given this statement, made laughingly, no importance at the time when it was uttered.

The jury had been appointed by drawing lots, and M. Moriaud, as I have said before, was acting as counsel for the defence.

Luccheni persistently denied throughout the long trial having had any accomplices, but repeatedly declared that he was glad to have killed the Empress, adding, with an ugly scowl:

"I did my utmost to succeed in the attempt, and I meant to kill the Empress, that is certain! Human suffering is the motive of my act."

Thereupon the president pointed out to him that he himself had never been in want, and could, therefore, have had no such motive in view. The prisoner rubbed his hands and, smiling blandly, replied:

"On the day of my birth, or soon after, my mother herself renounced me; that is enough of untold suffering!"

The public prosecutor delivered an eloquent address to the jury, laying stress upon the fact that Luccheni openly gloried in his crime, and that although he denied the existence of accomplices it was quite certain that he had been aided and abetted by other anarchists, which, however, in no sense diminished the full responsibility borne by Luccheni himself for a crime so odious that no words could describe the fulness of its horror. He said further that the time had passed for psychological study of the anarchist breed, or for investigating the origin and the cause of so dreadful a movement. The time had come indeed, he thundered on, when society ought to get up *en masse* to annihilate and repress this ever-growing danger, this many-headed hydra which threatens to encompass in its many tentacles the entire system of our modern civilization.

"Only a few weeks ago," said the public prosecutor, in conclusion, "in a dark vault under the Church of the Capuchin in Vienna, the grave closed forever upon the prisoner's victim. May it close as heavily to-night at Geneva on the foot-steps of the murderer when he has crossed the threshold of our penal prison, and may he pass into everlasting oblivion. Let this be his punishment."

To the procureur's address the prisoner listened with the greatest attention. At one point, where M. Navazza alluded to the fact that the prisoner had attempted to escape from those who held him in arrest, Luccheni turned towards his counsel and exclaimed, with a great show of firmness, "That is not true!"

Again, when the procureur pointed out that the late Empress had never concerned herself with politics, the accused remarked, in mocking tones, "She was always a worker, perhaps." The public prosecutor, commenting on this interruption, said that the prisoner's doctrine appeared to be that no one who did not work should be allowed to live, to which the prisoner responded loudly, "That's right."

When M. Moriaud addressed the jury for the defence, he sought to minimize the prisoner's responsibility and attempted to move and touch his audience, and especially the jury, by theatrically appealing to the dead Empress's spirit, saying that from heaven, where she was now enthroned, she pitied her murderer, and that could she but do so, she would intercede for him, for during her life she had always pleaded the cause of the condemned and had obtained the pardon of many! This magnificently pompous peroration fell rather flat, for in very justly exalting the virtues of the victim the worthy counsel entirely lost sight of the fact that he was emphasizing still more all the odiousness of the murderer's crime. There were at that moment murmurs and mutterings among his hearers, who had, until then, remained very quiet and peaceable.

Baron Giskra, the representative of the Emperor of Austria, seemed deeply affected by the lawyer's allusion to the dead Empress, and changed color several times in rapid succession.

Three questions were put to the jury: 1. Is Luccheni guilty of having assassinated the Empress? 2. Did he act with premeditation? 3. Did he lie in wait to commit the crime?

The jury retired to consider their verdict. After an absence of twenty minutes they brought in a reply to all three questions in the affirmative, finding no extenuating circumstances.

The procureur-general then rose and demanded the penalty of imprisonment for life, whereupon the president asked the prisoner whether he had anything to say why this sentence should not be pronounced. Luccheni smilingly replied that he had nothing to add.

The court retired to consider the sentence, but returned in a few minutes and imposed the full penalty allowed by the law of Switzerland—imprisonment for life. The prisoner, when the sentence was delivered, cried, "Long live anarchy! Death to the aristocracy! Let there be only two hundred such brave men as myself and all the thrones of the world will be empty!" Then, smiling serenely upon the assistants, he followed his escort of gendarmes out of the court-room.

Luccheni is now in a subterranean cell reached by a staircase of twenty steps and a corridor so dark that the jailer who led him had to carry a lantern. At the end of the corridor is a strong door signed with the letter C. with a hole for air and light at the bottom. Then another yard of corridor and a second door, strong like the first, with holes at the top for light, which leads directly into the cell. This cell is without a window and is quite dark; on the ground a sack filled with straw, to serve for a seat by day and a bed by night. No other thing in the cell. Here the Empress's assassin is to pass the first six months of his imprisonment only, being taken out for a breath of fresh air once in every fortnight.

He was transferred to his cell in the following fashion: A little before eleven o'clock at night, Luccheni, who was in a deep sleep, was awakened by M. Lafond, governor of the prison of St.-Antoine, and told to dress himself. Though aware of the fate in store for him, he had not been told of the date of his departure, and he was clearly much affected now that the hour had come. M. Lafond then explained to him the regulations to which he would be subjected. When informed that he would be allowed to receive visitors four times a year, and that he would be visited every week by the prison chaplain, Luccheni expressed his gratitude for these concessions. He was then intrusted to a guard of five gendarmes. Under their escort, and preceded by two warders carrying lanterns, he traversed on foot the short distance that separates the prison of St.-Antoine from that of the Evêché. The streets through which he passed were quite deserted, and in a few minutes he had reached his destination. At the gate of the Evêché he stood still for an instant, and cast an inquiring glance around as if in expectation of some sign that an effort was to be made to rescue him, but not a sound broke the silence, and his escort pressing him forward, he angrily shrugged his shoulders and entered the prison. After being made to put on the costume of prisoners condemned to life sentences, he was conducted to a cell. He will remain in this prison until his death a mere number—No. 1144.

This form of punishment needs no comments. Perchance its advocates are right when they claim that it is far worse than capital punishment itself, for in the gloom of this sinister cell the mind of the caged assassin will need to be very strong indeed not to totter and fail him. Everlastingly upon the curtain of deep shadows which will press upon his sight he will see appearing before him his beautiful victim, the woman he so odiously killed; and upon his ears in that palpable, oppressive, wellnigh unbearable silence of dungeons will fall nothing but the imaginary sound of the sobs which his revolting deed has caused. He will then mayhap regret this deed so quickly executed, and for which there is no expiation possible.

> "There are swift hours in life—
> strong, rushing hours
> That do the work of tempests
> in their might!"

And so no more of the fiend now entombed in the prison of the Evêché, excepting the heart-felt hope that he will now and hereafter reap his sowing.

That may not sound like a very Christian wish, but one's softer and better feelings are apt to become weakened by the thought that the old Mosaic law was not applied, and that Luccheni escaped the *Lex talionis* of the ancients, be his present predicament ever so dreadful.

And now, in the crypt of the Capuchin church, the Empress lies at rest till the consummation of time, side by side with her beloved son. The coffin in which she was borne from Switzerland to Vienna has been placed in a sarcophagus of gold and silver, adorned by a large cross—the last she will ever bear—beneath which, framed in a beautifully chased garland of flowers and buds, the following inscription is engraved:

"ELISABETH AMALIA EUGENIA, IMPERATRIX AUSTRIAE ET REGINA HUNGARIAE, MAXIMILIANI JOSEPHI ET LUDOVICAE, DUCUM IN BAVARIA, FILIA. NATA IN VILLA POSSENHOFEN DIE XXIV. MENSIS DECEMBRIS ANNI MDCCCXXXVII. NUPTA FRANCISCO-JOSEPHO I. IMPERATORI VINDOBONAE DIE XXIV. M. APRILIS A. MDCCCLIV. CORONATA REGINA, BUDAE DIE VIII. M. JUNII A. MDCCCLXVII. DENATA GENEVAE DIE X. M. SEPTEMBRIS A. MDCCCXCVIII.   H. S. E."

("ELISABETH AMALIA EUGENIA, EMPRESS OF AUSTRIA AND QUEEN OF HUNGARY, DAUGHTER OF MAXIMILIAN JOSEPH AND LUDOVICA, DUKE (AND DUCHESS) OF BAVARIA. BORN IN THE VILLA POS- SENHOFEN ON THE TWENTY-FOURTH DAY OF THE MONTH OF DECEMBER IN THE YEAR 1837. MARRIED IN VIENNA TO FRANZ-JOSEPH I, THE EMPEROR, ON THE TWENTY-FOURTH DAY OF THE MONTH OF APRIL IN THE YEAR 1854. CROWNED QUEEN AT BUDA ON THE EIGHTH DAY OF THE MONTH OF JUNE IN THE YEAR 1867. DIED IN GENEVA ON THE TENTH DAY OF THE MONTH OF SEPTEMBER IN THE YEAR 1898. HERE SHE LIES.")

FINIS

THE EMPRESS REINCARNATED—
ELIZABETH CLARE WULF, AGE 4,
BORN APRIL 8, 1939, RED BANK, NEW JERSEY

A Letter to My Friends
Who "Forget Me Not"

I am always
Elizabeth

To My Intrepid Companions
Who Still Dare to Call Themselves—
"My Friends"—
When a love between two people spans the centuries, is lost and found again, sparkles in the depths of soul-memory only to surface upon the sea of life by the mighty yearning of hearts' mutual affection—such a love deserves to be immortalized, not alone in the memory of God who gave it but in the lives of other people who have also loved as the saints have loved—purely, serenely—and are yet in the process of reforming those ancient friendships as Christ would have them—formed and reformed in Him.

Our partings—from one lifetime to the next— seem life's sweet sorrows. And our findings of one another must surely be the sheer bliss of discovering rare wildflowers in the fields of life as we gather a bouquet of souls for their enshrining at the feet of the Blessed Mother.

The story you have read is an insight into my life as Elisabeth of Austria. It was written by a friend—then and now. One who has been my very own beloved soul-friend for many episodes in the earthly journey. To me it illustrates as much about the devotion of a precious soul and her immaculate concept of the one who represented to her the highest virtue in Life, as it serves to unfold perhaps a hidden lining in the mysterious garment that was given to me to wear.

As to my worthiness of her undying affection, I am grateful to have been born again to speak of her own purity of heart and blessed friendship, to know her now as then as the indomitable defender of the honor both of the person and the office of my flame, and to say that only God is worthy of such praise and loyalty—and that He so shone through the aperture of my selfhood may be attributed solely to His grace. It is the Light rather than the vessel that must be extolled.

The beauty of this heart's rendering of our experiences together is for me in the soul-knowing of her intimate appreciation for the light, her total absence of that most loathsome beast of idolatry, and her own personal sense of integrity that has made possible and joyous our friendship of the ages.

I have chosen to republish this out-of-print book for my students throughout the world (and those who may come after we have left the passing scene) as an insight into my soul. Surely it is a window on a phase of experience at once necessary for one's personal evolution and ordained by God as a mission in itself.

Many are the threads that crisscross our lifetimes as the evolving soul strives, however imperfectly, to externalize the God flame. Though it move in and out of the sine waves of illusion, the Presence of the Rock is always felt as the highest expression of selfhood we must one day meet and know as our own Real Self.

True friends endure because they catch the vision of that higher realm where they see one another in the perfect light. They read each other's thoughts and feeling , ups and downs, in the knowing of the inner self that is one with the Rock inscrutable. Such friends hold the balance as we pass through life's stormy seas and finally return, by way of the Lighthouse "steadfast, serene, immovable" to the eternal Bourne.

In this book, you will feel the depth of love between a spiritual mother and daughter that has always been and always will be—because it is necessary to our very soul's expression and because God willed it so.

It is a love I would openly proclaim for all to see because I believe it is a love that all should share and one day know—if they do not already. To me it portrays what ought to be the fount of our sisterhood on earth—holy orders we have served with saints East and West. It should typify and transcend the needs of women expressed in recent decades, as our liberation from our former selves has led us into new relationships—with God, with man, and with each other.

The two women who come out of the pages of this book and the last century are alive and well and happy. Our message as co-authors of our life, then and now, is that this experience we shared so personally and painfully is for us not a dark compartment where the memory weeps. Ah, no. Not at all. It is a springboard to new life and joyous fulfillment as God has given to us new opportunity to love and serve his purposes in this century.

We are no worse and far better for the lessons of that tragic drama. Our souls are satisfied that it was a cup He gave us to drink. And in witness to His life we drank—gladly—"all of it."

We do not rebel against our past or the obligations it brings us, even to the present hour. We would share our soul experience, our memory as déjà vu, with women all over the world who are searching for that thread of contact with Life in its totality as it stretches across the centuries of our evolving self-awareness.

We would share our realization of the soul of woman who, through the travail of giving birth to herself, is becoming more real every day. In that certainty of soul knowing we would share this ongoingness of Life in all the richness of its tapestry: As treasures of heart year upon year, as the eventual tragedy born of misplaced hopes, and as the testing and the testing again that leads to Christ's triumph over us and ours over the lesser self—until at last we reach the eternal Self, the source of our own tributary but never of our tribulation.

It is our hope that this insight into our previous life lived side by side, bound by the iron bands of karmic law, will provide many with an understanding of the experiences we are all having today. The search for our identity as women goes on. Our need for independence from the unredeemed masculine self—whether within ourselves or objectified in society or soul mates—is very great. Then, too, the fallen woman as 'femme fatale' can and must be redeemed in a heightened self-awareness that can be known only through a direct relationship with God the Father, God the Son, and God the Holy Spirit.

The untransmuted male as the bullish, boorish brute intensifies the reactionary nature of the untransmuted female—wily, deceitful and self-deceived. But the true polarity of the ascendant self (of Man reborn in the image of Christ and of Woman resurrected from the tomb of mortality) gives birth to the liberating experience of being woman in the fullest sense that Life itself has mandated—and the even greater joy of seeing man in all of his regal majesty discover himself in the full light of a burgeoning Godhood intended from the Beginning.

My life with Franz-Joseph, Sophie, Rudolph and all the other players on that Austrian stage has finally fulfilled itself through Love's own perfect transmutation. But death was not our liberation. It never is. We had to meet again and love again, more selflessly, in order to reach that resolution in which there are no more tears or death consciousness, neither sorrow nor crying nor pain, as John the Revelator says, "for the former things are passed away." And those former things, we come to realize, are karmic ties that tie tightly until cut by the love of Christ and consumed by the sacred fire of the Holy Spirit.

We learn that the love we bear one another, when pure, is never lost but moves through and beyond our temporary affections to the heart of the living Word. Love's labor is not lost but endures until that perfect love He has for us is ours for one another. Thus, out of this round of my life experience, the real love that has endured is the love of the disciple in us all for the Great Teacher and Giver of Life—and His love for us—all-encompassing, self-transcending and forgiving. It is this love I would extol and bid you to find and allow yourself to be conquered by. It is the greatest love of all and the one that pulls us past the tracks of time and space to the trackless reaches of Infinity.

Elizabeth Clare Prophet

All Saints' Day
November 1, 1981

For a list of books by Elizabeth Clare Prophet, write or call: Summit University, Box A, Malibu, California 90265 (213) 880-5300.